Text, photographs & artwork copyright 2016 SCSTyrrell
First published 2016
Set in Garamond 12 on 15
Published by Pasticcio Ltd. Registered in England No 5125728
01326 340153   www.pasticcio.co.uk
ISBN 978-0-9570311-7-3

Pasticcio

Sir James Tillie

His Life, Houses, and Eccentric Burial

Stephen Tyrrell

Pentillie Castle, in winter, from the west.
Picture Courtesy Pentillie Castle Estate

Contents

Introduction   7

Sir James Tillie
  1. Rumours and Reputation   9
  2. The Life of Sir James Tillie   23
  3. A Wife, Lead Mine and Dispute:
      James Tillie and the Vanes   65
  4. Murder, Theft and a Stolen Wife?
      James Tillie and the Corytons 75
  5. The Dispute at the Court of Chivalry   99
  6. Sir James Tillie's Will   109
  7. A Brief Introduction to the Period   123

His Buildings
  8. Pentillie Castle   135
  9. Gardens and Grounds at Pentillie   163
  10. The Tower on Mount Ararat   181
  11. The Building of Belle Cour   207
  12. Comparative Architecture
      and the Design of Pentillie 241

Conclusion   253

Sources and Acknowledgements   257

Ce' que Mars et venus, Minerve ont de parfait,
Brave Jacques Tilli se voit dans ton portrait.
The young James Tillie, here referred to as Jacques Tilli, in an un-
dated engraving whose original was 'sculpsit' by FH van Houe.
Reproduced from 'Cornish Characters and Strange Events' by S Baring-Gould.

Introduction

Sir James Tillie was long famous for his eccentric funeral, for stories of a misspent life and for his wish that, following his death in 1713, his body should be left sitting in the vault of the three storey tower he built, looking over the Tamar. The tower, where his life size statue can be seen through a small window, is to the north of Pentillie Castle, Cornwall. This was built by Sir James as a house which was never a castle but, rather, a villa designed to suggest an owner of high status and ancient lineage. Sir James Tillie married into the Coryton family, who still live in the building that was part of Sir James Tillie's original 'palace'.

Pentillie Castle is renowned for its dramatic position above the river Tamar. Described as an 'elegant and beautifully situated mansion on a commanding eminence above the river', it is not only magnificent as seen from the river but also has acres of garden, valleys and hills of park and woodland. Pentillie was restored in 2009 by the Coryton family who brought new energy to the house and grounds after long decline and generations of neglect. Today, Pentillie is not only visited by many, but the house, outbuildings and grounds are steadily being restored. Not only does the castle's position mean that it's been admired for some 300 years but the 'wondrous stories' which have accumulated about the notorious life of Sir James Tillie have created a curious reputation for the man, his life and his death.

However, Sir James Tillie was also notable because, having been brought up on a small holding in Wiltshire, he rose to success, to be knighted and become a rich man and the possessor of much land. In middle life he bought land in the village of his father and ancestors and built another eccentric house, Belle Cour, to justify his place of birth as one of family status and antiquity.

Sir James married twice, and despite rumours, seems to have been a loyal family man. Certainly a man of ambition, he was also responsible for the building of two country houses of some originality and eccentricity in design and at both Pentillie and Belle Cour, he built tower retreats, which were among the first of their type in the country.

Finally he was one of the first to be buried in a purpose built mausoleum outside a churchyard, the mausoleum and burial itself being of some eccentricity.

While his reputation suggests that he was a man of dubious character, his life was more interesting than that reputation, and Sir James deserves to be remembered not only for his life and buildings, but also for being one of those who managed to rise during a period of social upheaval, changing society and opportunity.

Notes

1 Endnotes at the end of each chapter provide references and research information. A further list of references is included in the 'Sources and Acknowledgements' section at the end of the book.

2 The dates of events, legal actions, births, deaths and marriages were recorded in the late 17th century under the convention by which the legal year began on Ladyday, that is the 25th March each year, a convention which ran until change from the Julian to the Gregorian calendar was enacted in 1750.

During the life of Sir James Tillie, an event in, for instance, February 1667 would be recorded as of February 1666, because the year did not end until March 25th of the year we call 1667. To add to the confusion this was often written as 1666/67. A modernised date would be February 1667, and where possible we have adopted the modern equivalent.

Chapter 1

Rumours and Reputation

Sir James Tillie is a man of whom it is difficult to get a clear picture. We know when he lived, because an inscription in his mausoleum states that he was born around 1647 and died on 15 November 1713, in the 67th year of his life.

His death and mausoleum became the subject of much gossipy speculation. The lack of surviving direct family meant there were no advocates to counter the wilder stories of his life and death.

One notable culprit was the 'unreliable' early 18th Century historian, Hals, who wrote at length only shortly after Sir James' death. Hals described him, with scorn, as the son of a labourer and a man who was little more than a thief, alleging that his steward, a Mr Eliot, and a confederate, Mr Popjoye, were found guilty of making counterfeit money. He alleged that Sir James had robbed his former client, Sir John Coryton, perhaps poisoned Sir John, and stolen his wife and lands. Finally, he suggested that in his new house at Pentillie Castle, he:

liveth in much pleasure and content in this place, honoured of some, loved of none, admiring himself for the bulk of his riches and the arts and contrivances by which he got it, some of which were altogether unlawful.

Hals also exaggerated the story of his death and the instructions for his funeral. This dramatic tale caught the imagination, particularly the story that his decaying body remained strapped to his chair, looking over the Tamar, and awaiting resurrection.

It is these stories that have been remembered over the years and became repeated in the 18th and 19th century histories of Cornwall as

Number I.

Of the Weekly Publication of Four full Sheets

(Now printing at Truro)

OF THE

Compleat Hiſtory of *Cornwal,*

GENERAL and PAROCHIAL:

Written by **WILLIAM HALS**, Gent. deceas'd, a Native of that County, perfect Maſter of the Cornish, and very well vers'd in the Britiſh and Saxon, as well as the Learned Languages; and

Compos'd by him after Fifty Years ſtudy, and the moſt curious as well as induſtrious Search in Perſon, on the Spot, in the ſeveral Pariſhes and Places.

The GENERAL PART

Is comprehended in an INTRODUCTORY DISCOURSE concerning the Original Habitation General, as among Kings, their Laws, Wars, &c. &c. with an Account of the Old Britiſh Druids, or Prieſts of their Towns, their Towns, Dioceſes, &c. and the ſtrange Superſtitious Worſhip of the Inhabitants, their Manner of Living, Cuſtoms, Ceremonies, Marriages, Funerals, &c.

In the PAROCHIAL PART

(Which is Alphabetically digeſted) is given the exact Account of the Number of CHURCHES in the County, with their ſeveral Dedications, Endowments, Patronages, ancient and preſent Value, Monumental Inſcriptions, Lords of the Soens to whom dedicated, and Hiſtorical Fragments relating to the ſame.

The ANTIQUITIES and uncommon CURIOSITIES in every Pariſh.

The Ancient CHARTERS of the Body and Seminary of Cornwal, with the Liberties, Privileges, and Cuſtoms of the Tinners, at large.

A particular Hiſtory of St. Michael's Mount, with a true and perfect Deſcription of it, very remarkable Occurrences relating to the ſame, and an Account of ſeveral divers Metals and liquid ſtones, within above Five Hundred Years ago.

A nice Account of the Names, Arms, and Deſcents of moſt of the Ancient Corniſh GENTLEMEN.

The whole illuſtrated with great Variety of Hiſtorical Obſervations, and interſpers'd with uſeful Entertainments, Divine, Moral, Natural, Medical, and Political, collected from the moſt ancient Records and ancient Manuſcripts.

In which innumerable, Errors and Miſrepreſentations in Carew's SURVEY of CORNWALL, and Camden's BRITANNIA (which Authors turn too much on Truth) are detected, confuted, and corrected.

It is all exact and to be added.

An Etymological *Corniſh* VOCABULARY;

Serving no only to explain the ancient Britiſh and Corniſh Words mentioned in the foregoing Hiſtory, but may be of conſiderable Uſe to a like Purpoſe, with regard to Familiar Names, and other Parts of England.

And of the ſeveral uncommon Curioſities, belonging &c. will be printed a proper Plate, and a very correct Map of the County will be prefix'd to the Whole, to be deliver'd with the laſt Number.

This History will be comprized in One Volume, conſiſting of Two Hundred Theets, to be deliver'd in Weekly Numbers of Four Sheets each, (at Three pence proper, if Printed in Blue Covers, Price Six pence) Sewing. The Money to be paid as the Old Methods and manner.

The History conſiſts only of the full Impreſſion, that only the other Weeks Pariſhes, (if both paſs'd in bed in this Nature or order of the Place where the Ministers are ſettled &c. may be proved.)

The Numbers are deliver'd at Mr. Thomas Palmer's, Bookſeller, over the road in the Stairs, at Biſhopſgate Street, London; at Mr. Baſket's Printing Office in Exeter; and at the Houſe of Mr. Philip Chriſtian and Mr. of the Bible, and Proprietor of this Work, at his Houſe in Truro.

N. B. If Gentlemen, &c. in other Towns pleaſe to have the ſaid Numbers to ſerve Cuſtomers, they may be had of Booksellers in the ſeveral Country Programs, according to Directions, and the ſaid Profit as above to them.

*** If any Gentlemen pleaſe to communicate any Thing relating to their reſpective Pariſhes, their Arms, &c. in a ſhort time the History of the ſame, they are earneſtly deſired that their Intelligence, if it pleaſe this certain may eaſy, poſt this Author, (Enquiry is not Name, but probable to aſk and in their proper Places, if ſuch more Page are to proper of above to the Manuscript may more at arm in hand &c. A Way of Advertiſe at the ſuitable. In the next Numbers any in ſeveral ranges the News of the ancient Inhabitants of the ſeveral Pariſhes, &c. &c. All the Arms and Affairs at any place may be in order, if pleaſed ask at the Proprietor attend and that the ſaid Profit is above before ſaid.

N. B. We hope Purchasers with the laſt two Parts of the Work, will note becauſe the proper Proceedings for the laſt Part are not yet completed, but as Corn for their Relations are preparing for a new Good Field.

The title page to the parts issue of Hals' *'Compleat History of Cornwal'*
some sections of which were published posthumously, from 1750.

an example of an evil and eccentric man. This view became accepted and repeated in other books about Cornwall. Even today, I have heard it repeated that he was a 'bad man', a heretic who stole someone else's money, and then his wife, before dying an eccentric death.

William Hals

This reputation arose because the first printed record of his life was written by William Hals, (1655–1737), an early local historian and antiquary who wrote for a planned parochial history of Cornwall from about 1685 until his death, which although continually revised was yet never finished, and his original manuscripts are now in the British Museum. It was not until after his death that some of the parish histories were published, in sections from 1750. Notes on the life of Sir James Tillie are found in the passages written on the parishes of St Mellion and Pillaton, which themselves suggest that part was written while Sir James was still alive and the rest perhaps four years after his death.

However, publication soon ceased, perhaps because the work was considered scandalous and unreliable. Despite this, the text was quoted by many 19th century writers. Hals recording of the life of Sir James Tillie is therefore the best and indeed only place to start considering a biography of Sir James and is here as printed in Lake's Parochial History.[1]

Pentillie is a house built and so named by one James Tyley, son of ----, in the parish of S. Keverne, labourer, who, as I am informed, was placed by him as a servant or horseman to Sir John Coryton, Bart., the elder; who afterwards by his assistance, learning the inferior practice of the law, under an attorney, became his steward. In which capacity, by his art and industry he soon grew rich, so that he married Sir Henry Vane's daughter, by whom he had a good fortune or estate, but no issue.

At length after the death of his master, he became a guardian in trust for his younger children, and steward to their elder brother Sir John, that married

Chiverton; whereby he augmented his wealth and fame to a greater pitch; when, soon after King James II. came to the crown, this gentleman, by a great sum of money, and false representations of himself, obtained the favour of knighthood at his hands. But that king, some short time after, being informed that Mr. Tyley was but first but a groom or horseman to Sir John Coryton,- that he was no gentleman of blood or arms, and yet gave for his coat armour the arms of Count Tille of Germany, ordered the heralds to enquire into this matter; who, finding this information true, by the king's order, entered his chamber at London took down his arms, tore others in pieces, and fastened them all to horses tails, and drew them through the streets of London to his perpetual disgrace, and degraded him from the dignity of that bearing, and imposed a fine of £500 upon him, for so doing, as I am informed. But alas ! maugre all those proceedings, after the death of his then master, Sir John Coryton the younger, not without suspicion of being poisoned, he soon married one, with whom, common fame said he was too familiar before, so that he became possessed of her goods and chattels, and a great jointure.

Whereby he liveth in much pleasure and content in this place, honoured of some, loved of none, admiring himself for the bulk of his riches, and the arts and contrivances by which he got it ; some of which were altogether unlawful.

Witness his steward Mr. Elliot, being indited for a mint, and coining false money for his use, who, on notice thereof, forsook this land, and fled beyond the seas; though his other agent and confederate, Car alias Popjoye, indited for the same crime of high treason, committed at Saltash, was taken, tried, found guilty, and executed at Launceston, 1695.

At which time, the writer of these lines was one of the grand jury, for the body of this county, that found the bills; when William Williams, of Treworgye, in Probus, Esq. was sheriff, and John Wadden, Esq. foreman of that inquest.

In this parish [of St Mellion] is Pentyley, or Pentillie, a house and church built and so named by Mr James Tillie, afterwards knighted, and married the widow of Sir John Coryton.

Since the writing of the above premises, about the year 1712, Sir James Tillie died, and as I am informed, by his last will and testament, obliged his adopted heir, one Woolley his sister's son, not only to assume his name (having no legitimate issue) but that he should not inter his body after death in the earth, but fasten it in the chair where he died with iron, his hat, wig, rings, gloves, and best apparel on, shoes and stockings, and surround the same with an oak chest, box, or coffin which his books and papers should be laid, with pen and ink also ; and build for reception thereof, in a certain field of his lands, a walled vault or grot, to be arched with moonstones; in which repository it should be laid without Christian burial ; for that as he said but a hour before he died, in two years he would be at Pentillie again ; over this vault his heir likewise was obliged to build a fine chamber, and set up therein the picture of him, his lady, and adopted heir for ever ; and at the end of this vault and chamber to erect a spire or lofty monument of stone, from thence for spectators to overlook the contiguous country, Plymouth Sound and Harbour; all which as I am told is accordingly performed by his heir, whose successors are obliged to repair the same for ever out of his lands and rents, under penalty of losing both.

However, I hear lately, notwithstanding this his promise of returning in two years space to Pentilly, that Sir James's body is eaten out with worms, and his bones or skeleton fallen down to the ground from the chair wherein it was seated, about four years after it was set up; his wig, books, wearing apparel, also rotten in the box or chair where it was first laid.

Later Writers

This early 18th century passage was the source for most references to Sir James Tillie. It was used in nearly all works on the history of Cornwall and accepted without further research. Robert Clutterbuck[2], for instance, repeated the story, although adding that Tillie was buried in a vault below the tower.

One example of how the story grew is the passage quoted by Richard Gough, an antiquary and publisher (1735-1809), who in his manuscript *'Tour of Cornwall in 1765'*, held in the Bodleian library, included a letter from the Revd. Benjamin Forster of 1775. This, in writing of the caves of the south west near Landsend at Whitsand Bay, reported that: *'In the rocks hereabouts the body of Sir John Tilly was inclos'd by his own order, drest in his cloaths, seated in a chair, his face to the door of a cell hewn in the rock, the key put under the door. He died above fifty years ago'.*[3]

Gough repeated this story in his version of Camden's Britannia 1789.

Others who repeated the story of the Sir James Tillie's evil life and eccentric death included: Gilpin[4] in *'Observations on the West Parts of England* 1798, and the Reverend Richard Polwhele[5], who in his History of 1816, includes the story of Sir James Tillie. Although disagreeing with the suggestions of Mr Gough, Polwhele then repeated the story as told by Hals.

'Sir James Tillie of Pentillie Castle, who died in 1712 was an eccentric person who directed by his will that his body should be deposed in a chair draped in his clothes and sitting in the lower apartment of a small building erected for the purpose on an eminence overlooking the Tamar which he called Mount Ararat. His strange will was not punctually complied with, for he was buried in the usual way, but an effigy of him in marble was placed in the apartment'.

Fortescue Hitchins[6] was another who repeated Hals' story, together with some additions such as that Sir James' heirs should maintain the vault in repair under the threat of losing the inheritance. Fortescue Hitchins also quoted passages of moral fervour by the rector of Ruanlanihorne, the Revd. John Whitaker, 1735-1808, who was an early local historian with a number of publications to his credit and had plans for a parochial history of Cornwall. He was famous for his strong and sometimes unusual views on history, government and religion. Whitaker added a condemnation of Tillie as non-Christian:

'This ...Tilley, of Pentilley, was one of those persons whom we frequently see rising up in life: men born in a low situation, from their earliest years looking up to grandeur with a foolish feeling of admiration, and as they grow in manhood, aspiring to procure, what they have so long envied. Then, unawed by any dread of God, for want of religion, and exerting the powers of intellect that God has given them for better purposes, they become men of business, clever, dexterous, cunning, and knavish; practising every enormity, that is safe from the sword of the law, and wading successfully through guilt into wealth. Such seems James Tilley to have been! He had thus lived, until he feared to die. His fear at last operated so powerfully, as to stupify his understanding, and extinguish his common sense. He felt he must die, but he persuaded himself he should soon revive.'

Like many a good story, it continued to be told and indeed grow.

Another writer[7] wrote, adverting to these circumstances: *"Mr. Tilly was a man of wit, and had by rote, all the ribaldry and common-place jests against religion and scripture, which are well suited to display pertness and folly, and to unsettle a giddy mind. In general, the witty atheist is satisfied with entertaining his contemporaries; but Mr. Tilly wished to have his sprightliness known to posterity. With this view, in ridicule of the resurrection, be obliged his executors to place his dead body, in his usual garb, and in his elbow chair, upon the top of a hill, and to arrange on a table before him, bottles, glasses, pipes, and tobacco. In this situation he ordered himself to be immured in a tower of such dimensions as be prescribed, where he proposed, he said, patiently to await the event. All this was done; and the tower, still enclosing its tenant, remains as a monument of his impiety and profaneness.'*

This popular view is summarised in an exceptionally lengthy tour guide written as a poem of five cantos by George Woodley, published in 1819. This described the Pentillie Tower as:

Nigh where St Mellon's unassuming fame
Casts a faint shadow o'er the wat'ry plain
Pentillie's noble pile, in gothic guise,
Starts from th'embracing groves that charm the eyes
With rich variety of light and shade,
As struggling rays-bright gleaming through the glade,
Vainly essay to pierce th'impervious wood,
Whose leafy arms have long the storm withstood.
Behind, yet ah! Too prominent to view,
In evil eminence, if Fame say true,
Rais'd on a lofty and romantic mound.
Discern'd afar amidst the op'ning ground,
The unbeliever's tow'r offends the eye,
And shuddering nature chills while passing by.
Why thus it rose, why stands the impious swell,
Th'indignant, blushing Muse declines to tell.

The poem has much on the beauties of nature. Indeed it is

the sort of poetry which suggests that the poet was paid by the line. However, I particularly like the reference to 'the unbeliever's tower' which 'offends the eye' and which 'shuddering nature chills, while passing by', when 'the indignant blushing muse' is too embarrassed to tell why this impious tower was raised. Following first publication, a lengthy note was added on the story of the infidel Sir James Tillie.[8]

In the 'Devonshire and Cornwall Illustrated' of 1832, the story of Sir James was that: *His burial-place is distinguished by a small tower, erected on a conspicuous eminence at a short distance from the mansion, northwards; and which hill, according to Lysons, he used to call Mount Ararat. Gilpin, in his "Observations on the Western Counties," characterises Tillie as "a celebrated atheist of the last age;" and states, that, "in ridicule of the Resurrection, he obliged his executors to place his dead body, in his usual garb, and in his elbow-chair, upon the top of a hill, and to arrange on a table before him, bottles, glasses, pipes, and tobacco; and, in this situation, ordered himself to be immured in a tower of such dimensions as he prescribed, where he proposed, he said, patiently to wait the event.—All this was done, and the tower, still enclosing its tenant, remains as a monument of his impiety and profaneness. The country people shudder as they go near it:—*

"Religio pavidos terrebat agrestes
Dira loci ;—sylvam, saxumque tremebant."

Gilbert and Drewe, in their recent "History of Cornwall," say, "Nothing can be more false than this account of the body being placed in a chair, with a table laid out before it, with bottles, glasses," &c.; and that, "on the contrary, the body was placed in a coffin, and deposited in a vault." Hals, however, who was a contemporary with Tillie, has stated circumstances which partly correspond with the statement of Gilpin; and, in conclusion, says, "I hear lately, notwithstanding his promise of returning in two years' space to Pentyley, that Sir James's body is eaten with worms, and his bones, or skeleton, fallen down to the ground from the chair wherein it was seated, about four years after it was set up."

Gilbert[9] had not only queried the story, but having established that Tillie was in fact in a vault suggested that *far from being Atheistial [his arrangements] breathe throughout a disposition fraught with the utmost submission to the will of divine providence and a perfect confidence in the mercies of the creator').*

Although some antiquarians had therefore queried the truth of Hals' account, his version continued to be told and believed. It set the tone for reports on the life of Tillie right through to modern times.

The 20th Century

S Baring Gould, a popular and respected author of the time, added fuel to the notoriety of Sir James Tillie, when his story was included in *'Cornish Characters and Strange Events'*, published in 1908. Baring Gould wrote well of Tillie's life, but based his 'facts' on Hals' account and queried little.

A well written example of the story is that retold in a delightful book of travels written by Charles G Harper[10], published in 1910. Charles Harper writes well of the walk to Pentillie, of the grounds there and of *'Mount Ararat, a weird 'folly' or monument, rather famous in its way, in which was buried, under peculiar conditions, the body of a former owner of Pentillie, who died in 1713. …..It is well worth seeing…'* Charles Harper was also told by the gardener at Pentillie that if visiting the tower containing a *'forbidding statue of Sir James Tillie'*

"An' if ye look through a peephole in the wall,
ye can see th' owd twoad quite plainly."

Charles Harper summarised Hal's story without precise allegation and without further research. His essay included:

'How all these things came to pass does not exactly appear…. Wild and fantastic legends fill up the mysterious lack of facts here and there in Tillie's life. ….. The brick tower of " Mount Ararat," now open to the sky and plentifully overgrown with ivy, is approached by moss-grown stone steps, A lobby at the summit of them ends in a blank wall with a kind of peep-hole into the space within, not at all easy to get at. Any stranger peering through, and not knowing what to expect, would be considerably startled by what he saw; for directly facing the observer is the life-size effigy of a ferociously ugly, undersized man, with scowling countenance and great protruding paunch, seated in a chair and wearing the costume of the

DO MYSTERIOUS REMAINS BELONG TO CORNWALL'S 'RICHARD III'?

Sir James Tillie mystery solved ?

Human remains discovered at Pentillie Castle

Pentillie Castle: Body found in knight's grave hunt

Is Sir James Tillie's body buried in his mausoleum?

The aristocrat who planned for his own resurrection: Mausoleum excavation uncovers body of stately home owner buried 300 years ago in his best clothes (and brought wine every day by servants). Excavation of a mausoleum in grounds of Pentillie Castle in Cornwall uncovered body of Sir James Tillie who built home in 1698, died in 1713. He asked to be dressed, bound to chair and placed with wine and books, but mystery has surrounded his final resting place for three centuries.

MISSING CORNISH LORD FOUND IN HIS OWN GRAVE

Sir James Tillie, whose dying wish was that his corpse be brought food and wine daily, found buried in vaulted chamber

The Mystery of Sir James Tillie's Missing Corpse

Sir James Tillie was, by all accounts, a slightly strange chap. An eccentric Cornish landowner, he had a rather unique burial after his death, and to this day the location of his final resting place is a myth. Grave robbers need not fear, however; a new restoration of his mausoleum looks set to reveal the location of Britain's most eccentric and elusive corpse.

Born to fairly humble surroundings in Gloucestershire in 1645, James Tillie rose through the ranks of the Newton Ferrers estate run by the Coryton family, ending up as the manager of the estate while John Coryton played at being a politician in Westminster. (See, even in those days MPs had two homes.) When Sir John suddenly died at the tender age of 58, his faithful servant James did what any ambitious commoner did in those days – married the grieving widow – and became owner of the Newton Ferrers estate. Wasting no time in spending his new-found riches, Sir James commissioned the building of Pentillie Castle (because you can't be a true nobleman without a castle to call your own), and lived happily ever after. An Englishman's home is, literally, his castle. His eccentricity shined through in his will, however. Rather than being buried like most respectful, God-fearing folk of the time, Sir James just couldn't let go of his estate. His will stated that he should be "dressed in his best clothes, hat and pipe; bound to a stout chair, surrounded by his books and wine, and then placed at the top of Mount Ararat, a hill overlooking his estate, to await resurrection". His loyal servants dutifully did as instructed for the next two years, bringing food to the slowly-decomposing corpse, until someone saw sense/they got bored, and the body was buried. Problem is, no one knows where the besuited corpse was moved to, and to this day the location of his final resting place is a mystery.

A selection of Newspaper reports from 2013
summarise Sir James Tillie's modern reputation.

early eighteenth century. The statue is of a light sandstone, capable of high finish in sculpture; and every detail is rendered with great care and minuteness, so that, in spite of the damp, and of the ferns and moss that grow so plentifully about its feet, the statue has a certain, and eerie, close resemblance to life. It is so ugly and repellent that the sculptor was evidently more concerned about the likeness than to flatter the original of it'.

Modern Times

The stories of Tillie's eccentricity have expanded over the years and now usually include the suggestion that he was buried in his best clothes with hat on his head, his hands on his knees and his body then secured with iron bands. He had an oak chest containing books and other personal effects placed with him and a final roast dinner cooked and placed on the table in front of him together with a glass and bottle of the finest port. He was to await resurrection and return in two years, some stories adding the suggestion that his servants were to provide him with meals during this period of two years.

His reputation as some sort of Mafia chief of piratical character has so expanded that, when speaking to older local residents of the area in 2009, I was told with assurance that the decorative garden folly towers of Pentillie were the remnants of raiding towers from which his servants would set out on raids of neighbours, retiring to the towers to defend themselves against reprisals. There is, so far as I can find, no truth in these tales, but they endorse the perception that he should not be remembered as worthy of respect or admiration.

Modern historians suggest that much of what Hals wrote should be ignored. It is said that Hals retold rumour and relied on ill substantiated stories and gossip rather than balanced research. However, there is no avoiding the fact that Hals wrote contemporaneously with some of these events, and that some of his facts are supported by later discoveries. The difficulty is therefore to separate out the useful from the gossip and rumour. It was the tales and rumours which grew and, for Sir James Tillie, had included varying reports of where his body

Sir James Tillie's statue could only be glimpsed through a small opening in the forgotten, distant tower and it ensured that Sir James became known only for the decaying stone of a big bellied rogue, *"th' owd twoad.."*

actually lay, from distant coast to differing churchs, removals by the family and so on.

Nevertheless, the story as told by Hals survived and lives today in the popular knowledge of the life and character of Sir James Tillie.

The newspaper reports, internet essays, even serious histories, all refer to Sir James as an eccentric man who had himself buried sitting up, supplied with food for two years, after an immoral and irreligious life. The stories usually repeat how he had stolen from his employer, and then poisoned him and taken his wife.

By the end of the 20th century, Sir James was renowned as a man who had not only stolen his way to wealth, but in his eccentric death had defied belief and the established religion. He was not only irreligious but evil. Today, the story of the eccentric bad man has spread to the internet, and the stories continue to grow, just as they did in the 19th century, perhaps because the story as told makes such a good story. The normally irreproachable History of Parliament, for instance, refers in an unsourced comment on Sir Christopher Vane, to '*his brother in law, Sir James Tillie, an attorney who later defrauded [Sir Christopher Vane]*'. This is an opinion which I can not verify anywhere else and which surviving records do not support.

So was Sir James a man who stole from his employer, and then stole his wife? Was he a despoiler of goods, was he not Christian, did he lie and steal his way to wealth, did he run false coin operations?

Quite a few details in Hals story are demonstrably false. But is the impression of an unpleasant rogue really true? I had long understood that the work of Hals was 'unreliable', and that even his contemporaries looked at his writings with some suspicion. Can we therefore accept that our impression of an unpleasant rogue with an eccentric irreligious death be really true?

We must start with what we know, and look at his life anew.

Endnotes

1 Lake's Parochial History of Cornwall by Joseph Polsue, Published 1867-1872: Pillaton Volume lV p.79, continued in Volume lll St Mellion pp 305-6:]

2 Clutterbuck, Robert: Journal of a Tour through the Western Counties of England during the Summer of 1796 pp 305-7, MS3 277 Cardiff University Library

3 Richard Gough's Tour of Cornwall in 1765, as edited by John Gough and O.J.Padel for the Journal of the Royal Institution of Cornwall, 2009, p.79. Richard Gough (1735-1809) was an antiquarian who travelled with the intention of producing an antiquarian guide to Britannia.

4 As referenced by Baring Gould

5 The Revd. Richard Polwhele History of Cornwall etc…Enlarged ed., Seven Vols, 1816 inc Supplement pp 44/45

6 Fortescue Hitchins, edited by Samuel Drew. The History of Cornwall (2 vols), Helston. 1824. Vol 2 pp 559-563

7 'Another Writer': This is an un-referenced quotation from Fortescue Hitchins, q.v.

8 *"Th'indignant, blushing Muse declines to tell." After much investigation—(resulting from some doubts lately thrown on the testimony of other writers who have noticed the object to which the above line alludes)—I am enabled to give the following as a correct statement of the facts connected with the tower at Pentillie: Sir James Tillie, the former proprietor of the estate, was an atheist; and, like other infidels, being unable to shake the truths of Christianity by reasoning, he had recourse to ridicule. As a perpetual jest against the doctrine of the Resurrection, he ordered by his will that after his decease his body should be placed, sitting in a chair, in his customary dress, in the lower apartment of a tower which he had erected for that purpose, on an eminence overlooking the Tamer, where he intended, he said, to await the event. He further directed that a table, with bottles, glasses, pipes, and tobacco, should be placed before him. Sir James died about the year 1712, and it was generally understood that his profane injunctions had been complied with: The tower, consequently, was regarded with horror by the inhabitants of the surrounding district; but on its being opened, some years since, it was reported that the body had been interred therein, in a coffin, in the usual manner, but that the effigy of the infidel, in white marble, remained in a room above.*

The above was ' Note 4, page 19, line 12 of *Cornubia, a Poem in five cantos descriptive of the most interesting scenery, natural and artificial in the County of Cornwall, interspersed with historical Anecdotes and Legendary tales* by George Woodley, London and Truro 1819

9 Gilbert, C.S. An Historical Survey of Cornwall, Ackerman, London. 2 vols. 1817 & 1820

10 Charles G Harper, The Cornish Coast, (South) and the Isles of Scilly London: Chapman & Hall, 1910

Chapter 2

The Life of Sir James Tillie

'It is certain that Mr Tillie was one of those persons, most justly esteemed, who advance themselves in the world without being beholden in any considerable degree to their ancestors'. (Davies Gilbert 1838)

Sir James Tillie has long been seen as a man who rose from nothing to become a man of wealth and status, knighted by the king, builder of a great house, and a man who married twice, but had no children. Davies Gilbert suggested that James Tillie had done this without any help from a rich family, and it is true that he rose from being a clerk to someone of considerable wealth, and that he did this through his own efforts.

However it is not true to say that he was from nowhere or had no family. When he was knighted, he wished to tell those in the Parish where he had grown up, how well he had done, and at the same time suggest that he came from a family of gentility.

Winfield or Wingfield is a small parish west of Trowbridge, Wiltshire, only two miles south of Bradford, and it was there that in 1687 James Tillie had a plaque affixed just by the south door of the parish church.

Erected Anno Dom: 1687 By Sr: Iames Tillie Kt:
To the Memory of his Ancestors who in this Parish lived vertuously & died Piously and lie interred under the Two Opposite Tombstones viz Under the Nearest Stone John Tillie the elder and Mary his Wife and Severall of their Children And under the remotest Stone John Tillie the Younger and Susanna his wife and Severall of their Children.

Ce' que Mars et venus, Minerve ont de parfait,
Brave Jacques Tilli se voit dans ton portrait.
The young James Tillie, here referred to as Jacques Tilli,
in an undated engraving whose original was 'sculpsit' by FH van Houe.
Reproduced from 'Cornish Characters and Strange Events' by S Baring-Gould.

Family Origins and Connections

Sir James Tillie was born into a family of small farmers in Winfield, Wiltshire, who had, it seems many connections around Bristol. The name Tillie was common among tradesmen of 17th century Bristol. Modern directories show that the name Tilley is still found in Somerset. In Shropshire there is a village called Tilley, and it has been suggested that the name derives from a word for wood clearing, or a corruption of 'tilie', which was a word for a husbandman or farm labourer. The name was spelt in more than one way, but the spelling James Tillie favoured was with a double 'l' and 'ie' at the end of the word.

The Tillie family of Wiltshire may have been related to many in Bristol[1], but save for the connection of the name, their exact relationship is uncertain. Such connections could have included Sir John Tilley who bore arms around 1600 and was said to be a man of substance in Bristol. It was his coat of arms which James Tillie took for his family coat. Another John Tilley has an impressive 1658 Bristol monument recording his death. Sir Joseph Tillie, (1654-1708) MP for Exeter in 1695, may also have been a relation. However, Joseph may have been a person to avoid, since he was a chancer of dubious morality, a conspirator who took part in various plots, including the rebellion of the Duke of Monmouth, and spent time abroad before rehabilitation in the time of William and Mary.

Known family connections in Bristol included James Tillie's brother Jeremiah, who in 1673 was referred to as a 'cordwainer' but was by 1680 described as a merchant in Bristol, and was later involved with the West Indian Trade. Sir James Tillie includes as beneficiaries of his will some who lived in the West Indies. Thus Jeremiah Tillie's daughter, Susannah, had married a West Indian Trader called Elletson. Edmund Edlyn, of Jamaica, whose wife Ann may have been another daughter of Jeremiah, was another West Indian merchant who benefited under Sir James Tillie's will.

Other connections included the Gotley family, who were

John Tillie 1 = Mary
of Wingfield
d.1662?

Sir Henry Vane = Frances Wray
1613-1662

Christopher Vane,
Baron Barnard 1653-1723

John Tillie 2 =(1) Susannah =(2) Mistress Thomson Cox
or 'Tiley'   *d. 1658*
of Wingfield

Margaret (1) = **Sir James Tillie** =(2) Elizabeth (1) = Sir John Coryton
9th of 13? Children   *of Pentille*   *Daughter and Co- heir of*   *1648-1690*
c 1655-04.1682   *1647-1713*   *Sir Richard Chiverton*
Buried Shipbourne,   *1653(?)- 9 Sept 1717*
Kent   No children

Susannah
1655-8?
One of two?
daughters bap-
tised in 1658

Jeremiah Tillie
Bristol Merchant
Brother d by 1711

Christopher and Elizabeth
Batt received no Tillie
legacy. See text re disputes
over Chiverton trust.

Chris. = Elizabeth Batt
m.1692

Mary = Richard Gotley
1685-1737   *b.1680 m.1700/1*

William = Mary
Woolley   *Baptized 1658*
A Quaker   *Sister of*
     Sir James Tillie

Susannah = Richard Elletson
[Tillie]   *d. by 1713?*

Jeremiah Tillie Elletson

Elizabeth = Mayne

Chris. Batt

Albinia Tillie Gotley
Goddaughter of
Sir James Tillie

Elizabeth   John   Esther = James Woolley   William Woolley
     Changed name to
     James Tillie II
     1690-1746
     Called 'Jezzie' by Sir James Tillie

James Tillie III = Mary   Robert   Mary   William
1722-1772   *1728-1809*   *c1725-1742*   *Both died young*

John Coryton = Mary Jemima
1740-1803   *1750-1779*
of Crocadon   *Daughter &*
Heir of John Coryton   *Heiress of James Tillie*
1648-1690   *of Pentillie*

John Tillie Coryton = Elizabeth
1773-1843   *1784-1724*

Other relatives or 'kinsmen', of uncertain relationship to
Sir James, mentioned in legal documents or codicil, includ[...]
'Kinsman' John Bailward
'Kinsman' Henry Mitchell
'Cousin' Mary Love (daughter of Kinsman John Love and Cecilia Lov[...]
'Cousin' Albinia Jones
Edmund Edlyn, Island of Jamaica, esquire and wife Ann
     Was Ann another daughter of Jeremiah Tillie?
Stephen Tillie, Gentleman of Pillaton, witnesses many documents
     and is trustee but receives no direct legacy. *Was he a relative?*

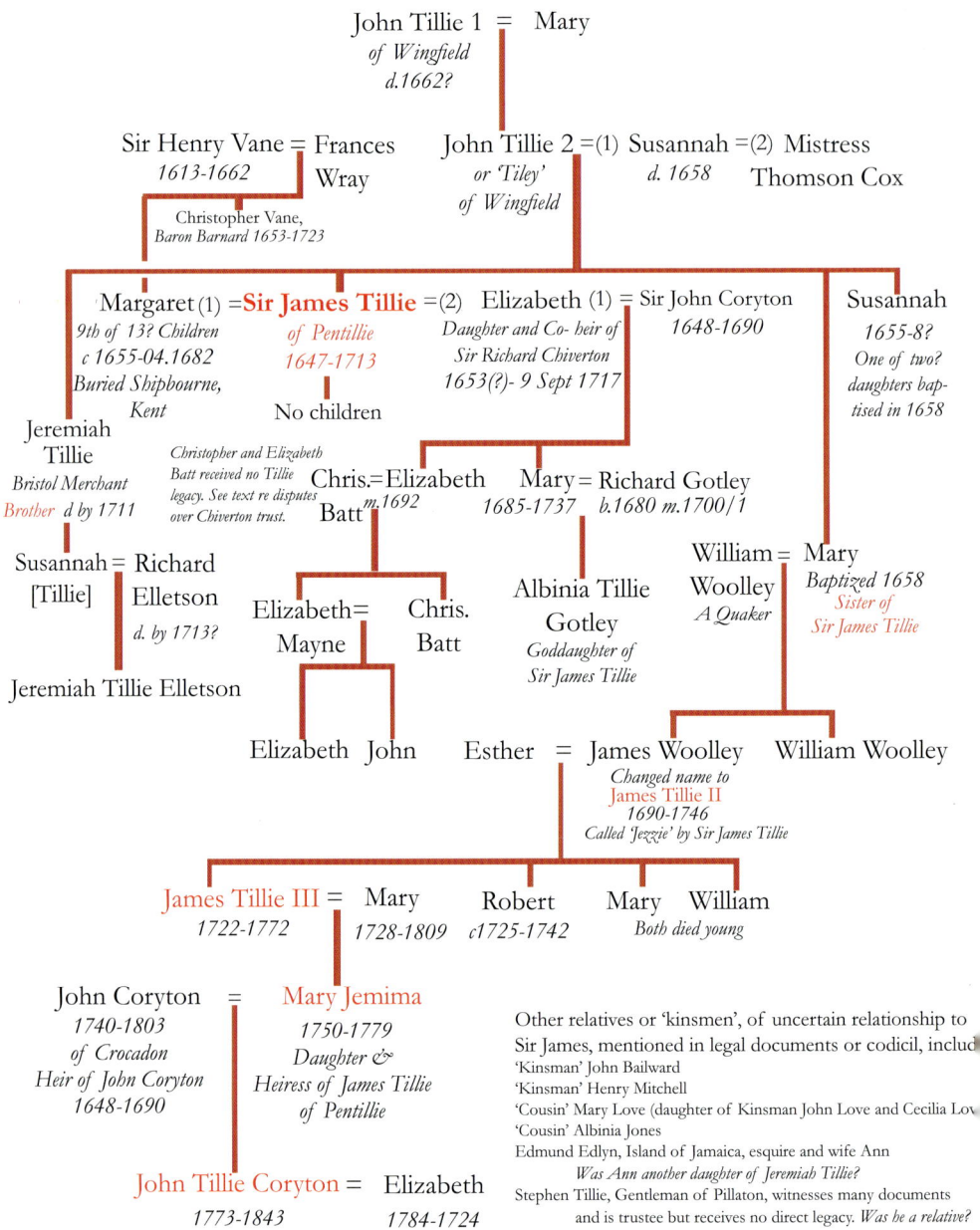

The Family of Sir James Tillie of Pentillie Castle
Only principal names and children are shown.

Quaker merchants of Bristol, to whom Sir James married his stepdaughter, and William Woolley, to whom Sir James Tillie's sister was married. William Woolley was from another family of Bristol merchants and also a Quaker. It was a member of the Woolley family who eventually inherited Sir James Tillie's estate, (although having to change his name from Woolley to Tillie to do so).

Hals had suggested that James Tilley had come from the St Keverne area of West Cornwall, but there is no record of him on the Lizard peninsula. There are, however, records of several families with the name Tillie in the East Cornwall area at the end of the 17th Century and there is also a Tillie street in Callington. Any connection to Bristol or to James Tillie is unknown. Even the connection of Sir James and one Stephen Tillie, who was a frequent witness to transactions of Sir James, remains an enigma.

Although it seems possible that the Tillie family had originated in or had relations in Bristol, John Tillie, the grandfather of Sir James Tillie, first comes to notice as a small holder or farmer in Winfield, Wiltshire, in the mid-17th century. Their status remains confused, since they appear to have been copyholders, but were also described as 'gentlemen'.

Early Life

We have no information at all on James Tillie's life before he went to London, where, as he wrote, he was 'Educated in the society of the Middle Temple'. As the son of a copyhold farmer related to tradesmen in Bristol, he must have had some schooling. Although there may have been a parish school run by the Curate, I could find no records of grammar schools, or indeed other schools existing at the time in Bradford or Trowbridge. It seems possible that before going away for school perhaps to Bristol, he learnt his letters at home. There is a record that Mary Tillie, thought to be James' grandmother, was witnessing, and signing documents, rather than making a mark, in the second half of the 17th century. He could not have started at the

The Tillies may have been related to David Tilly and Christopher Tylly who in 1632 lived in Wraxall and pledged sums towards the repair of St Paul's Cathedral, as shown in this page from the ledger.

The page for the Parish of Wraxall gives the names and pledges of those giving money as shown, at one page per parish for twenty pages, in the 'Account book of sums collected in the hundreds of Bedminster with Hartcliffe, and Portbury, county Somerset by Sir Ferdinando Gorges, Sir Robert Gorges, knts., Thomas Smith, Rice Davys and Richard Cole, esqs., Justices of the Peace for Somerset, towards the repair of St.Paul's Church, London'. Bristol Records Office document AC/36074/36214:

Temple unless he could read and write. With Quaker and merchant family connections we can assume that he could do so, and that James Tillie went to London to work at the Temple, perhaps when he was as young as 15 years old. However this, like many an apprenticeship, was expensive, and it could be that he started as a clerk, rather than student. Whichever it was, he would have needed good quality introductions and money to establish himself there, particularly at the respectable Middle Temple; it is likely that he had funds from home during much of that early training, and until he could earn money for himself. This was probably when he was about 20 years old, since he was writing estate schedules for Sir John Coryton when 22 years old.

Later in life, he is thought to have been a man who could get on with others and have been good company. He must have had some social skills and graces to retain clients, and join in their interests. Whether when he was a student at the Temple, he was the working nerd who did everyone's work, or whether he joined in the games, antics, gambling and drunkenness, is unknown, though the latter does not fit with what we know of him in later life.

Education at The Temple, London

An education at one of the Inns of Chancery was the first step towards becoming a barrister and such an education was not unlike attendance at one of the colleges of Oxford or Cambridge. A student joined one of the Inns of Chancery, where he would be taught legal basics. These Inns not only provided training but also lodgings and offices for members. Having joined an Inn, a student would then have to be 'read in', that is pass a series of interviews, before being 'admitted'. This signalled the end of training and allowed a lawyer to speak in court. Although there are now only four Inns of Court, there were at the end of the 17th century several such Inns, of which the Middle Temple was perhaps the most prestigious, with good connections, activities, entertainments and a particularly fine Elizabethan hall. Around such halls there were chambers, suites, residences and many regulations. According to the minutes for the 1670s there was much difficulty with drunken or gambling students, with students not paying their fees, not wearing gowns or not proceeding to be called. There were also endless disputes about who owned the lease to each set of rooms in the many buildings around the hall, the fees for rooms, the fees payable during vacation, or for eating in hall, for 'reading' and so on. Many students fell by the wayside and did not proceed to be called.

During the civil war and Protectorate the system for training lawyers had broken down and formal training had been replaced by a system of student registration or listing which allowed people to have their names listed and use time without presence as a qualification.

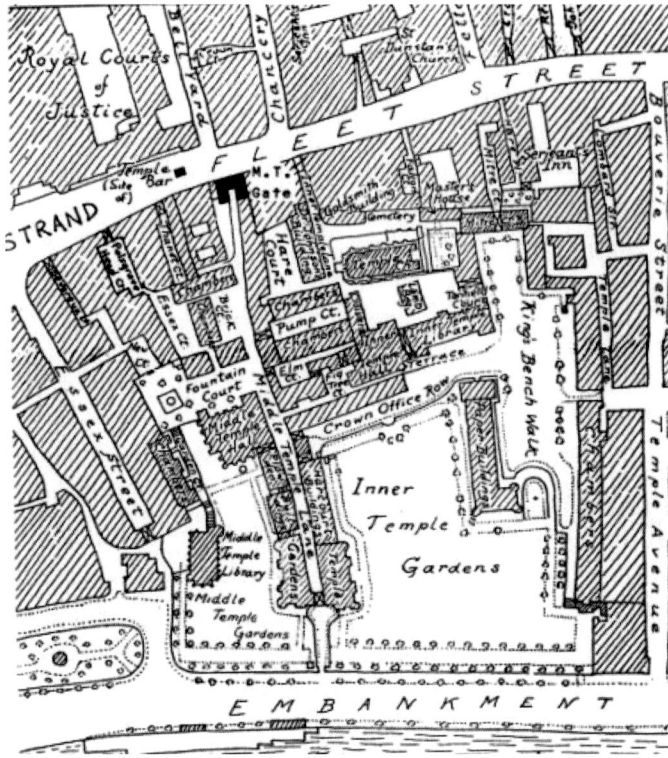

The Temple in a map of about 1900, after the new embankment had removed river access. Middle Temple gate, where James Tillie worked, is marked in black.

The years after the Restoration of 1660 brought improvement, but the number of students who did not attend or did not proceed to be called may have meant that those actually working at the Inns received good introductions to clients and a disproportionate amount of the work available. This recent tradition of disinterested students and the social nature of an Inn should have helped James Tillie to many introductions, which may in turn help explain the early rise of James Tillie.

I imagine that it was through the Temple that James Tillie was introduced to both the Coryton and Wray families and indeed to a network of friends, fellow lawyers, merchants and contacts from Bristol and the West Country. Although Christopher Wray was noted on one legal transaction as being of the Temple there is no record of him having been called to the Middle Temple. Sir John Coryton II does not appear on the records of the Middle Temple either although, as was his younger brother, it seems possible that he had been a student there, or at an another Inn, after he had left Exeter College Oxford. William Coryton was admitted to the Middle Temple on 20 March 1669 and called to the bar in May 1675, two years after James Tillie.

By 1669, the date of the earliest transaction which refers to him, James Tillie would have been 22 years old and it must be assumed that he would have started as a clerk some years before, perhaps around 1662, when he was 15 or so. He was admitted[2] to the Middle Temple in 1673 and had lodgings or offices over the Gate of the Middle Temple.

It was an achievement for James Tillie to be 'called'. Not only did it prove that you had passed the many readings before the benchers of the Inn, but it was not cheap to be one of the students at Middle Temple, of which there were 400 in the late 17th century. In addition to fees for lodging, food, living and 'reading', most students had to post a bond, or deposit, against behaviour and rent. Complaints about the fees for 'reading' resulted in their being set in 1678 to a maximum of 'only £300'. This was a very considerable sum, particularly when compared with average incomes at the end of the 17th century. According to calculations of the time these averaged £650 for a knight, £450 for an esquire and £280 for a gentleman. Clerks and legal staff only averaged £154 a year, and such clerks were relatively well paid[3].

Unless James Tillie had some support for the bond, and sufficient sums about him to pay his lodging, his food and Temple fees, he is unlikely to have been able to afford to be a student. Since a student would also have had to be competent in reading and writing I believe we can assume that Tillie had had some education and had sufficient financial support to study at the Middle Temple. He is unlikely to have started, as Hals had suggested, as a menial horse holder for Sir John Coryton.

James Tillie's Early Progress

There is no doubt that he must have been a man with much ambition and self-importance, since it seems unusual that a young lawyer should have an adulatory print published describing his own vertues. This early print shows him as a young man in fashionable dress, described in exceptionally flattering terms.

'Ce' que Mars et venus, Minerve ont de parfait,
Brave Jacques Tilli se voit dans ton portrait'

This extravagant inscription translates roughly as: 'That which the gods of war, love and wisdom consider or have, of perfection, the great Jacques Tilli sees [of] himself in your portrait'. There are few who could, unblushing, accept such flattery nowadays.

We do not have a date for this print, but it might have been done about the time of his marriage to Margaret Vane. The lines in French could suggest that he might have visited France, or had spent some time on the continent, as did others of his acquaintance when in their 'teens. It is possible to find hints of French influence in his designs for Pentillie Castle, but the use of French in this picture may be nothing but cultural boasting, and we shall probably never know anything of his early travels, although others from Bristol were sent to Paris, as was the young Penn when 18 years old. The printing of such a picture seems to be a relatively rare, ambitious and boastful action by the young James Tillie and also an act that would have required some funds to finance.

We have some idea of how James Tillie viewed his own social progression and status by the way in which he was described in documents[4]. These not only chart his advance as a professional lawyer but also as a person of means and standing. When first admitted to the Middle Temple he is recorded as being the son of a gentleman, which may have been pushing it a bit. In summary, he proceeds from a man with no recorded status to being described as 'of the Middle Temple', to then being first a 'gentleman' and then the higher ranked 'esquire', before using the description 'Sir James Tillie of Pentillie

Castle'. Although he once or twice describes himself as of Winfield, or Belle Cour in Wiltshire, these were always in relation to transactions in Winfield. In the 1670s he gave his address as in the Parish of St Mellion, Cornwall, which suggests that he was spending much time there in 1673-5, presumably working for Sir John Coryton as steward.

The Vane and Coryton Families.

Although the earliest records show connection with the Coryton family, he was also a friend and agent for Sir Christopher Vane. Sir Christopher's father had been executed in 1662 and when Sir Christopher came of age in 1674, there was much to do in restoring the family fortune which, despite the holdings in the north, were based in Kent. There we understand James Tillie was of some aid, presumably having met Christopher through the Temple. He certainly became a good enough friend to be considered an appropriate bride for Christopher's next nearest and younger sister, Margaret, who became James Tillie's first wife.

It would be good to fill in the background to such a first marriage, but we know too little to speculate. We have no picture of Margaret, no details of her birth life or death. We do not know why the marriage was arranged, where they lived, why or when she died, or why in Kent. Speculation has suggested small pox or childbirth as a cause of death, but as with the rest of her life, there is no evidence for anything, save that she is said to be buried in the Vane family church at Shipbourne in Kent.

The friendship with Christopher must have been solid for many years and also, for James, a source of fees, and, of course, with the marriage, a dowry of lands in the North of England which he did not sell until he was able to buy more land around Pentillie after 1700. The relationship broke down in disputes about the management of the northern estates, as described in a later chapter.

The earliest work of James Tillie of which we have record is the inventory or rental list prepared for Sir John Coryton in 1669. He

34

Sir James Tillie, shortly after he had been knighted in 1687
An engraving of a painting by Kneller

*The truely loyall Sir James Tillie Knight borne at Winfield, Educated in the Societie of ye Middle Temple
London and now Resident at his Castle of Pentillie in the Country of Cornwall. Jan.1686/7' and
'G.Kneller pinx. I.Beckett fec.'*
Original in Department Prints and Drawings, British Museum
Isaac Beckett; printmaker c.1653-1688 after Sir Godfrey Kneller, 1646-1723

later acted as the steward for Sir John, first baronet, and for his son, the second Sir John. He must have made himself useful since he is soon described as 'steward'; the fact that for some years he described himself as of St Mellion, in Cornwall, suggests he was spending time working there. He then progressed from being a steward and witness to a business man arranging mortgages, loans and signing documents on behalf of his employer. A steward could have had a fee, but more usually took a percentage of rents received. If that figure were the figure common today, then 10% might be reasonable and would accumulate a considerable sum to Tillie in a relatively short time, particularly if he was taking commissions on loans and new agreements.

He appears on Coryton documents from the 1670s, including the marriage settlement for Elizabeth Chiverton, when she married Sir John Coryton. By 1687, when he was made a knight, he seems to have ceased the drudgery of steward and rent collecting, and although he fell out with Sir John Coryton II, his brother William continued to use him from 1690-1694. He continued to behave honourably, so far as we can see, in handling the funds of his step daughters, confused as they were by William's tenancy of lands.

His relationship with the Coryton family is described in a later chapter. It is usually alleged that he had enriched himself at the expense of the Corytons, but there is no surviving evidence of such enrichment and the schedule of properties that he owned suggests that he didn't in fact take over any Coryton property without the specific approval of Sir John and Sir William Coryton.

A Knighthood for James Tillie

His work and marriage ensured that he quickly became a man of wealth. He was able, when only 35 years old, to buy a knighthood from James II. This was said to have cost him £10,000, although I have seen no evidence for the amount of the sum paid. £10,000 would have been an enormous sum, greater than the estate, for instance, that a rich Lord Mayor of London, Sir Richard Chiverton, left his daughter

Domina Elizabetha Coryton, Vxor Johannis Coryton, Baronett, Filia et Cohares Richardi Chiverton, Militis Aurati, Aldermani Patris & Pretoris Civitatis Londini. &c.

G. Kneller pinx. I. Beckett fec.

Elizabeth Lady Coryton, later Lady Tillie

Beckett, Isaac; printmaker; British artist, c.1653-1688 after Kneller, Godfrey, 1646-1723
Reproduction by permission of the Syndics of The Fitzwilliam Museum, Cambridge;
© The Fitzwilliam Museum, Cambridge

at this time. The cost of other honours helps set parameters for how much it may really have cost. First, Charles I had, fifty years earlier, sold a baronetcy, a higher honour than a knighthood, for 2000 marks, which is about £1,320. James Tillie's friend Christopher Vane bought a barony in 1698, a transaction referred to in a letter from Joanna Cutts "'tis not known yet who has got his money, but most think it went into the bargain with his father-in-law the Duke of Newcastle's Garter, which he gave six thousand guineas for to a friend of yours, which, with Vane's money, they say paid for [Twickenham] Park'[5]. This suggests that a garter, a greater honour, cost £6000.

James Tillie was not the only person to gain a knighthood having risen from a humble start. A list of a few names not only shows that gaining a knighthood was possible, but records the rise of a merchant and professional class[6].

Whether it was the king, a minister, placeman or intermediary who benefited from the fee, Sir James Tillie was delighted with the award. He had a portrait done by Kneller, and a print made of that portrait which noted:

Knighted at Westminster Hall Jan 4th 1686.
The Truly Loyall Knight Sir James Tillie borne at Winfield
Educated in the society of the Middle Temple and now resident at his castle of
Pentillie in the County of Cornwall   Jan 1686/7

He also arranged with the vicar of Winfield to have a plaque erected by the south door of the church, recording his achievement and origins, and also erected two splendid new tombs for his 'forebears' right by that entrance.

It seems that pride in his new achievement overcame him, because the coat of arms shown in the print became the reason for a rare action taken against him by the Court of Chivalry, who maintained that he was not entitled to the arms, nor to the the crest and supporters. The case is discussed further on, but the impression left is that Sir James Tillie had taken a step too far, assumed too much, and must have seriously upset establishment figures.

The two monograms in the two top corners of Sir James Tillie's dream design for Pentillie are thought to be those of himself and his wife, and intended to celebrate their 1692 marriage. We know from lettering in Tillie's tenant survey of 1669 that he enjoyed embellished capital letters and these monograms show not only the entwined initials of his name, but the same letters reversed. The JT at top is reasonably easy to see. The monogram below is, I think, EC for Elizabeth Chiverton (her maiden name), or Coryton. Suggestions are welcome. The colours have been added to emphasize initials.

The knighthood itself may also have created some difficulties when the reign of James II was succeeded by that of William, who removed many who had favoured or been favoured by James. The Stuart Court had relied heavily on patronage and making available court 'places' which carried income and support. The number of 'placemen' varied through the years and under the Stuarts had gone up and down. Such court offices were sold but not necessarily by the crown. The holding of an office was seen as a license to make money. In 1688 there were 864 'placemen' holding office at the court of James II; William had over 1000 such offices, but the holders were not the same men since half of the old holders associated with James were dispensed with.

The change in the Crown, the change in contacts and placemen, and the upset caused by the Court of Chivalry may have explained why he appears to have spent more and more time outside London from around 1690 onwards, although a letter of 1709 suggests that he still retained interests and business in London.

Marriage to Elizabeth Coryton, née Chiverton.

It looks as though Sir John Coryton II was in considerable financial difficulty for the last ten to fifteen years of his life. He may also have been ill and was certainly not on good terms with his wife. The relationship of the Corytons and Sir James Tillie is explained further in a later chapter, but it seems that during the time when, perhaps, Elizabeth remained in Cornwall, where she had her own estate, she had got friendly with Sir James. It was Sir James who was accused of helping her escape a husband who sounds as though he had become violent.

The gossip of the time was that they had been on 'familiar' terms before his death and it would be nice to say that following the death of Sir John, the romance between Elizabeth and Sir James was a true love story. However, all we know is that it was some two years later that they married, in 1692. In that marriage Sir James gained access to

There are two statues of Sir James Tillie: *Top* Sir James Tilley stands in full pride, circa 1700. Once placed in a niche over the front door, it stands, restored, in the west courtyard. *Lower:* The restored statue in the mausoleum shows a much older man sitting in his chair.

the income attributed to Elizabeth from those lands which (with the exception of some bought back by Sir William Coryton), were part of her original dowry. He also took over managing the land and monies intended for Elizabeth's two daughters. There is some evidence that their use had been abused by Sir John Coryton and some of the lands were certainly in the hands of Sir William Coryton, with others being the subject of mortgage to Sir James.

This second marriage could not have promised Sir James his much desired children and it is possible therefore that it was an arrangement of genuine affection.

One clue to that being so is in the artist's design prepared for the new house at Pentillie.

The Artist's Impression of Pentillie

Perhaps it was as part of his courtship, or to celebrate his marriage, that he arranged for a bird's eye view to be prepared showing the design and landscape for his new house at Pentillie. Such drawings usually had the coat of arms of the owner at the top. The one of Pentillie not only shows a house that was not then built but also has the initials of the owners in the top corners, with additional shells, what might be a moustached 'green man' below each cartouche, and with winged cupids above and winged putti to each side, representing non-secular passion.

Hours have been spent deciphering the initials. The clue seems to be that the lettering is balanced by a duplicate mirror image of the initials. The monogram on the left of the picture is therefore JT for James Tillie, with a second JT reversed; that on the right has I or L (for Liz?), C for Coryton or for her maiden name Chiverton, and is also duplicated in reverse. This monogram was for Elizabeth Coryton.

The detail in the picture has to have been dictated by Tillie, since the picture is a mixture of design and the realistic. The engraver shows the retention of the cow yard, a hay or straw stack and other service areas, all of which are recognised as important for the house.

The quarry by the road to the wharf, the wharves and dock buildings, even a lime kiln are shown. Figures include a shepherd, a packhorse being led down to the wharf, a dog, carriage and horses a lowered garden surrounded by walkways, balled decoration and little oval windows. It is a fascinating picture. The main access uses the original road in the valley which was extended to run round the hill and come up a ramp between the house and the river to a grand set of steps before a windowed lodge. The picture does not show any tower proposed for the strange rock stump on the adjoining hill, although some deer have been added, and a place of status, possibly Crocadon or the hamlet of St Mellion, is drawn in the distance.

Work on the Pentillie site had probably started in the 1680s but the design in this picture shows a concept, but a design which incorporated what had already been started. The building shown in the print was built between 1692 and 1707, and is discussed in a later chapter.

He was proud of Pentillie Castle. He added dates to the seven bells he put in the bell tower, all of which bells still survive today. He had a statue made for a niche over the west entrance. He arranged that Pentillie and his ownership would be marked on the map of Cornwall produced in 1699 by Joel Gascoyne which shows Pentillie Castle as in the ownership of Sir James 'Tilly' and which also marks the sites of Pentearr and Pentearr Cross.

He subscribed to a map by Blome of the entire county of Cornwall, where the only house illustrated was Pentillie[7]. This drawing was based on that of the bird's eye view print, but was different in several details, and omitted many of the images of people. Blome also produced a History of the Bible[8], whose maps were marked with those who had subscribed. Subscribers included Sir James Tillie, although I have been unable to find a copy of the subscribed print.

Personal Details for Sir James Tillie

A difficulty in writing of Sir James' life is that we have little to go on save for documents of property transactions or law suits. We know nothing, for instance, of his presumably convivial life while studying at the Middle Temple. We have, save for one page of a letter book, no surviving correspondence. We have almost no contemporaneous report, and although there was talk of him after his death, much of this has to be dismissed as scurrilous or without basis. The earliest surviving example of his handwriting is the schedule of estates and tenants prepared for Sir John Coryton in 1669, which shows only that he prepared careful lists and records and may have liked the odd flourish in his handwriting.

In Leeds University Library[9] there is an almanac for 1690, on the blank pages of which Sir James Tillie has kept household accounts. An almanac was a mixture of useful information, an annual calendar containing important dates and statistical information such as astronomical data, tide tables, notes on the phases of the moon and some planets and a horoscope for the month. We can read into this rare survival that he was interested in almanacs, kept good accounts and did not waste paper, but this is not a lot to go on.

We have two sides of a sheet of paper, illustrated on page 52, which survives from a letter book of Sir James for the 14 June 1709. Such letter books took the place of modern photocopies and were a file copy of both letters and transactions, although they were often in shortened form. They suggest a careful, recording nature. These surviving notes show a man supporting his family, advancing them money, and include report of a day spent in London, during which there were meetings with a number of clients.

We know that he was ambitious and pushy. We know that he had the latest of carriages, in a county where the roads were normally considered too bad, at his time, for wheeled traffic, since he left his wife in his will his coach, chariot and calash[10] and a set of 6 horses. Such wheeled vehicles were ambitious and powerful statements of wealth.

We also have two portraits of him, a possible third still at

Portraits of Sir James Tillie

Top Left: Print of Jacques Tillie as a young man.
Top Right: Print of Sir James Tillie from 1687 after Geoffrey Kneller.
Above Left: Detail from the statue that stands before Pentillie Castle.
Above Right: Detail from the statue that stands over the vault in the mausoleum.

A reference to another print may be a 'lost print' or one of those above. *See footnote 11.*
The two prints and two statues show that Sir Jame Tillie has some individuality
and it is clear that the four representations shown above are all of the same person.

Pentillie and a reference to one that has not been identified[11]. There are also two fine statues, one now restored and in the mausoleum and the other, made of lead, also now restored and standing on a plinth in the court before Pentillie. The statue before the house shows him in a pose fairly typical for the time and 'classical' in showing a man of importance. The dress detail is interesting, and includes what may have been a sash perhaps painted around his body. The coat, the buttons, his clothing the buckled shoes are all in great detail. He stands with his left hand on his hip and his right thrust forward holding a scroll[12].

The statue is life size, and although Tillie was said to be a short man, his height, as near as I can measure, was 5' 6" in his socks, perhaps even a bit more – but he has got a wig on. His shoes are low heeled, suggesting that contrary to rumour he was not concerned about his height. Since I had always understood he was a short man, this statue suggests he was the same height as everyone else. Indeed he was above the average of men's height for the time which was around 5'5".

Although he looks overweight in the last statue of him, he lived well and to a relatively good age. There is suspicion that at some time he had had either a bad fall or been hit over the head, because, although there has been no pathological examination of his remains, investigation of the burial vault showed that his skull had a bad head injury, which had healed.

We also have an example of the bottles into which he transferred his wine. Like many another landowner his wine was kept in his own named bottles since wine was usually bought in barrel for secondary bottling by the owner. In 1663, the politician and diarist Samuel Pepys recorded visiting a tavern to admire 'my New bottles, made with my Crest upon them, filled with wine'. The surviving example has as a seal the words 'Sir James Tillie of Pentillie' written around a castle tower, rather than the more normal coat of arms. Perhaps the bottle can be taken to attest to his conviviality.

The codicil to his will gives further glimpses of his character when it makes clear that he wished to avoid dispute about his will, and

'Portrait of a gentleman in wig and blue gown'.
This is said to be a portrait of Sir James Tillie and has been attributed to Sir Godrey Kneller (1646-1723). Despite some similarity to the four known figures of Sir James Tillie, it may not be him. There is some damage around the face, but it is speculation to suggest that this picture may be the one that once hung in the Mausoleum.

Since it is not certain that the portrait is of Sir James Tillie, the portrait at the top of this page has been reversed so that comparison can be made with a known likeness.

directed that just as he had been punctual in payments to others, so too should be his executors. He wished to avoid a display of 'expensive and useless mourning nor the pompous solemnity of an extravagant funeral' and asked that his coffin should be carried not by professional mourners but the men he had known. Frankly, I find the character that shines through the codicil to be rather attractive.

Today he is often referred to as 'Jimmy', but since James was often shortened to 'Jas.' that seems an unlikely term of affection. His nephew, named after him, was known as Jezzie, so perhaps we could refer to Sir James as 'Jez', which gives some humanity to a man of whom we still know little.

Surviving Legal Documents

In addition to the few personal surviving details above, we have a quantity of legal documents which are the primary source for the events of his life[13]. The details of those law cases that have survived are primarily those that were retained because they were important in later court cases of the Coryton family, particularly since they fought a case from 1740 to 1772 with the Hellyar family over the Coryton inheritance. We cannot therefore assume that these were the only cases in which Sir James Tillie was concerned. Most surviving documents refer to land transactions, purchases or disposals and leases and the odd case seeking recovery of money. A fair number of legal cases could be expected in any property management organisation and the very considerable number of surviving documents appear few when considered against the number of years and properties to which they refer[14].

The surviving legal documents, the most significant record of James Tillie's life, therefore present a skewed picture of his life and legal practice. There are, for instance, almost no documents relating to the transactions he must have undertaken for third parties, or those in which he had no property interest himself. A review of surviving transactions and legal documents suggests that Tillie was reasonable

A page (10" x 7") from Richard Blome's Map of Cornwall, from *Speed's Maps Epitomised*, 1715 edition. *Scale 12 miles to 21/32 inches.* The map not only has a picture of Pentillie Castle, but also marks Pentillie on the map. This print has Pentillie Castle in a slightly different version to that of an earlier large proposal print. Pentillie Castle does not figure in earlier maps by Blome. *Archive X438/64   This photograph taken from a print in private collection.*

and careful. I have found no evidence that he was outrageous in behaviour or morality. Indeed my impression is that, compared with the standards of the day, he was different, even 'proper' in his handling of money, loans and transactions, and that he did not work alone, but worked with a group of other lawyers, friends and merchants, some of whom were Quakers, but all of whom seem to have been of some standing.

In his own name, the legal actions often seem to have been what we would consider ordinary management, and also give an idea of how difficult it was to control property in an era of leases and sub-leases. In 1693, Tillie had bought property in Padreda, and the tithes and income from the River Lynher. However, despite it being allegedly 'free of encumbrance', he had to sue various tenants and the vendor for occupation and for the collusion between the two. The defence brings the people to life, but is implausible, and the case sounds a tedious mess. This was probably an expensive litigation to obtain what was already Tillie's. Interestingly, John Lanyon, former steward to Sir John Coryton, is a witness to the issuing of the complaint, showing he was still alive in 1693 (CY/7097).

We know that Sir James Tillie owned property in Devon, in Plymouth and that he had property in Kingston and on the Medway. We know little of how these were acquired or managed, and it remains the case that a knowledge of someone's life, if seen only through a selection of law cases, can only give a partial view of a life and activities.

Difficulties with Step Children

Elizabeth Coryton had two children who both benefited from the trust set up by Elizabeth's father for her and her children. However, the management of the estate appears to have gone through some difficulty as Sir John Coryton looked for money. Some land was held by Sir William Coryton, and Sir James Tillie had lent money to the Corytons on the security of some of the land. It was, I think, difficult to turn over the sums due the two girls when they got married. The

A surviving page for June 14th, 1709, from Sir James Tillie's letter book has copies of letters sent out. It is believed to be in his handwriting.

There are five copied letters on the two sides of the sheet, in an abbreviation of the originals sent. The letters include a note to his niece Susanna Elletson, with a bill of exchange for Richard Elletson, her husband for £25, with notes on 'Christianitie[and] humanity'; another letter which appears to be declining business; a letter to a shipper [in Plymouth?]to say that 'a large chest with two iron hoops, there being brittle ware in it' will arrive in Monsieur Andart's ship, and should be carried to his wife at Pentillie; Another letter, written to an anonymous 'ladyship', is of some length, retails gossip about people's health, mentions a number of visits and transactions in London, talks of the need to 'rage and storm' at one meeting, hopes to travel to the west and then 'to your ladyship in the north', and includes in the letter 'On saturday last I ended my severall businesses by a value of several thousands and hope shall tomorrow and now in a little finish my affairs in town..'

CRO CY/6850.

elder of the two, also called Elizabeth, married Chris Batt, who appears to have been wealthy in his own right. Chris Batt instituted a number of cases against the trustees, including both Sir William Coryton and Sir James Tillie, about the money and property his wife should have. These disputes seem to have outlasted the life of both James and his wife Elizabeth and continued after their death[15]. The disputes may have become quite bitter, since relations between the generations seem to have broken down, unless it was simply that Elizabeth Batt died young and connection was lost. It is notable that the Batts were not mentioned in Sir James' will.

Mary Coryton, the younger of the two daughters of Elizabeth Coryton, married Richard Gotley by license in London in March 1700/1. Richard Gotley, a Quaker, was from a community of Bristol based merchants, many of them Quakers. His father, also Richard, was a Quaker, and traded in the new world, having sailed to Virginia at least twice. It is probable that Mary met Richard Gotley, born in 1680, through introduction from another Quaker family, the Woolleys, since it was William Woolley who had married Sir James Tillie's sister and whose son inherited Pentillie.

Like her elder sister and her husband Christopher Batt, Richard and Mary Gotley sought to obtain more funds from the trust set up by Sir Richard Chiverton and there were further court cases between the Gotleys and Sir James Tillie and Dame Elizabeth. However, the disputes may have been influenced by the difficulties of Richard Gotley who with his partner Thomas Perrin filed for bankruptcy. Richard ended up in the Fleet prison in 1712, but then may have 'turned in' his partner so that he could avoid a prison sentence. The debts arose from difficulties in a tobacco trade which was glutted after 1690. Re-export or resale meant difficulties with excise duty and at the same time duty was tripled. Tobacco merchants were in trouble from 1702 and since they all guaranteed each other and their trade and businesses were related it seems that when one fell, all fell. Although Gotley was said to owe the crown the enormous sum of £31,000 in

'Broad Quay, Bristol'.
This 18th century painting is attributed to Philip Vandyke (c.1729-1808) and although not painted during the life of Sir James Tillie shows Bristol as a busy trade centre, considered the second place in the country, after London, at the end of the 17th century.
Reproduction: Society of Merchant Venturers, Bristol.

duty, he was released from prison. The Crown probably recovered funds and tobacco from his associates. Along the way he had sold some of his lands, and it seems that his brother in law, Christopher Batt, had bought them, perhaps to help out. Richard Gotley later set up as a brewer in Putney, Surrey and then moved to Gloucestershire.

There are a number of cases involving the two daughters of Elizabeth, but it appears that there were genuine difficulties in finding the cash the daughters were due when lands were on long lease, an arrangement which had been a requirement of the original Chiverton will[16]. My impression is that all went well, but that one of the couples, the Batts, may have become impatient.

James Tillie's Family.

For a man who had no children of his own, and who had long been thought of as without relations, Sir James turned out to have many relations and cousins. His will refers to cousins, which may be a term of affection rather than relationship. However, whether 'kinsman' or 'cousin', it is clear that there were many to whom he was related. Rather than list these relations it is easier to refer to the family tree on page 26. This sets out an extensive network and includes some who he claimed as relations but where the connection is unknown. First he had a brother, Jeremiah, who had daughters, the families of both of whom were remembered in his will. Jeremiah's son in law, Richard Elletson, was a Jamaica merchant and it is possible that Edmund Edlyn was another Jamaica son in law of Jeremiah. Although there was a case taken against Tillie about the estate of his deceased brother Jeremiah when he died in 1711, he remained on good terms with his extended family, as he did with his step-children.

It brings Sir James Tillie to life to find that he writes to ask after his nephew James Woolley, who was called 'Jezzie'. Sir James' great nephew Jeremiah Tillie Elletson and Richard and Mary Gotley's daughter Albinia Tillie Gotley, a goddaughter, were both named after Sir James.

A rare survival is this late 17th century wine bottle with the Pentillie mark. Into such a bottle was transferred a gentleman's wine from his barrels. It is interesting that he uses a design for Pentillie Castle rather than a coat of Arms or Crest. *Private Collection.*

Friendships

Not only did Sir James Tillie have an extensive family but he also had friends and business partners. Throughout the documents of forty years the same names keep cropping up. They tend to be a mix of solicitors and of merchants from Bristol and Bradford. Daniel Defoe, in 'A Tour Thro'... Great Britain' visited west Wiltshire in 1725, and described Bradford and Trowbridge as 'the two most eminent towns in that part of the vale for the making of fine Spanish cloths of the nicest mixtures'. Bradford was only two miles from Winfield and was the home of John Bailward who built a fine town house there. John Bailward appears in many documents both as witness and as intermediary to smooth property transactions. It was John Bailward who engaged in the purchase of some parts of Pentillie in July 1698 (CY671), for instance. He is called a 'kinsman' in James Tillie's will, is also appointed executor and trustee and gets a substantial legacy. This is a friendship that must have started when Tillie was a young man.

Another name that reoccurs often is that of Richard Asshe. Richard Asshe was another lawyer, based at the less prestigious Lyons Inn. He acted as the purchaser or 'querant' in transactions between Christopher Vane and Tillie in 1687, and was one of the three 'partners' against whom Christopher Vane took action over the accounts of the manors of Raby and Barnard Castle, Durham, in 1702.

A third name that often occurs is Henry Mitchell. He was described as a grocer, fruiterer or merchant of London, but must long have been a friend of Tillie's because he acts for him in the earliest transactions undertaken to buy land in Winfield. He continues to act in transactions with Tillie throughout his life and was the third defendant in the action instituted by Christopher Vane in 1702. He must have been in poor health towards the end of his life, because he came to live with the Tillies at Pentillie Castle, making a will[17] in February 1707 that left everything to Sir James Tillie, with nothing to anyone else. This looks as though it was a substantial estate since it included his 'Mannors Messuages Lands Tenements and hereditaments' and all

Pentillie Castle from the west still has Sir James' original Loggia arches, his statue in the courtyard, and the gardens descending to the river Tamar to the east.

his chattels. Sir James was also the executor of Henry Mitchell's will, which was witnessed by Stephen Tillie, Richard Lawrence and by 'the signe of Joane Tackaberrie'.

The transactions that survive suggest that Sir James not only had connections in London but friendships among the merchants of Bristol and Wiltshire, many of which were of long standing.

Many of these were Quakers[18], a sect who had grown during the century from a group of dissenting Anglicans. Despite their very considerable numbers, two restricting Acts of Parliament in the 1660s encouraged them to emigrate, thus cementing the close connection between Bristol, North America, and other lands overseas. Quaker merchants were well respected and renowned for straight dealing. They had a reputation for honourable trade; that James Tillie could count Quakers among his friends suggests that his business deals were also honourable.

It appears that James Tillie was part of a network of interlinked families, in which the same names turn up among interlinked activities. Examples of the connections include Mary Tillie who signed a Quaker marriage certificate in 1682 as a relative and James Tillie senior who did the same for Rachel Dowling and the senior Richard Gotley. The extensive Perrin family were also close since the Quaker Edward Perrin of Bristol was a witness to deeds of Coryton and Tillie in 1681.

Sir James Tillie had written his will in 1704, and added a codicil when he was near death in 1713. For the last twenty years of his life, he appears to have lived in some contentment with his wife Elizabeth, and enjoyed both the building and occupation of his houses at Pentillie Castle and Belle Cour. He had obtained a knighthood, lived in a 'castle' designed by himself and had a 'beautiful place' in the village of his childhood. I like to think too, that he was fortunate in having good friends, and by the sound of it, good staff, and was able to look back on his life with some satisfaction and pleasure.

58

Endnotes

1. Tillie connections in Bristol:

a. Miss M E Williams, formerly City Archivist, Bristol, recorded that there were many Tillies engaged in various trades in Bristol, between 1656 and 1685.

b. The Wall memorial in St Mary Redcliffe, Bristol, to John Tilley d.1658, is an aedicule with panelled pilasters and a ramped top to a shield and urn.

c. In 1632 a family called Tylly, who lived in Wraxall, Somerset, contributed to a collection for the repair of St Paul's cathedral in London. Bristol Records Office document AC/36074/36214

d. That his brother Jeremiah was a cordwainer of Bristol in 1673 was recorded by K H Rogers, formerly of the Wiltshire Record Office. A cordwainer was tradesman who made, rather than repaired, new shoes and provided or worked on new shoes usually of higher quality. Jeremiah was later referred to as a merchant as CY/1218, CY/1223, CY/1230.

2. The Archives of the Middle Temple provide records of all those called to the bar at the Middle Temple and these records area publicly available through their library archive. The entry for the admission of James Tillie on 4 November 1673 reads: 'JAMES TILLIE, son and heir of John T., of Winfield, Wilts., gent.'.

3. Gregory King Natural and Political Observations and Conclusions upon the State and Condition of England 1696 (1801) quoted in The English: A Social History Christopher Hibbert, Guild Publishing London 1987 pp 257-8

4. The earliest documents have no description of his job, title or status.

a. In 1673, Tillie was recorded as a 'steward and meniall servant of Sir John Coryton'. The last part of the description does not match well with the fact that James Tillie was called to the bar in November of that year 1673, which automatically gave him some status, and I suspect phrase 'meniall servant' was included as a matter of pragmatic politics since James Tillie was not only witnessing a deed but, as a listed 'life', gaining access to the granting of a lease of three lives, which could be of value.

b. When he was admitted to the Middle Temple in that same year, 1673, he was described as the son of John Tillie, Gentleman, of Winfield. In this description he was therefore claiming that his father had the 'rank' of gentleman.

c.   1673 was also the year when he commenced buying property in Wingfield, Wiltshire, although he was in this year noted as resident 'of Mellin', that is St Mellion in Cornwall, which is a parish north west of Pentillie. Another transaction in Wiltshire of 1675 also describes him 'of Ms Mellion, Gentleman' and does not describe him as of the Temple. Both these references suggest that in 1673 and 1675 he was spending time in Cornwall, presumably acting as steward for Sir John Coryton.

d.   By 1681, James Tillie was described as 'of the Middle Temple, gentleman'

e.   In 1683 he was still a 'gentleman', although his colleague and client, William Coryton was, in the same document noted as 'of the Middle Temple, Esquire', the latter being of higher rank than a gentleman.

f.   Then in 1684 and 1685 documents show that he had given himself promotion from being a mere gentleman to being 'of Middle Temple, esquire'.

g.   During 1687, he was either 'of the Middle Temple, London, Knight' or of Pentillie Castle, referred to in 1690 as just Pentillie.

h.   Although there was a transaction of 1695 when he was referred to as 'of Belle Cour, Knight', he was from the 1690s onwards usually described in documents and for legal transcations as 'Sir James Tillie, Knight'.

5.   Joanna Cutts to her brother Lord Cutts, about 20 July 1698. HMC Report on the Manuscripts of Mrs Frankland-Russell-Astley of Chequers Court, Bucks. London 1900, page 92-3

6.   'A number of merchants were knighted, some of them men who had risen to wealth and position from humble origins. Examples are John Langham, a Yeoman's son, who made a fortune from the Levant trade; Sir William Thompson, of obscure origin who became a wealthy London merchant; Sir Richard Crumpe, another Yeoman's son who became prominent in Bristol's administration and commerce; Richard Browne I of unknown parentage who became a London merchant and eventually Lord Mayor and Sir William Bucknall, also of obscure background, who made a fortune as a merchant and excise commissioner. Sir Robert Clayton, the son of a carpenter, became a highly successful land agent and financier, or usurer'. The House of Commons 1660-1690 Volume 1 by Basil Duke Henning 1983

7.   Richard Blome (1635-1705) published county maps which were based on those of John Speed, and were financed by including a subscribers arms or plate on one of the maps or illustrations. The illustrations and subscribers changed through different editions, particularly when a 'renewal fee' was declined. Pentillie is not on the 1673 edition and was thought to be from the 1693 edition which would agree

well with the assumed date for the engraving. The illustration may however have been in the edition 'Speed's Maps Epitomised 1715'. The map is 10" x 7" and at a scale of 12 miles to 1 and 21/32 inches (CRO X43864) It should be noted that the drawing of Pentillie is not identical to that ascribed to Jan Kip and Leonard Knyff, in that there are some differences; most obviously, many characters and divertissements have been removed.

8.   Richard Blome published a History of the Bible, London 1712 with lists of subscribers, maps and discourses on the Bible. Several plates were dedicated to members of the Royal Family, presumably raising the status for other subscribers.   It was to this volume that, in a reference of 1806 as note 1 above, it was recorded that Sir James Tillie had 'contributed a plate'.

9.   Notes and accounts for 1689-90, kept by Sir James Tillie, written on the blank leaves of *John Partridge, Merlinus liberatus: being an almanack for ... 1690 London: printed by R.R. for the Company of Stationers, 1690.* Leeds University Library, GB 206 MS 176.

Merlinus Liberatus. …. Wherein are all things fitting and useful for such a Work; as an Ephemeris of the Longitudes, Latitudes, and Southings, of the Planets, with their Configurations, and Aspects ; Lunations, Eclipses, Astrological, and other Observations; the rising and setting of the Sun and Moon; Tables of the Tides, Terms, and Holidays at Public Offices; Length and Break, Increase and Decrease, of Days; Judgments of the Eclipses and Seasons. Also a correct Table of the Elements of the Newtonian System; a brief Chronology of English Sovereigns; an Excellent Table for valuing Annuities on Lives, &c

10.   A coach had large wheels and a small body swung on straps. A chariot was a lighter, probably two wheeled, coach and a calash was a light low trap with a folding hood.

11.   The 'A Biographical History of England from the Revolution to the end of George I's reign….. with anecdotes and memoirs of a great number of persons' by The Rev. J Granger as edited by The Rev Mark Noble 1806. This book lists but does not illustrate published prints. On page 205, Volume I   there is reference to a print of Sir James Tillie, as 'with wig, laced neck cloth, a proof, scarce mezz.' I have been unable to trace the print to which this entry refers.

12.   The statue that now stands in the court before the west front of Pentillie, has been repaired and restored.

          The print of the house from 1770 shows that it then stood in a niche on the first floor of this west front, which explains the rough edge to the back of the statue's plinth. It was moved from that position when the house was altered from 1812, and had then stood in what appears from photographs to be a rather neglected corner of an internal courtyard near a service wing. When much of the Georgian house was demolished in the 1960s it was moved to its present position. The statue is lead. Repair of the statue has allowed Andrew Mitchell to provide details of how it was made. First it is possible that lead was chosen because Sir James had an interest in a lead mine in Durham, which he owned in partnership with his first wife's brother, Sir Christopher Vane, following a lease signed in 1687.

The sculpture was made using the 'lost wax' technique, although using a mixture of plaster and brick dust as filler. The figure was cast as one piece and during earlier repairs had been filled with concrete and scaffold poles. The repair was a considerable technical achievement of what was a poor quality hollow lead casting of variable thickness. The base was a piece of Carrera marble. It appears that the sculpture was always painted, first with an overcoating of brown, which was perhaps to give the impression that, like the statue of King Charles in London, it was of bronze. There are also traces of other paint, a flesh colour and a trace of red on the lips. *'Restoration of a life size lead sculpture of Sir James Tillie: 2008' : Andrew Mitchell*

13.   Difficulties in understanding legal transactions: Claims and law suits could be entered as part of some other underlying process. I confess that it has sometimes been difficult to follow the underlying intent in an often incomplete series of documents.

• One way of transferring property was to enter into a fictitious law suit for the property, which when undefended by the existing owner or 'deforciant' meant that the property was gained by the applicant (often known as 'the querent') and the 'compromise' agreed by the court. Such a law suit avoided some dues and requirements and restrictions on entail, trusts or dowries. In the days before land was registered, this method of transfer ensured that the transaction and ownership had been registered at a court. Such a transaction was called a 'fine of lands', a 'final concord', a term usually shortened to just 'a fine'.

• Another common method of land transfer was called 'lease and release'. Again this allowed a swift transfer without the difficulties of a conveyance. In a lease and release, the vendor entered into a lease for the property, signed by the purchaser, and then, either a year later, or in many cases, the next day, when the purchaser was therefore in possession, the vendor or lessor released the tenant from his obligations and released any interest the landlord might have in the property. This type of transaction, which had started in response to new laws to raise money by Henry VIII, was apparently the most common form of conveyance from the late 1600s onwards. Because any one case could be part of a number of transactions and also involve third parties who might hold property, represent trustees or be acting to agree terms, such transactions can appear complex.

14.   Notes of some legal cases undertaken by Sir James Tillie

1.   1691   Lease and release and redemption of a mortgage for property in St Kew Cornwall. 69/M/2/604

2.   1691   Sir James Tillie is leasing lands from the Rashleigh estate CY/1007

3.   1692   An action by which Sir James sought to recover money from defendants in Middlesex. C7/339/21

4.   1696   Sir James was the defendant in relation to some property in Kingston upon Thames C72224/34

5.   1697   Sir James took action against John Nance about some property in Warleggan, Cornwall.

         C 7/334/14 Actions against Nance continued after his death

6.   1697   Sir James was again the defendant in relation to some property in Kingston Upon Thames [C 7/135/65]

         A Second transaction in 1698 [C 5/609/12] suggests this was a purchase.

7.   1698   Yet another transaction in Kingston upon Thames C 7/336/24

8.   1698   Sir James Tillie was the plaintiff in an action about land in Altarnun Cornwall. C7/340/75

9.   1699   A transaction about money in Middlesex   C 7/90/41

10.   1700   With a further transaction in 1700   C 7/90/20

11.   1700   A further transaction about Kinston upon Thames C 7/332/40

12.   1700   A transaction in relation to money due in Surrey C 7/332/40, with a matching transaction reversing plaintiffs and defendants. C 7/141/93

13.   1701 A case between Sir James and his wife against John Cheeley and others Cornwall   C7/605/102

14.   1701   Two further cases with the same people about property in Kingston upon Thames C7/338/1

15.   The purchase of a Brewhouse?   C 7/605/102   C 7/334/19

16.   1703   A series of transactions where it appears that Sir James was buying two small holdings, some acres of land, and some 10 properties in Plymouth for £2100.00   CY/431-432

17.   1706   A case about the recovery of money due to JT   C 7/633/90

18.   1707   A case about ownership of the copyhold of the manor of Leigh Durant C 7/339/42

19.   1708   A case against Sir James ref a manor at Mutton Cornwall   C 7/292/75

20.   1709   Estate of Ceeley, Plymouth Devon Tilley v Edgcumbe C 7/339/45

21.   1711   A case against Sir James for money in Cornwall   C 7/661/45

22.   1711   Tilley and wife v Owen and Sarah Betley re property in Quethiock being Wife's dowry C5/633/127

23.   1711   against others ref Middlesex   C 7/657/35

24.   1712   against Sir Henry Furness for money in Cornwall C 7/659/50

25.   1712   For money against Sir James in Middlesex   C 7/361/6

26.   1712   for money against various ref estate of Edward Haistwell   C 7/343/80

15.   8 Mar 1739 Abstract of Christopher Batt's marriage settlement and will: '....To James Tillie £50 on trust to pay some to his sister-in-law Mary Gotley for her own separate use. To James Tillie £100 on trust to pay to Rachael Elizabeth and Albania Maria Gotley, daughter of sister-in-law Mary Gotley'…. 'Note at end `I have perused this Abstract, as also the abstract of ye Title to the other moiety of this estate purchased of Mr Gotley, And as it appears that the Lady Tillie, daughter of Sir Richard Chiverton died without issue male, I am of opinion that by the Recovery mentioned to be suffered last term Mr Batt hath enabled himself to make a good title to ye other moiety to a purchaser'. CY/1694

16.   A receipt for £3000 from Mary Coryton of Pillaton, 'gentlewoman to Sir Wm Coryton who following arrangemnts of 1692 came of age 11 April 1699 witnessed by Jas. Tillie. CY/1570 1 February 1700

17.   Will of Henry Mitchell of Pentillie Castle, 1707: Source: The National Archives Ref: PROB 11/506/257 Transcribed by Angela Wood.

18.   Richard Perrin A Perrin History 4th Edition July 2014 copyright Richard Perrin 2014. This summarises considerable research on the Quaker and merchant families of 17th century Bristol and Wiltshire and provides sources for information therein noted.

Lady Elizabeth and Sir Christopher Vane, First Baron Barnard
Reproduced with permission of Pentillie Castle Estate

These two portraits had long been identified as Lady Elizabeth and Sir James Tillie. However, the man does not look like Sir James Tillie, and the portrait of the lady, who would have to have been over 40 years old (her age at marriage to Sir James) to be referred to as Lady Elizabeth Tillie, is not similar to the only authentic portrait of Lady Elizabeth Tillie. She would not have been addressed as Lady Tillie until after marriage, which was well after the death of both artists concerned.

The portrait of the man is in fact identical to one at Raby Castle, which is of Sir Christopher Vane, Lord Barnard. It is illustrated on the next page. This pair of paintings should be more correctly identified as Lady Elizabeth and Sir Christopher Vane, First Baron Barnard

The portrait of the lady is attributed to Sir Peter Lely (1618- 1680) and that of the man to Willem Wessing (1656-1687). Wessing was one of Lely's principal pupils and took over the latter's work after his death in 1680, which explains the similarities in the paintings and cartouche.

Chapter 3
A Wife, Lead Mine and Dispute:
James Tillie and the Vanes

One of the friends that James Tillie made at the Middle
Temple was Christopher Vane, who had an estate in Kent and
Durham. Christopher Vane, born in 1653, was some six years younger
than James Tillie, and came from a well-known family who had been
among the greatest in the land. The friendship between James and
Christopher led to a first marriage for James Tillie, the obtaining of
land in Durham, including a lead mine, but ended in a dispute between
the two friends.

The Vane Family of Fairlawne, Kent and Raby Castle, Durham

The Vane family had risen high during the reigns of the early
Stuarts. Sir Henry Vane the Elder (1589-1655) became a trusted
advisor of King Charles I and held high office under him. Although
from a family of little importance, he managed to achieve great wealth
and power. He bought the Fairlawne Estate in Kent and Raby Castle
and lands in Durham.

His son, Sir Henry Vane (the Younger) (1613-1662), was one of
the great figures of mid-17thC England. He remains a romantic figure,
regarded as someone of principle. He wrote on religious and political
matters and believed in the overriding power of Parliament. When still
in his twenties, he travelled to New England, and helped establish the
puritan colony of Massachusetts, of which he was elected Governor
in 1636. It was during his time that Harvard College was founded,

The portrait of a man at Pentillie is identical to one at Raby Castle, identified as 'Lord Barnard', [Sir Christopher Vane, (1653-1723)]. He was brother to Sir James Tillie's first wife and Tillie's client, friend and business partner. It is therefore likely that the lady's portrait is another Lady Elizabeth, the wife of Sir Christopher. Lady Elizabeth Vane was daughter of Gilbert Holles, 3rd Earl of Clare. She married Vane in May 1676. The picture at Raby was painted by Mary Beale (1633-1699), a respected late 17th century court painter. She often used the same cartouche as at top, and worked with Sir Peter Lely, (d.1680), to whose studio the other two portraits are attributed. I suggest that all three portraits were painted between 1676 and 1680.

Reproduced with permission of Curator, Raby Castle.

ensuring that Vane remains a person of interest in the United States. When he returned to England, he became an MP and a loyal cavalier, knighted by Charles I in 1640, shortly before he married the wealthy heiress, Frances Wray. Although he had been a royalist, he espoused a free Parliament and, despite a pardon from Charles II, was, in 1662, executed on Tower Hill. Following Vane's skilful defence of the rights of Parliament, Charles II thought that Vane was 'too dangerous a man to let live'. "He died", recorded Pepys, "as much a martyr and saint as ever man did".

Sir Christopher Vane

His son, Christopher Vane (1653-1723), was only 9 years old when his father was executed. He is not thought to have studied at Oxford or Cambridge but rather to have been educated at the Temple in 1671. He inherited the family property in both Kent and Durham and lived mainly on the family estates in Kent, a county where he held many offices.

In 1676, at the age of 23, he married the wealthy Lady Elizabeth Holles, daughter and co heir of the 3rd Earl of Clare. The family house at Fairlawne, rebuilt for his grandfather, was altered and extended in 1680. He became an MP and seems to have been well regarded but not of primary political importance. A supporter of King James II, even being an executor of that King's will, he also supported the revolution that brought William III to power in England. Made a privy councillor in 1688, he bought a peerage in 1698, and became first Baron Barnard[1].

At his funeral in 1723, a lengthy sermon and obsequious panegyric[2] reported that he had long been in poor health. The sermon went on to suggest a man of easy going character and great generosity, so generous that, when there was a run on the Bank of England in 1711, he had sent the bank large sums to sustain public credit. 'He was a man of excellent understanding, but of retired habits, a great economist, a most exact manager of his private affairs…yet, on special occasions, he shewed instances of a very generous liberality, to a degree uncommon, and, in a word, as much concealed from the world as possible...His temper was generally even, free from the ruffles of passion, and excellent in itself...'

An understanding of Vane's character is necessary to assess his dispute with Sir James Tillie. The sermon at Vane's funeral suggests he was a saint, which could indicate that Sir James was properly vilified by Sir Christopher. However that funeral oration conflicts with what we know of Vane's life.

That oration made no mention of the famous disputes with his sons, both of which ended in court[3]. First, his son William Vane took Christopher to court in the House of Lords in 1703 after a dispute between Christopher's wife and his daughter-in-law. Christopher refused to pay an inheritance annuity to William, who was to be given the Fairlawne Estate, and when Christopher was living at Raby Castle.

Then, when his son Gilbert married Mary Randyll, Elizabeth quarrelled with her daughter-in-law, which forced Christopher and Elizabeth to move back to Fairlawne. This dispute rolled on until Christopher made it worse in 1712, when, in order to ruin the inheritance for his son, he hired the steward of Raby Castle to get 200 workmen to strip the castle so that it lost 'its lead, glass, doors, and furniture, even pulling up the floors, cutting down the timber, and destroying the deer, and 'of a sudden in three days' did damage to the tune of £3000, holding a sale at which the household goods, lead, etc., were sold for what they would fetch'[4]. In response, Gilbert sued Christopher for the damages to the castle.

These two family disputes do not suggest a man of equable or conciliatory behaviour.

Christopher's relationship and fondness for disputes may have been a factor in some clauses of his will[5], which first set out to ensure that there should be no dispute about his wishes, and further on referred to his daughter-in-law as a 'scandalous mother'.

It may also have been that Sir Christopher, despite the panegyric heard at his funeral, was a difficult man and poor businessman. When he was living in Durham it was said that he was a litigious and irritating neighbour or landlord, and that his neighbours regarded him as 'a sort of plague of Egypt upon us'[6].

Sir James Tillie's Marriage to Margaret Vane

Sir Christopher Vane's friendship with James Tillie presumably dates from the time when, aged 18 or so, Christopher had studied at the Temple, where James Tillie was working. Their relationship became so good that it was to Margaret Vane, a sister of Christopher that James Tillie was married.

Christopher had been one of 13, 14 or, in some sources, 16 children, not all of whom survived infancy. Margaret was born in 1655 and since Christopher had been born in 1653, she may have been his closest sibling. Although Tillie's wife is in some sources referred to as Mary, a deed of 1681[7] refers to her as Margaret. It is pure speculation to suppose that Christopher encouraged the marriage about the time of his own marriage in 1676, when Margaret would have been about 20, but we know little of Margaret save that she was still alive in 1681 and because she is referred to in a document as Tillie's wife in that year. It would appear that unless James and Margaret had fallen out, they spent time at the Vane estate in Kent, because that was where she died in or about 1682. She was buried at Shipbourne, the church of her brother's estate in Kent, possibly in the Vane family tomb. We have no knowledge of why she died.

This marriage was an achievement for James Tillie, the son of a copyholder from Wiltshire. His wife's dowry also brought him an estate in Durham. The friendship of James Tillie and Christopher Vane was therefore important, indeed central to James' advance up the social and financial ladder.

The few deeds and records of legal or property transactions[7] involving Christopher Vane and James Tillie suggest that the friendship, indeed trust, between the two was considerable.

First, James Tillie acted for Christopher Vane in some legal matters and there are references to him assisting on the Fairlawne, Kent, estate.

Second, the two seem also to have acted together in processing property transactions. In 1681, it looks as though Sir John Coryton was short of money and had raised funds, provided by James Tillie. In due course the properties were transferred to Christopher Vane who was acting on behalf of Tillie or as facilitator of the purchase by Tillie. There appears to have been a similar transaction in 1687 for a rather larger estate over three counties. Sir James had also bought Ley in St Ive from Sir Christopher Wrey, Vane's first cousin. Trustees, who included Sir William Coryton, had added this land to Elizabeth's Trust.

Third, Sir James was appointed Christopher Vane's agents for his estates in the north of England, and some cases show the administration of that and the purchase of additional lands.

Fourth, it was to Sir Christopher Vane that a letter for Sir James was sent when Sir John Coryton was making difficulties for his wife, Elizabeth, and her steward felt that both his and her life were threatened. John Lanyon, the steward, enclosed his letter to Sir James in an envelope addressed to Sir Christopher Vane. This suggests that Vane and Tillie must have been close friends.

Lead Mines, the North and Dispute: Was Sir James an unjust Steward?

Our understanding of the land in Margaret Vane's dowry, the land held by Sir James, and of transactions for Durham properties is not clear. We know that James Tillie acquired land both for Vane and for himself. Tillie had also set up a smelting mill and a consortium to work lead mines, an operating business more demanding than the simple leasing of ground.

Historians of the Vane family claim that Sir Christopher Vane, Lord Barnard, had been defrauded by his steward, Sir James Tillie. Vane accused Tillie of denying Vane his rights and of making inappropriate profits in an abuse of position. In 1702, Vane commenced proceedings, together with a number of other claimants, against Sir James.

It is not easy to sort out what was behind the quarrel and law suit. This complex case starts with Vane's claim that Sir James, who had acted for Vane for many years without being checked or reviewed by Vane, was asked to buy property for Vane. When this was done, it was alleged that Tillie had used Vane's own rental account to fund the purchases which were then put in Tillie's name. Tillie then proceeded to sell or transfer them to Vane, for a substantial profit.

Lead mines and their assumed profitability may have been an element in the claim, although for these operations, both freehold and mining rights had to be purchased, together with minority shares. There may also have been confusion between land that Sir James already owned through the dowry of his dead wife Margaret Vane, the investments that Sir James made in the lead mine operation and the rental properties of Sir Christopher Vane. It is thought Tillie made substantial sums from his interests in the lead mine which may also have provided the lead for the statue at Pentillie Castle although this theory is not supported by any evidence.

The claimants with Vane included others who were presumably tenants or mine venturers and the defendants were not only Sir James Tillie but also two of his London 'partners', Richard Ash and Henry Mitchell. This complex case involved many parties, and had an enormously lengthy defence.

Sir James' defence was that the income of the Barnard estate was far lower than that stated by Lord Barnard and that there were charges, jointures, (that is, mortgages in favour of surviving wives or relatives) and so on, which all drained the available income. Tillie also claimed that he was owed money by Lord Barnard, and that he had taken on the role of steward partly as a way of trying to realise these loans through making the estates more profitable and better managed. Tillie was Vane's agent and presumably entitled to an agent's fees, and I see that one batch of documents[7] transferring lands to Vane allows James Tillie an annuity of £100 per year a reasonable sum, but not a fortune.

Christopher Vane, Lord Barnard, issued a writ against Sir James Tillie in 1702 for the return of rents and other monies. The complaint and defence cover four large Vellum sheets of great and illegible length. The picture shows part of the defence.
National Archives C6/333/13 provided photographs of the complaint and defence.

The dispute between Vane and Tillie had ended by 1704, when Tillie notes in his will that he had exchanged his lands in Durham for lands more convenient to Cornwall, which had previously been held by Vane[8]. There is record of one further action in 1711, but it seems that after 1704 there was no connection or dispute between the two former friends. Sir James is not mentioned in Sir Christopher's will.

It is difficult to assess whether Sir James had, as Sir Christopher suggested, been fraudulent. Standards for business were different and commissions and a profit margin expected and accepted. Even today, property agents can take substantial percentages to manage property, a cost which it appears Sir Christopher was disputing. Much of the defence sounds reasonable and fits with what we know of both Tillie and Lord Barnard. I am not certain that the case came to court.

In the end, the matter seems to have been resolved by an exchange of property whereby Sir James gained land in the south west in exchange for land in Durham, suggesting that not all of Sir Christopher's claim can have had merit.

Endnotes

1.   In July 1698 Joanna, sister of Lord Cutts, reported that 'my cousin [Christopher] Vane, to the surprise of everybody, is a peer of England. It is not known yet who has got his money, but most think it went into the bargain with his father-in-law the Duke of Newcastle's Garter.' Joanna Cutts to her brother Lord Cutts, about 20 July 1698. HMC Report on the Manuscripts of Mrs Frankland-Russell-Astley of Chequers Court, Bucks. London 1900 page 92-3

2.   Funeral Sermon, preached at the church of Wrotham, in Kent, by the Rev. Thomas Curteis, as recorded in the journal *La Belle Assemblée or Bell's Court and Fashionable Magazine Addressed Particularly to the Ladies,* June 1823.

3.   Mounsey, Chris. Christopher Smart: Clown of God. London: Bucknell University Press, 2001.

4.   Handbook to the Bowes Museum, Barnard Castle (1893) by Owen Stanley Scott Reprinted Barnard Castle

5.   Extract from will of Christopher Vane, Lord Barnard:

"In the name of God Amen I Christopher Lord Barnard do declare this to be my last Will and Testament consisting of one sheet of paper made and written all with my hand and published in the presence of several credible witnesses whose names are underwritten in the presence of me the testator ....

"In primis I give unto my grandson Henry Vane the sum of five hundred pounds to be paid him when he shall arrive at the full age of one and twenty years and not sooner lest it should fall into the hands of his scandalous mother who has brought by her carriage so much misfortune upon my family and by which means has deprived her said son of a very considerable part of my personal estate I had otherwise designed him.

"Item - I give to my younger son William Vane the sum of five hundred pounds for mourning for himself, wife and children as also my library of books and manuscripts after the decease of his mother the Lady Barnard.

Item – I give unto each of my servants one year's wages over and above what shall be due to them for wages at the time of my death" Probate copy of Will of Sir Christopher Vane 11 November 1723   PROB 11/592/427

6   Undetailed reference.

7   Archive references give some idea of transactions and of the relationship between Christopher Vane and James Tillie:

1681   Complex of transactions where Christopher Vane (of Fairlawne) had bought property in Callington, Cornwall from Sir John Coryton, William Coryton and another, but acting in Trust for James Tillie and using money provided by James Tillie, so confirms that the property is that of James Tillie. CY/87. Note Transaction refers to James Tillie and Margaret his wife

1684   The Plaintiffs were Christopher Vane and James Tillie who sued a number of people in relation to property in Middleton in Teesdale. C 7/354/33

1687   A Concord or transfer of land in Cornwall Dorset and Wiltshire between Christopher Vane with Richard Asshe on the one hand and James Tillie on the other for the sum of £1080. CY/7

1687 (24 March) Christopher Vane, Raby Castle, Durham, esquire, and Sir James Tillie, Middle Temple, London, knight agree with eight merchants, gentlemen and yeoman for a lease of 21 years on the property being only Seven eighths of groves, mines rakes and veins of lead ore in Middleton in Teesdale, County Durham, the rent being 1/5 of ore raised and. CY/1195

1690 Sir James Tillie of Pentillie Castle Kt sold to Christopher Vane of Rabie Castle in return for Annuity of £100 for life, properties in Cockfield and Middleton in Teesdale. Sir James Tillie has poss. of front stead and toft in Rabie town, Durham, Cowley in Woolland in Cockfield, Durham. Manor in Woodland, Cockfield (with closes named). Smelting mill lately erected for lead ore on Cockfield Common or Fell, near Gaundles Beck with two acres of common adjg. Bradshaw close in Cockfield. Cutt Road close, Cockfield. All occ. Jn. Mackarist of Cockfield as tent. to Sir James. Close (6a.) in Cockfield, ruins of house to south. 1/6 of Teesdale common, 'the Great Common in Teasdale' in Middleton in Teesdale. Close called Bowlers in same parish bt. by James Tillie of Jn. Race & Anth. Voysey. CY/1196-1198

1698   Christopher Vane, plaintiff against Sir James Tillie kt. defendant about property in Middleton, Teesdale, Cockfield, Durham etc. C7/349/56

1702   A serious claim by Lord Barnard (and others) of Sir James Tillie, Richard Ash and Henry Mitchell, (note this was presumably Tillie's Wiltshire friend who queried the accounts over many years presented by Sir James Tillie for the accounts of the manors of Raby and Barnard Castle Durham, and accused him of using Vane's money to buy property, which he then sold to Vane.. C 6/333/13

1711 Vane v Tillie ref Property in Middleton Teedale Cockfield Durham etc   C 7/349/56

8   A recital in the Tillie will of 1704 notes that 'since [the marriage] settlement, land sold called Softlie and Hinton Hill and several other lands in the county of Durham of yearly value of £100'.

Chapter 4

Murder, Theft and a Stolen Wife? James Tillie and the Corytons

Under the picture of himself by Kneller that the newly knighted Sir James Tillie had had painted, were the words 'Educated in the Societie of ye Middle Temple London'. It was probably at the Temple that he found the contacts that provided him with business through his life. The historian Hals had described Tillie as a 'labourer, [from West Cornwall] who, as I am informed, was placed by him as a servant or horseman to Sir John Coryton, Bart., the elder; who afterwards by his assistance, learning the inferior practice of the law, under an attorney, became his steward'. This description of Tillie's career start must be wrong, not only because he came from Wiltshire, but also because reading and writing, abilities not normally available to labourers or junior servants, would have been so important an attribute for any work at the Temple.

However, it does suggest that his first client may well have been the Coryton family. It is possible that, just as Christopher Vane studied at the Temple, so may have Sir John Coryton's son, the second Sir John, who was a year younger than James Tillie. Friendships among young men studying at the Temple may have been the source of introduction to both the Vane and Coryton families.

The first documentary record we have of Tillie is the property inventory he made for Sir John Coryton in 1669, when Tillie was about 22 years old. The progression through documents shows him acting as a junior clerk, a witness and, in 1672, actually signing for Sir John. In

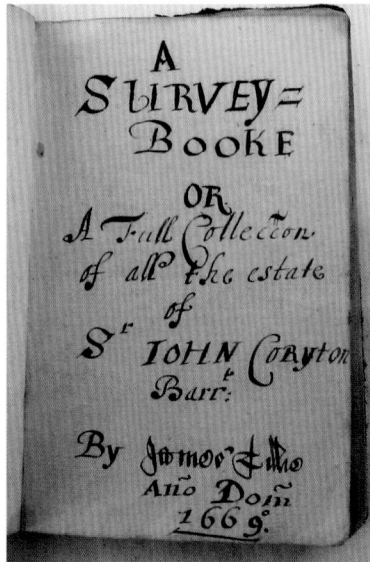

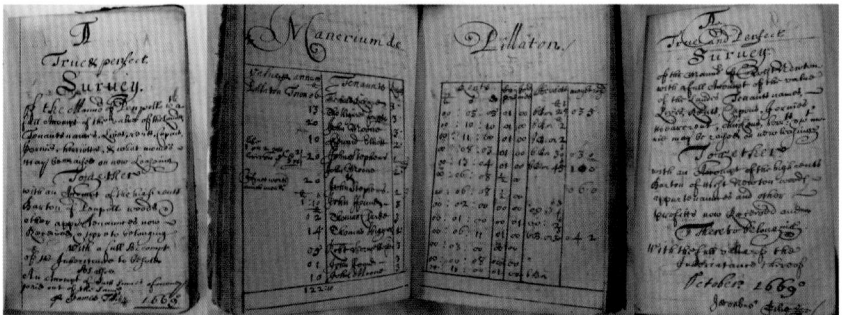

A survey of the properties of Sir John Coryton, first baronet.
In November 1669, James Tillie prepared an inventory of properties in the Estate of Sir John Coryton. This noted some 449 tenants divided into 22 areas or manors. The final abstract of worth, if an immediate sale had been required, was £45,763. 1s. 0d. The lists were detailed and it would seem that this must be the product of some years of management, since otherwise the information would not have been easily or readily available. The schedules are in a small book about 6" x 4" and cover many pages, including calculations of different forms of rent and the value of the estate at a distress sale. It appears to be in James Tillie's handwriting as a young man of 22 years. Later in the book are notes in a different hand, possibly Sir John's, recording some land transactions and notes on farming, and even a recipe for a pottage soup. *Cornwall Record Office CY 6549*

1673 he placed himself as one of the 'lives' (or possible beneficiaries) in a lease, and was called 'steward and meniall servant of the said John Coryton', also witnessing the same document. Although Hals continued in his essay to refer to Tillie as someone who had started out as 'but a groom or horseman to Sir John Coryton' and although the phrase 'menial servant' suggests that James Tillie was at this time a very lowly servant indeed, the conjunction with the title Steward suggests a different sort of status.

In any event, James Tillie was admitted to the Middle Temple in 1673, a sign of recognition and achievement and a date from which he was able to work as an independent lawyer and appear in court. His career progressed steadily and included considerable work for the Coryton family. Having worked for the first Sir John Coryton, he went on to represent each of his two sons, at the same time managing to acquire, negotiate, and deal his way to owning land on his own account.

Many of the property transactions in which he was involved have survived because they were retained in the Coryton family archive. These documents are held in the Cornwall Record Office, from whose records a schedule of some cases relevant to Sir James Tillie and the Corytons has been added as endnote 1, and that note should be referred to for other legal references in this chapter.

Sir John Coryton, the First and Second Baronets

Sir John Coryton, 1st Bt (1621-1680) had been a royalist Colonel who, after the Restoration, was appointed a 'Gentleman of the Privy Chamber' and then made baronet in 1662. Although the family's origins had been in Coryton, Devon, they were now based at West Newton Ferrers in East Cornwall. When he inherited in 1651, the estate was of considerable size; his grandfather had inherited some 9000 acres, mostly in Cornwall, and it had then grown over the years.

However, it would seem that although Sir John's estates were extensive, he remained short of funds. He married twice, and after his first wife's death, married a widow, by license, only three months

Sir John Coryton: This Portrait is said to be of
Sir John Coryton (1648-1690).
Pentillie Castle

before his own death. He was four times a Member of Parliament and played a part in the politics not just of Cornwall, but of the country. In 1677, Shaftesbury, in a comment on his character and politics marked him as 'doubly vile'. Coryton was granted an Excise pension of £400 per year in 1677 but, as was probably in accord with the morality of the time, was accused by contemporaries of cheating the Prize office[2].

The first record we have of James Tillie in connection with the Corytons is a little book, about 6" x 4", prepared for Sir John Coryton I and which recorded the extent of Sir John's estate and rents in 1669. This document is held in the Cornwall Record Office, from whose records a schedule of some cases relevant to Sir James Tillie and the Corytons has been added an endnote[1].

The first Sir John was succeeded by his heir, the second Sir John Coryton (1648-1690). He had studied at Exeter College, Oxford in 1666 and may then, like his brother William, have spent time at the Temple. When he inherited he described himself as 'of Newton Ferrers' rather than using his father's title 'of Coryton and Newton Ferrers', which suggests that lands in Devon were now of less importance. In February 1672, this second Sir John married well, since his wife, Elizabeth, was the daughter and co-heir of the wealthy Cornish landowner and former London Mayor, Sir Richard Chiverton. She brought with her a very considerable dowry of lands in Cornwall and elsewhere which, although hers, were tied up in trusts.

Sir John Coryton II held a number of offices in Cornwall, including that of Sheriff, and was also a Member of Parliament four times. He 'owned' the seat of Callington and although nominated for that seat in 1685 never took the seat, probably because of ill health.

This may be relevant to the troubles recorded in his family over the next five years, and perhaps his early death in 1690[2]. It seems that the second Sir John was in financial difficulty for much of the last two decades of his life. Surviving legal transactions show that he was mortgaging and selling property. James Tillie appears to have been advancing him money on the security of property. It is also possible that he had mismanaged his wife's dowry which was not available for his daughters after his death.

This position cannot have been eased when he started on the rebuilding of the great house at Newton Ferrers, some five years before his death. He died in 1690 when only 42 years old, leaving his wife, Lady Elizabeth Coryton, with two daughters, Elizabeth and Mary, who were both under age.

Sir William Coryton

He was succeeded by his brother, Sir William Coryton, 3rd Bt. (1650-1711), who was of Newton Ferrers and Crocadon in Cornwall and, since he was a professional lawyer, of the Middle Temple in

William Coryton: this portrait is said to be of William Coryton (1650-1711),
painted around 1680, before he inherited from his brother, John.
Pentillie Castle

London. Sir William had been at Exeter College, Oxford, and then joined the Middle Temple in 1669, being called to the bar in 1675. Despite his inheritance of the Coryton family estates, he continued working as a lawyer. He too held offices in Cornwall and was eleven times returned as a Member of Parliament. Active as a member during the reign of James II, his legal training was later made use of when he drafted a number of bills. He took some part in the activities of the House of Commons, but was granted leave of absence on the grounds of ill health for the years 1706, 1707, 1709, and 1711 before dying at the end of that year.

It is Sir William who is credited with building the magnificent new mansion at Newton Ferrers, although the work, which included the fine stables dated 1688, had been started by his brother in 1685 but is thought to have proceeded slowly until his death in 1690.

The Newton Ferrers Mansion was built between 1685 and 1701. The stable block has a date stone of 1688, and gate piers bear the dates 1688 and 1695. Building accounts show that much of the work was done by Sir William whose building accounts date between 1695 and 1701. As in many a modernisation of the time, it was built in front of and to the east of the earlier house which remained as a rear wing to the north-west. The new house is one of the earliest Cornish mansions of classical design. It was intended to sit in an extensive formal landscape of terraces, ornaments and gardens and it was even said that some terraces were laid out 'by an Italian'. Burnt in 1940, the house was restored by new owners in the 1990s.

Rather than settle at Newton Ferrers, Sir William had his own house at Crocadon, in East Cornwall, which he bought in 1704. This was then a towered mansion, just by St Mellion church, and although now much reduced and altered, is still within the Pentillie estate.

Sir William married Susanna, daughter of Sir Edward Littleton, in 1688. She died in 1695. His second marriage was to Sarah, the 'elderly but rich' widow of Thomas Williams, a London Banker. An untraced commentator of the time wrote:

Refues noe women nere soe old
Whose marriage bringeth store of gold.

After Sir William's death, the rich widow married yet again.

Sir William's will, dated 1711[3], is interesting not only because it throws light on his friendships, his servants, his life and habits, but also because there is no reference to Sir James Tillie.

Sir William comes across as a pleasant fellow. He made good and amusing arrangements for his wife, including the suggestion that should she not wish to live with her son at Newton, she could use Crocadon as long as she remained unmarried. It was this will that set out that if the estate descended to John Goodall, his nephew, then

Newton Ferrers, Cornwall
Drawing by Edmund Prideaux c 1717.
Reproduced with permission

John would be required to change his name to Coryton.

William also wrote off sums owed by Rich.Smith 'who has long served me' and who was to receive £200 and the write off of: '…debts he owed his master through negligence in accounts especially in the matter and concern of my new building [at Newton Ferrers] which was as it seems an undertaking too hard for him'. Richard Smith was also given 'clothes, lines, woollen hats and periwigs and the little black mare he usually rode on'.

William had already settled everything on his son when he had first married but added: 'I leave behind me in cash and unquestionable debts on good securitys a much greater personal estate than will pay and satisfy the same with a considerable overplus'. This accumulation of wealth was achieved despite the cost of rebuilding Newton Ferrers.

A splendid monument erected after William's death, which

is illustrated in Chapter 12 on the Mausoleum, shows him and his first wife, but also demonstrates how different from the norm was Sir James Tillie in his funeral arrangements.

The Tillie and Coryton Families join in Marriage

Some time after the deaths of both Sir James Tillie and Sir William Coryton, the close connections between the Tillie and Coryton families became more closely entangled, not only by lawsuits and the sorting out of various trusts, but also by changes of name.

First, in the Tillie family, Sir James Tillie had left Pentillie to his sister's son, James Woolley, on the condition that he change his name from Woolley to Tillie. This he did, and James Tillie II, formerly Woolley, (1690-1746) took over Pentillie and Belle Cour. He was Sheriff of Cornwall in 1734. On his death in 1746, the estates were inherited by his son James Tillie III (1722-1772). The daughter of James III was called Mary Jemima (1750-1779, and it was she who married into the Coryton family, thereby combining both estates.

Second, William Coryton's will had also ensured that the family name remained Coryton, even if it descended through a female line. Peter Goodall therefore changed his name to Coryton in order to inherit and took over the Coryton estates in 1739. His management of the estate was blighted by a Chancery dispute with the Hellyar family who, through marriage, claimed much of the estate. The law suit started in 1743 and lasted nearly 40 years. Peter and his son, John Coryton (1740-1803), continued to live at Crocadon rather than Newton Ferrers, the original family home whose ownership was disputed by the Hellyars.

It was John Coryton who married Mary Jemima, and so combined the interests of the Tillie and Coryton families. Their son, John Tillie Coryton (1773-1843), inherited both Pentillie and Crocadon, only moving to Pentillie from Crocadon on the death of his widowed mother. John Tillie Coryton rebuilt Pentillie Castle and made Pentillie the chief Coryton residence.

The original complaint by Sir John Coryton about the flight of his wife
includes the added suggestions of his Lawyer: 26 July 1689.
First page: CRO CY/7197

Elizabeth Coryton, née Chiverton: Sir James Tillie's Second Wife

Elizabeth Chiverton was one of two children of the wealthy Sir Richard Chiverton, who had been Lord Mayor of London, Sheriff of Cornwall and was knighted by Charles II in 1663. Although spending much time in Clerkenwell, London, the Chivertons had considerable estates around Trehunsey in Quethiock parish, Cornwall, close to the Coryton lands there. Elizabeth's first marriage was to Sir John Coryton, in February 1672. She brought with her a rich dowry which remained for her and her children's benefit[4].

We assume that James Tillie had made her acquaintance by 1680, the year Sir John Coryton inherited from his father and the year when James Tillie became involved in documents relating to the Chiverton Marriage Settlement, to which he was the leading witness. James Tillie is first referred to as 'Steward' to Sir John Coryton as early as 1673, and continued to act for him through that decade, a job that covered the management of the estate and the collection of rents.

However, by 1683 he was not only described as a 'gentleman' but was also acting as a principal in transactions with both Sir John and his brother William. James is noted as arranging the sale of property, the arranging of loans and finding of mortgages. Indeed James Tillie appears to have granted mortgages to both the Coryton brothers. This suggests that James Tillie was no longer acting as the steward of Sir John Coryton and that someone else had taken over the day to day running of affairs for Sir John, including the collection of rents and moneys. We know that in 1689, John Lanyon was the steward, and that James Tillie, by now knighted to become Sir James Tillie, was regarded as a family friend of Elizabeth Coryton.

One transaction gives a flavour of Sir James' activities. A deed dated 2 April 1689, (that is only a month before the complaint set out below) records that some property in Devon was held in trust by Richard Asshe, of Lyon's Inne, a legal friend of James Tillie's. It appears that Sir John Coryton had borrowed £500 from Sir James Tillie and had to repay £530, the Devon property being held by Richard Asshe as security. Interestingly, Sir James Tillie does not seem to have been present. The deed suggests that Sir James directed that he, Sir James was acting for Sir John Coryton. Among the three witnesses was John Lanyon, Coryton's steward[5].

Murder Attempts and an Absconding Wife

Central to the stories about Sir James was the description by Hals that Sir James stole from his master, Sir John Coryton, that he may well have poisoned him and then made off with his wife. In the middle of a lengthy passage abusing Sir James, Hals wrote: '..after the death of his then master, Sir John Coryton the younger, not without suspicion of being poisoned, he soon married one, with whom, common fame said he was too familiar before, so that he became possessed of her goods and chattels, and a great jointure.'

Since much else of what Hals wrote about Sir James Tillie was exaggerated and incorrect, this sort of comment has to be taken with a pinch of salt. However, two documents that survive in the Cornwall Record Office hint at the story behind the rumours.

In 1689, Sir John Coryton wrote to request a legal opinion of what action he should take over what he had found when going through the papers of his steward John Lanyon. He was, in modern terms, seeking counsel's opinion on what action he could take against his Steward, John Lanyon, against Sir James Tillie, to whom he believed his wife had fled, and against his wife. The document asks eight questions which the lawyer, Tremayne, then answers, adding the date of his answers, 26 July 1689[6].

The complaint starts by summarising letters which had been found in Lanyon, the Steward's room and includes an allegation which, misunderstood, has been central to the reputation of Sir James Tillie. Sir John refers to a letter from John Lanyon the Steward to Sir James Tillie, in which Lanyon alleges that Sir John Coryton had tried to murder both his wife Elizabeth and 'himself', John Lanyon. Previous readings of the document had suggested that it was Tillie who was threatening the murder. However, that is not a correct reading of the grammar, does not agree with why Lanyon, whose handwriting Coryton claims to recognise, is writing to Tillie, nor is it supported by the wish of Sir John Coryton to sue Lanyon for libel. However, it does suggest that John Lanyon must have been acting in an unusual way, since, as his complaint goes on, it is clear that, with the aid of several helpers, his wife Elizabeth had fled from the house. Indeed, it would appear from Parliamentary records that Sir John had been unwell for some time. If, as is suggested, Elizabeth had been alone and carrying on the trade of brewer or 'Maulster' without her husband's knowledge, then they cannot have seen much of each other in their recent past.

Coryton also complains of deeds and rent demands for Coryton Property being left in Lanyon's study, although I would have thought that the fact that he left the items there, rather than take them with him, suggests a degree of innocence. One of Sir John's questions relates to a supply of malt which his wife had left behind when she fled, and which he wishes to sell. He appears to suggest that Lanyon had been working under Elizabeth's direction, which also confuses the matter. To my mind Coryton's question suggests that he was not sure that the 'mault' and corn were indeed his, and so were possibly the fruit of his wife's own dowered lands and businesses, since unless the product were his wife's I can see no need for the question. It also suggests that he was seriously short of money, a suggestion supported by his hope that he need no longer support his wife. We understand that when he died a few months later, his 'free' estate could not meet his liabilities.

The whole document is included at the notes at the end of this chapter, and deserves reading in the original, since there appear to be enough plot lines here to run a television soap for several episodes.

It is a bit difficult to know what situation the document describes, but it looks as though Elizabeth and Sir John had been on bad terms and that she may even have been supporting herself from her own funds. Lanyon the steward appears to have regarded Sir James

Tillie as a mentor and certainly as a friend and supporter of Elizabeth.

Clearly there had been difficulties for some time, since Lanyon's letter asking for help was addressed not directly to Tillie, but enclosed in a blank letter to Christopher Vane for him to forward. This suggests support from Vane, or is confirmation, that Vane knew of the affair, and that Sir John Coryton was not entirely blameless. Elizabeth's flight must have been sudden and the departure of John Lanyon, the steward, even more so.

Contrary to what was later said of Sir James, this letter shows that he was in not in charge of rent receipts and money, and that it was not he who had threated to murder anyone, but rather that the man making threats of murder may have been Sir John Coryton himself.

A Second Document

A second sheet was found folded inside the first complaint[7]. This second manuscript was undated and was also about seeking legal advice. It asked about the legal situation arising after a steward had died intestate but owing considerable sums to his master. It is thought, because this undated note had been enclosed in the other, that the note refers to John Lanyon, the Steward, who is understood to have died within a few years of the original complaint. Since the steward seems to have died leaving no funds, and because his only property seems to have been tied up in his wife's dowry, it would seem unlikely that, if this does refer to Lanyon, he had been making off with his master's money. The note may also be confirmation that Sir John Coryton, or his successor, Sir William, was seriously short of money and looking around for any means to find some.

We shall probably never know what happened. Sir John Coryton then died in July 1690, a year after the date of his complaint about the loss of his wife. The estate was then presumably in some turmoil, but our confidence in the abilities and honesty of Sir James Tillie is supported when it turns out that Sir William Coryton, who inherited, appoints Sir James as Steward a post he held until 1694.

In 1692, after a decent two year interval, and in an event which would delight the heart of many a romantic, Sir James married the widow Elizabeth, who we can assume he had been admiring for some years. Sir James' first wife is thought to have died 10 years earlier, and in an age when marriages were based on the acquiring of wealth and the producing of heirs, this marriage to Elizabeth was not obvious. First, Sir James could have married someone younger, particularly given his acknowledged wish to produce a dynasty. Elizabeth, who was probably born in 1653, was therefore around 40 years old at the time of this marriage, and cannot have been considered of realistic child bearing age. Although the possessor of a 'great fortune' her access to the sums due her from the Coryton estates appears to have become difficult and the subject of actions. The 'trust funds' due to her from her father's will also became the subject of dispute and thus in 1696 she, with James Tillie her husband, sued for the recovery of £2,000 held in trust under her father's will[8.]

It seems possible that this was a marriage not of convenience, but of understanding, even affection. I also find it difficult to believe, that, even in the different traditions and world of the 17th century, Elizabeth would have married someone who had stolen family money or endangered her husband. Her own fortune, even if reduced, should have been sufficient for her to be able to live alone. But then, I could be a romantic fool.

Although Sir James had no children of his own by either of his wives, he treated the two daughters of his wife Elizabeth as close family, not only being their trustee but looking after their interests. Sir James is also believed to have gained access to those lands which (with the exception of some bought back by Sir William Coryton) were part of his wife's original dowry, and also to the trusts, land and monies which went to the daughters and so to their husbands.

Sir James' lands included much in Plymouth, in Devon, and some estates he purchased in Cornwall. There is no evidence that he stole from the Coryton family. He was involved in transactions to which both Sir John and his brother William were party, but although he took mortgages and the security of land to support loans he had made to the Corytons, there appears no suggestion that he acted dishonourably. Sir James Tillie had accumulated a considerable estate, but unless transferred with the knowledge of Sir James or William Coryton, it does not seem that any had been part of the Coryton Estate.

There is a suggestion that Sir James had supported Sir John Coryton's children, who had died leaving insufficient funds to meet his liabilities. There is also evidence that he managed the affairs of those children to their best interests, although it is clear that he fell out with the husband of Elizabeth, the elder child. Deeds also suggest that Sir William had transferred monies to Sir James which were properly the property of Elizabeth, James' wife.

Sir William Coryton was a professional lawyer, a man who appears to have been a pleasant character, and one who had been involved as a principal in land transactions with James Tillie in earlier years and then, in 1690, on his brother's death appointed or re-confirmed Sir James Tillie to look after the estates. I think it unlikely that if Sir James had been cheating William's brother Sir John Coryton, William would have made that appointment.

It seems probable that Sir James had taken fees, may have made money from the purchase and sale of property, and may have managed the Chiverton marriage trust for a fee and some advantage but his continued employment by William suggests that William, believed to be a sensible lawyer and businessman, was content with his service.

The tales of malfeasance in Coryton lands were perhaps confused by the joining, at the end of the 18th century, of the two families of Tillie and Coryton, which also combined and confused the origin of their joint property.

Endnotes

1.   A selection of legal transactions involving James Tillie and the Coryton family. References are to the identification codes in the Cornwall Record Office.

1.1.   1669: 'A survey booke a Full Collection of all the estate of Sir John Coryton Barrt. By James Tillie Anno Dom 1669' prepared by Tillie when aged 22 years old for Sir John Coryton Senior. CY 6549

1.2.   01 September 1669 James Tillie is one of three witnesses to matters of the Hundred Court and the appointments sold by Sir John Coryton. CY/7255

1.3.   17 January 1672   Agreement of John Carpenter, vicar of Quethiock with James Tillie acting for Sir John Coryton. Latter to pay £2.10s. per year for small tithes and tithe woods and 6s. for Kitchin Parkes.

1.4.   30 May 1673   Lease of property in Quethock   and granting of lease by Sir John Coryton to Michael Allen on three lives security – the second life is James Tillie `steward and meniall servant of the said John Coryton'. James Tillie then witnesses the document   CY/2908

1.5.   9 October 1673   Re-entry/regain repair of some Mills.   Witnessed by Jas. Tillie and others   CY/5563

1.6.   27 December 1679   Receipt by Sir John Coryton from his son Wm. Coryton for £360 rent due for Carrybullock   witnessed by James Tillie and Hen. Bolt.   CY/5184

1.7.   3 August 1680 An assignment of trust in relation to financial arrangements made by Sir Richard Chiverton for his daughter Elizabeth and John Coryton. 'Jas. Tillie' the first of three witnesses. CY 1567

1.8.   1681 Complex of transactions where Christopher Vane (of Fairlawne) had bought property in Callington, Cornwall from Sir John Coryton, William Coryton and another, but acting in Trust for James Tillie and using money provided by James Tillie, so confirms that the property is that of James Tillie.   CY/87.

1.9.   1683   Kekewich Title Deeds Liskeard. Release. 1. Sir John Coryton of West Newton Ferrars, Cornwall, Bart. William Coryton of the Middle Temple, Esq. James Tillie of the Middle Temple, gentleman. Walter Hoskin of Durnaford, St. Ives Devon Heritage Centre 1926 B/K/T/3/90

1.10.   30 August 1683   Land in Colebrook mortgaged by William Coryton with trustees but James Tillie of the Middle Temple gentleman has put up the money and was to whom would be conveyed the manor   CY/1076

1.11.   3 Dec 1685 Warham, Stoke Climsland   Note by James Tillie to say papers relating to the manor of Landegay are in his hands. William Coryton, esquire is to have moiety of Warham (Stoke Climsland) and Grimscombe Woods in equal co-partnership with James Tillie. CY/6076

1.12.   23 December 1686 Receipt for £750 for portion of Katherine, youngest daughter of Sir John Coryton Bt from Manor of Landegay then vested in William Coryton. (Receipt from James Tillie to William Coryton. CY/5169

1.13.   2 April 1689 Declaration of trust, Puddington, Stockley English, Sandford and other lands, Devon.

Parties: 1) Richard Asshe, Lyons Inne, Middlesex, gentleman 2) Sir James Tillie, Middle Temple, London, knight. Recites of release by Sir John Coryton of West Newton Ferrers, baronet by direction of Sir James Tillie. £500 Tillie to Coryton 25 March 1689 - Richard Ashe. Mansion house and barton of Piend, held by Richard Chaunter - - Bounsdon in Puddington held by George Westland alias Bainsdon - - Spreetwell in Stockley English held by - Blackmore - - 2 messuage or tenement in Sandford - - messuage in Colebrooke. Mortgage of premises for 1000 years [from] 20 December 1681. £530 owing by Sir J Coryton - Richard Asshe was acting in trust for James Tillie who had paid £500 consideration money. Witnessed: William Perry, Timothy Goodwin, John Lanyon. CY/1187

1.14.   1690 - 1694 James Tillie's account as steward to Sir William Coryton (Rent accounts for manors of Colebrooke, Caradon, Dinnerdake, Frogwell mills, Greston, Hammet, Moiety of Hopsland, Kerrybullock Landegay   CY/5189

1.15.   Not dated (temp. William Third.) Conveyance, Callington. Parties: 1) Sir W Coryton of West Newton Ferrers, baronet 2) Sir James Tillie of Pentillie, knight 3) Arthur Squier of Clements Inn, gentleman. Draft, 5 shillings.(3-2). Recites deeds (Lease and Release) of 27 and 28 April 1694 of 1) and 2) of several messuage or lands in Callington. Those below in some dispute. 2) -3)- Pickleton meadow (1a) with common of pasture on Hingston Down; Great Broome Down close (6 acres) with common of pasture on Hingston Down. (All parish of Callington) Hay tenement in borough of Callington. Zuggar meadow (3 and a half acres) with common on Hingston Down. CY/8814

1.16.   January 1691. Another deed relating to the Trust affairs of Dame Elizabeth Coryton, (widow of Sir John Coryton). Witnessed by 'Jas.Tillie' CY/1568

1.17.   3 Feb 1692.   The marriage Settlement for Elizabeth Coryton's eldest daughter Elizabeth for £4000 had set out lands in Chiverton. Under the trust and purchases, Sir James Tillie agrees to pass over all the lands left by her father to his, Tillie's, wife. Many of relevant lands actually in possession of Sir William Coryton. This deed notes that: Sir John Coryton died in Debt, including mortgage and his personal estate among other items not sufficient to pay some of debts related to diet, apparel, schooling and education of E and M Coryton.   J Tillie has a mortgage of £1500. A series of complex transactions were proposed to clear up a mess. However, difficulties continued and some of the property meant to be sold in order to settle John Coryton's debts was not done and this became a factor in 1743 Coryton/Hellyar action. CY/1594

1.18.   21 June 1692 Receipt for £1000 from Sir Jas. Tillie of Pentillie, KT and his wife Dame Elizabeth and others to Sir William Coryton in relation to marriage settlement of 1672 on Chiverton daughters. Sir John Coryton had died 1690 leaving two daughters. Redistribution of trust and maintenance money including some to Sir J. Tillie. CY1569

1.19.   3rd November 1693   Sir James Tillie, Pentillie, Kt gives long lease of Outlands and bits in St Cleer   CY3561

1.20.   1 February 1700. Receipt for £3000 from Mary Coryton of Pillaton, 'gentlewoman', to Sir Wm Coryton who following arrangements of 1692 came of age on 11 April 1699. Witnessed by Jas Tillie. CY/1570

1.21.   1701. South Hill and Callington. Release. (i)Sir James Tillie, Pentillie, Kt. To (ii) Sir Wm. Coryton, West Newton Ferrers, Bt. (Rec. of release of same date of various unspecified properties ii-i). i - ii - mess., lands in Callington CY/89

1.22.   1696   Christopher and Elizabeth Batt, (Elizabeth is Tillie's step-daughter) take action against Sir JT and others (including Coryton) in relation to her mother's original Chiverton marriage settlement. There are a number of actions under this process: A) for properties in Tintagel. C7/36/9. B) Quethicok   C7/641/48.   C) Estate of Sir Richard Chiverton C7/334/9. D) 1700 for money C7/22/71.   1703 E) Property in Colebrooke etc. C7/27/8

1.23.   1703 and 1705 Both the Batts and Tillies are plaintiffs for the same property in different years.

1.24.   Sir JT and Dame Elizabeth sue Christopher and Elizabeth Batt for property in Romford   C7/335/6220

1.25.   Jan 1709 Colebrooke Devon For £256 Conveyance Sir James Tillie Kt and wife Dame Elizabeth to Sir Wm Coryton of West Newton Ferrers, Following a

Mortgage made by Sir John Coryton.

2.   The History of Parliament: the House of Commons 1690-1715, Eveline Cruickshanks ed. D. Hayton, E. Cruickshanks, S. Handley, 2002 gives information on the parliamentary careers of the Coryton family, and has provided information not available elsewhere.

3.   National Archives: Prob 11/530/59

4.   Extrct from summary for CRO CY 1593. 'Sir R Chiverton settled barton of Trehunsey, Trehunsey mills, Trehunsey Cottage, 234 acres, Quethiock Ven alias Taven, Vendowne, Treweese 200 acres, Quethiock, 2 houses in Quethiock and close called Venn Hills, 2 messuages, in Quethiock Church Town, other messuage or cottages in Quethiock. All part of manor of Landrake purchased of Henry Killigrew. Ley in St Ive - bought of Sir Chichester Wrey, baronet For use of Dame Elizabeth Tillie for life etc Dame E. Tillie had 2 daughters Elizabeth and Mary Coryton'.

5.   Cornwall Record Office CY/1187

6.   Sir John Coryton had written to request legal advice on any action he could take against his Steward, John Lanyon, and against Sir James Tillie for carrying off his wife, and for other matters. The original document first sets out the circumstances and then lists the questions, to which, alongside, the answers are written in a different handwriting. (CRO CY 7197)

I am indebted to Doctor Joanna Mattingly for her help in transcribing the document, which, save for three material amendments arising from study of the background, is as follows: Counsel's answers are shown in red.

'That the 21st of June last there being letters intercepted by Sir John Coryton Barronett after in the posts hands written by John Lanyon directed for Sir James Tillie, butt the corect [?] or outside letter directed for Christopher Vane esq a Member of Parliament but nothing written the inside of that letter to Mr Vane.

In that letter directed to Sir James Tillie, Lanyon doth question Sir John Coryton that he *[that is Sir John Coryton?]* togeather with others had endeavored? to murther his Lady^& himself?^ *[that is John Lanyon?]* and severall other oprobious based and scandalous expressions of simi[lar?] in the letters (Butt useth strange names as you will see by the letters, butt Sir John finds by severall other letters sent to Lanyon from Tillie tis the rev[er]saunce[?] of sens me[a]nt-------------See the letter

That the same day by the wickett designes and contrivances of Tillie, Lanyon & one Charlton and there Complices & without any provocation of Sir

Johns his Lady left him and was carried away, And Lanyon the same tyme fled Lanyon beinge thus fled Sir John seized his study and tooke into his possession the Deeds and writings therein most of them belonginge to himselfe, and ever since hath kept them.

That since Lanyon fled Sir John hath found lodgd in his study and Chamber severall of his goods to a Considerable vallue pact upp in Boxes and Trunckes and hidd under his bedd & other private places, and since gone out of Sir John's service hath endeavored by letters & threateninge law suites and by other wayes and meanes to gett the Rents of the tenants then due into his hands unknowne to Sir John.

Quest [ion] 1

Whether the words in the letters were [?] tantamount to accou[nt] att Comon Lawe or what course to be taken for the scandells therein the letter beinge well proved to be Lanyons writinge

you may proferr an Informacion for a libell

2 What course to be taken against the conturey *[Contrary? or country, that is neighbourhood?]* for getting away the Lady and deteyning and carryinge her off

you may bring an accon [action] against them for takeing & carrying her away

3 Whether Sir John Coryton shall hereafter be lyable to the Ladyes contracts towards her maintenance and how farr, more then a reasonable compensation accordinge to her quality

he is lyable to allow her reasonable mayntenance untill a divorce

4 How farr Sir John or his serv[an]ts by his ord[er]s that seized the study, chamber writings & other things therein (nott all beinge his owne) shall be lyable to an accon and what way they may proceed Sir John being a Member of Parliament, and whether hee may safely deliver upp those writings of other mens that were in Lanyons custody to those persons [?] they.belong to

Sir John was best keepe them ....his owne in his howse & not deliver them over to other persones

5 What way Sir John may p[ro]ceed ag[ains]t Lanyon for takinge away those goods that he found pact upp & hidd in the Study & Chamber (to be conveyed away) And after gone out of Sir Johns service endeavored to robb him of his rents as aforesaid

an accon [action] of trespass lyes ag[ains]t him

6 What way Sir John may proceed against Lanyon to call him to an Acc[oun]t for the many greate summes rec[eive]d for him from his rents & others hee havinge not

presented any Acc[oun]t these Severall yeeres with Sir J T *[? ie Tillie or 'M Joy' difficult to read but important]*

he must call him to Account in Chancery

7 The Lady hath some tymes last past drove the trade of A maulster in Sir Johns house, And Lanyon as then his serv[an]t ordred his corne to be converted to that use & bought in other corne & from tyme to tyme sold itt as shee pleased. Quere there beinge a stocke of mault layed by & other moneyes due from severall persons for mault sold & delivered Sit John may w[el]l dispose of the mault [crossing out] left & receive the money due on Account & to his [owne?] use (?)

he may dispose of the mault & receave ye mony

[Question 8 on the rear of the document]

Quere If the Lady should by vainst (?) wayes or meanes be begotten with childe with [a??] childe Sir John nott livinge with or nigh her (that sone shall inheritt) And if [so] what meanes to be taken to prevent itt

He must sue for a divor[ce] in ye spirituall court off[ice?] as he can in case he c[an] make out the Adultery he was best have full a[nd] Clere proofe before [ ] being [bringing] that suite

Tremayne 26 July 16[89]

[Note: 'from the late 17th century it was possible to divorce by private Act; but there were only 200 divorces by this route up to 1857, of which six were at the suit of women.' (Paul Carter & Kate Thompson, Sources for Local Historians (Phillimore, 2005), p.175.]

7.   This document is thought to be about John Lanyon's stewardship for Sir John Coryton. John Lanyon witnessed deeds in 1693 so it is thought to date from not too long after that. Below is an amended summary of the manuscript extracted from that provided by the Cornwall Record Office;

        The document is about a person called A, believed to be John Lanyon, being indebted to someone in mortgage, to others on bond, to others on simple contract including his master 'to whom he was steward' in a large sum of money which A had received in the year 'before his Death out of the Rents and profitts of has Masters estate'.

        A had died intestate, and so his widow took out letters of administration. It seems that A's only sister was his heir at Law. A had some personal estate and effects, but these were not sufficient to pay his debts. He was also seized in fee of several lands, but these were subject to one mortgage out of which the widow claimed dower.

The questions put to the advisor were: Was the sister to be compelled to sell lands as heir at law to pay debts of A? Should lands stand [remain] charged with payment of debts on simple contract as well as speciality?

Answer - these assets to be used by heir at law to pay debts due by speciality. However these assets can not be charged with debts due by simple.contracts. If personal estate not sufficient to pay all debts, then the court of equity will take real assets to make satisfaction to simple contract creditors for so much of personal estate exhausted in payment of bond debts. Last query about methods to be taken by debtors whether by speciality or contract etc.   CY/1798 [found inside CY/7197]

8.   National Record Office   PRO C/7/334/9.

The coat of arms claimed by Sir James Tillie

Chapter 5

The Dispute at the Court of Chivalry

Central to Sir James' wish to establish himself in society was his claim that he was a member of an old and armigerous family. The earliest picture of him shows him with a coat of arms which bears a blazon that never varies throughout his life. The phrases that normally accompanied the grant of a coat of arms include: '...These ancient Badges or Ensigns of Gentility, commonly called or known by the Name of Arms have heretofore been, and still are continued to be conferred upon deserving Persons, to distinguish them from the common sort of People who neither can nor may pretend to, use them without lawful Authority'.

It is certain that Sir James, newly knighted, would have wished to distinguish himself from the common people, and so adopted a coat of arms to which he claimed entitlement, and on which were also the arms of his first wife. However, his swift rise to prominence, his purchase of a knighthood and his legal work are likely to have made him enemies, and it is thought that it was either they or his legal opponents who, in 1687, reported him to The Court of Chivalry for bearing arms to which he was not entitled.

This resulted in a relatively rare court action initiated when, following the citation of 31st October 1687, the warrant was executed on November 4th 1687 by John Currey, an officer of the court, stating that Sir James Tillie did not have the right to bear the arms 'used in various places in his house and elsewhere' over the previous three years. The case, 'Oldys v Tillie[1] was promoted by William Oldys, LLD king's advocate, against Sir James Tyllie, knt, formerly known as James

The arms shown in the early picture of a young James Tillie,
with the engraving from which it is taken.

The arms in a 1687 portrait of Sir James Tillie show the Tillie Cross
fleurie top left, with four other blazons which can not be read, save
that one appears to be the open mailed hand of the Vanes, for his wife
Margaret Vane. The angel supporters and rising phoenix crest are also
shown. Motto illegible.

Tillie of Pentillie Castle esq, for unlawfully using arms and supporters.

The citation was issued on the 31st October 1687 and included, with Latin quotations from legal precedents and the general law of arms, the statement that no one below the rank of a Baron, except Knights of the Garter and Bannerets, ought to bear his arms without special license and authority first obtained. The case alleged that in 1685, 1686 and 1687, the defendant bore the arms and crest without any right; and what is more, that Sir James supported the arms with two angels with wings outstretched, the right to such supporters being restricted only to certain ranks, a crime that seems to have particularly irritated the court. Although the picture of the crest and the disputed arms is missing from the record, it is suggested that this crest was a rising phoenix, a crest appropriate for a rising Sir James and as shown in the picture of him now in the British Museum.

From the Latin documents, it is not clear that Sir James either entered a defence or appeared in his own defence.

The Earl Marshal pronounced sentence on Sir James, stating that the defendant had no right to the arms, crest or supporters. In January 1687/8 therefore, Sir James was 'monished' and ordered to pay a fine of £200 and £20 costs. Although probably within Sir James' means, this was a considerable sum, and we can imagine that the principal effect of the fine was a blow to the pride of the ambitious Sir James, and that the action may have been a factor in his decision to give up London ambitions.

It was probably because of this case that there are few examples of Sir James using an illustration or representation of these arms thereafter, and that the stamp on his wine bottles shows his name and Pentillie Castle, rather than a crest or other armorial bearing.

Heraldry describes the terms and way in which emblems identified those entitled to bear a 'coat of arms'. Such insignia were said to have started as a way of recognizing friends or foes in battle, but by the 17th century had become a matter of social status, and of pride, and also of showing off the families to which one was

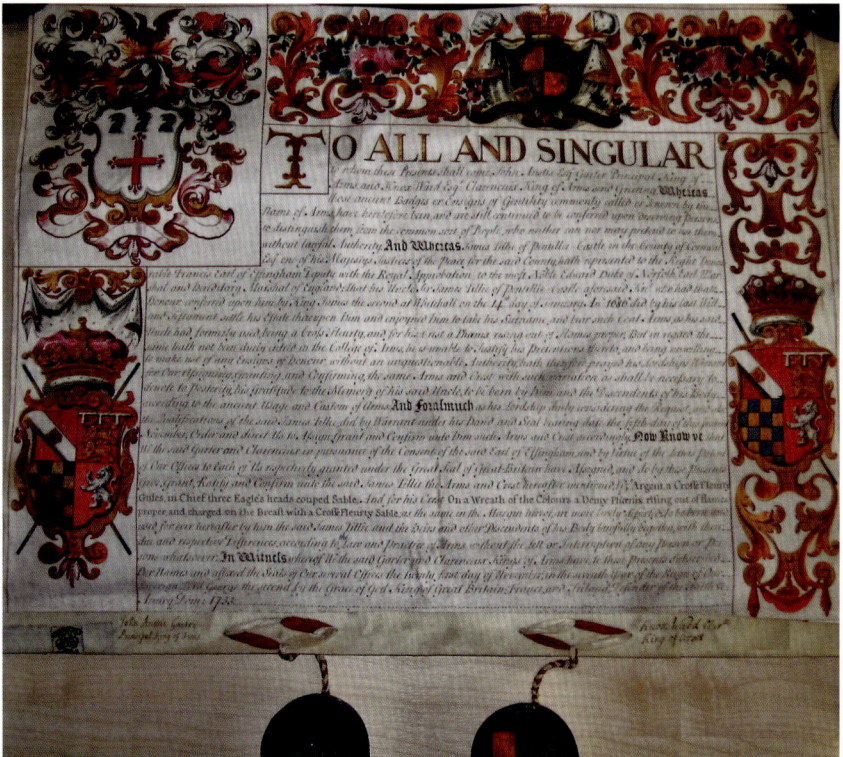

The Grant of Arms awarded to James Tillie on 21 November 1733

CY/7048

connected. Coats of Arms became the important definition of social status and position. Indeed, it became important to show that you were descended from the 'right people' in as many generations and from as many armigerous ancestors as possible.

One might suppose that a knight might be entitled to arms, but the bearing of such a coat of arms was regulated by the rules of heraldry and policed by the College of Arms. Inspectors made regular tours in an attempt to record and control the grant and use of arms, and the College of Arms, with its advisors or policemen called Heralds, still exists. The last such inspection of families and their arms for Cornwall took place in 1620.

This story of the arms assumed by James Tillie was first described in print by Hals, and thereafter followed by later writers. Hals suggested that Sir James was using a coat of arms from a continental count, presumably Johnann Tserclaes, Count of Tilly, known as the most successful general of the 'Thirty Years War' fifty years earlier. However, the arms that Sir James used were nothing like those of the Count of Tilly and this allegation was entirely without foundation.

In fact Sir James appears to have used the arms of a genuine Sir John Tilley (note spelling), a man of substance and importance in Bristol at the end of the previous century, whose arms were recorded in various heraldic and other documents around the year 1600. These same arms were also found as quarterings in the family of the Earl of Derby, which suggests that members of Sir John's family had married into Derby's. However, the arms and the family of Sir John Tilley appear to have died out in the male line, and it is therefore possible either that Sir James was an indirect member of the family of Sir John, or that he had taken the arms because of the similarity of name, arms which are similar in detail, even to the *patonce* on the cross. I am inclined to suspect, because of the Bristol connection and the number of Sir James' family based there as merchants and businessmen, that he was in fact some distant relation.

Much of the art of Heraldry is overlooked nowadays, but remains a useful tool in trying to identify building owners, phases and the occupiers of church tombs and the relationships of and between families. The colourful designs and complex imagery are fascinating. Pentillie Castle and the neighbouring churches retain many survivals and examples of Sir James Tillie's extended Coryton family.

The illustrations on page 100 show first the simple arms, included in the early picture we have of the young James Tillie. Then, at the bottom of the page, are the arms shown in the later engraving of Sir James Tillie, dated 1687. This print was done shortly after he had gained his knighthood and so shows the arms he claimed. These not only have the angelic supporters and the phoenix crest, but also

The arms adopted by James Tillie in 1733 (detail).

CY/7048

include in the quarterings the three mailed hands of his wife's Vane family. I have been unable to identify the other quarterings. The blazon he claimed for himself is identical to that recorded for Sir John Tilley of Bristol at the end of the previous century. It was the arms shown in this engraving that created the dispute at the court of Chivalry.

The blazon or description of the Tilley blazon is: *'Argent, a cross Flory [gules], between four crescents gules'*. To you and me this means a red cross with flowery ends, with four red crescents in the corners on a silver background. Above the coat of arms was the crest of a phoenix rising from the flames. To each side of the shield was an angel acting as a 'supporter'. These arms are shown in the engraving of 1687.

It seems that Sir James never gave up on this coat of arms, and neither did his descendants, since, some 45 years later his family continued to use the blazon.

The illustration opposite shows the grant of arms made[3] on 21 November 1733 to James Tillie esquire, Pentillie Castle, which was based on that claimed by Sir James Tillie fifty years earlier, but 'differenced' by the addition of three griffin's heads 'in chief' across the top. This beautiful document refers to the earlier arms of Sir James as:

'..that his Uncle Sir James Tillie, aforesaid, Knt., who had that honour conferred on him by King James the second at Whitehall on the 14th day of January in 1686 did by his last Will and Testament settle his Estate thereupon him and enjoined him to take his surname and bear such Coat Arms as his Uncle had formerly used, being a Cross Fleurty and for his Crest a Phoenix rising out of flames proper, But in regard the same hath not been duely entred in the college of Arms, he is unable to justify his pretensions thereto and being unwilling to make use of any Ensigns of Honour without an unquestionable authority, hath therefore parayed his Lordships warrant for our Assigning, Granting and Confirming the same Arms and Crest with such variation as shall be necessary to denote to Posterity, his gratitude to the Memory of his said Uncle,

The heraldic description of the new blazon was:

'Argent, a Crosse Fleurty Gules, in Chief three Eagle's heads couped Sable. And for his Crest On a Wreath of the Colours a Demy Phoenix rising out of flames proper, and charged on the Breast with a Crosse Fleurty Sable'.

The document is a delightful piece of art with the Heraldic devices of the heralds, much coloured decoration and textual reasoning, including that justification mentioned earlier which we may today find amusing:

'Badges or Ensigns ... are ...conferred upon deserving persons to distinguish

Left: The Tillie arms recut (?) into a granite lintel at Pentillie.
Right: A sundial at Pentillie Castle, as reviewed in text.

them from the common sort of People...'

Even today, it seems that there are many of us among the 'common sort of people' who still hope and strive to have their rise from that common sort recognised by a grant of arms.

It is the 1733 coat of arms which can be found added above the granite door to the lime kiln down by the river at Pentillie, shown in the picture at the top of this page. It also has some Jacobean decoration, but the date of 1657, which is long before the grant in 1733, is a puzzle. Was the lintel recut? The same blazon is above the finely cut door to the well, also by the river.

Although no coats of arms or heraldic devices have been identified at Belle Cour, there are a number of date stones and heraldic shields around Pentillie, and at many houses these might refer to family or marriage connections. Such stones and shields can lead to confusion and dead ends. For instance a beautifully cut slate sun dial, engraved with the phrase *Quotidie Morior*, and the date 1693, now hangs on the 1968 south portico at Pentillie. It tells the 'correct' time, although this could be debated since Cornish time is apparently half an hour different to that of London. Its blazon has a chevron with three balls, which may be the arms of the Bond family who were from Erth, opposite Anthony House. The little crescent hanging above the chevron is the mark for a second son. I suspect that this sun dial has been re-sited from elsewhere and that it is nothing to do with the Tillie or Coryton families.

Sir James Tillie's family was in the end given the right to the arms he had claimed as a young man. There may have been some justifiable connection to the earlier 16th century Sir John, but whether or not Sir James was a distant member of that family remains at present a mystery.

Endnotes

1   Cur.Mil.Boxes X/12/1-3; X/23/5

2   N 1599 Smith's Ordinary, a manuscript, includes a reference to the arms of Sir John Tilley which could be blazoned as 'Argent a cross Flory between four crescent gules'. [Coll Arms Ms EDN22 f.75v]

An important ordinary complied by Robert Glover in 1584 and updated and expanded in the 17th Century includes the same arms for Sir John Tilly [Coll Arm Ms CGY74 f.490].

A further 5 volume manuscript known as the EDN Alphabet and compiled in the early 18th Century mentions the Arms of Tilley as 'Argent a Cross patonce between four Crescents Gules' and suggests that these were quartered by the Earl of Derby and by William Russell Earl of Bedford. [Coll Arm Ms EDN Alphabet Col 5/...]

Peter O'Donoghue: Report on Armorial Affairs of Sir James Tillie 29 July 2009 by Bluemantle Puirsuivant,

3   CY/7048 Cornish Record Library. The original Grant of Arms, complete with seals, is held in the original grant box. Photographs have been taken courtesy of the Cornish Record Office.

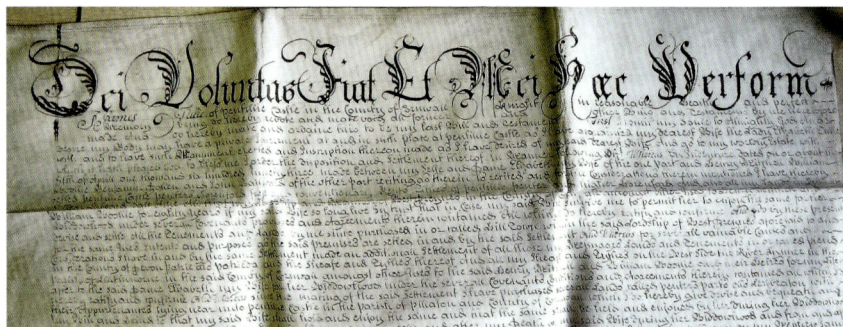

The first lines of the will as signed by Sir James Tillie
Cornwall Record Office CY/1676

Dei Voluntas Fiat mei hac performet.
The first lines of the will of Sir James Tillie, Pentillie Castle, KT., 22 March 1704
as copied into the probate records of the National Archives.
Photograph of Sir James Tillie's Will. National Archives Catalogue reference:
prob/11/537 Image reference 309

Chapter 6

Sir James Tillie's Will

Contrary to the legends that surround it, Sir James' will was relatively straightforward, even conventional. However, he added a codicil shortly before his death, when he was 'in his 67th year', and it is this codicil that sets out the more unusual arrangements for his burial. The burial is discussed in the chapter on the Mausoleum, as is the possibility that concerns about overcrowded churchyards may have helped persuade him to consider burial outside a churchyard.

The will is worth quoting in some detail, because it tells so much about the man, his wealth and wishes, and because it remains one of the few documents that gives us an idea of his character, with some flashes of what the man may have been like.

First, it lists much of his property by name, providing evidence of his considerable holdings. It sets out an inheritance sequence which suggests that, as a lawyer, he had had much experience of disputed wills and wished to avoid family disputes, detailing an order of succession for sons, daughters and so on.

Second, it suggests that the mausoleum was not then built, that is by 1704, since it refers to a monument yet to be erected, (although it is possible that he had a study or small tower already on the site). Although the will refers to a monument and inscription, these are in a separate sentence to the burial and it is not clear to me that this was intended to mean the building of a mausoleum.

Third, it is good to read inventory lists, particularly the 'fine coaches and the Calash' - a light carriage with seats for four. The list of wheeled vehicles is important simply because at this time such wheeled vehicles were still relatively rare in Cornwall, even in the extreme east of the county.

Fourth, it suggests a man who liked his own way, with incentives for the marriage of his wife's granddaughter Albinia Tillie Gotley and penalties for relatives who did not marry as he thought best; Sir James cannot have trusted Mary Mattock's beau William Parkes.

Fifth, there is no reference to any legacy for the Batts, his wife's elder daughter and husband, who had instituted legal proceedings about their marriage settlement against the Tillies. This confirms that a family dispute may have arisen in the Coryton trusts set up for his wife's children, combined with the probability that Sir John Coryton had been insolvent when he set up the trusts. Thus although Elizabeth Tillie, Sir James' wife, had two daughters, it is only the younger that figures in the will, the elder with her husband, having been cut out.

Sixth, it gives some details of a circle of long standing friends, and friendships such as those with Henry Mitchell and John Bailward that appear to have lasted most of his life. The will also refers to an extended family for Sir James of which we have no other knowledge.

Seventh, the will of 1704 appears to go beyond convention in confirming his Christian beliefs, contradicting the rumours that he was not of good Christian faith.

Eighth, the will reaffirms his wish to establish a family name, with a change of name required for inheritance. He also tries to encourage, or force, his wife's granddaughter, his god daughter, to marry one of the two Wooley sons, presumably to bind his family more closely together.

Finally, the will suggests a genuine affection for his men, and implies some respect for him by them. We would like to know why John Cory got a joint of mutton weekly for life.

There is a fair amount of detail in this will but it is worth taking the time to go through it, despite the abbreviations and references to legal procedures.

The Will of 1704

The following extracts from the 1704 will[1] are taken from the abbreviated summary of the will in the Cornish Record Office[1]. To this abbreviated summary have been inserted additions where it seemed necessary. The will started with the phrase:

'Dei Voluntas Fiat Et mei hac performet'

Interment and Burial

'And I do desire my body may have a private interrment at and in such place at Pentillie Castle as I have acquainted my dearest wife the Lady Elizabeth Tillie with and to have such Monument erected and Inscription thereon made as I have desired of my said dearest wife'.

Marriage Settlement and Support for Wife.

Recital of Settlement made on or about the 5 April 1693 between (a) testator and wife Dame Elizabeth (b) Henry Mitchell, William Wollie, Benjamin Dollen and John Bailward.
Pentillie Castle, Penters, Horenford, free and conventionary rents tithes of Pentillie, Penter and Higher Horenford. Testator's lands in Callington, St Cleer, Liskeard, Saltash. Manor of West Dreynes to Henry Mitchell and William Woollie for 80 years or if my wife so long live. In trust that in case my said wife survive me to permit her to enjoy that same for her widowhood…..

Lands since bought called Hill Town in manor of West Dreynes settled to uses of settlement. Recital of additional settlement of land etc at Piend in Devon. Patrieda (Linkinhorne) with sheaf and tithes and sheaf and tithes of west side of the river Lynher.
To wife during her widowhood: the central estate at Pentillie.

Pentillie

Since the [marriage] settlement of 1693, the testator had bought Penters Parks alias Leribeaton lying near unto Pentillie Castle, Pillaton). Last recited properties to wife during her widowhood,

Then to testator's son in tail male, in default his daughters, in default to James Tillie eldest son of testator's only sister Mary and his sons in default to William 2nd and youngest son etc, in default to sons of Mrs Mary Gotlie daughter-in-law by his cousin Richard Gotley,

Chargeable with £1500 for use of granddaughter cousin and goddaughter Albinia Tillie Gotley.

Other Lands

Land outside the marriage settlement includes land swapped after sale of Durham lands.

Recital since settlement land sold called Softlie and Hinton Hill and several other lands in the county of Durham of yearly value of £100). In lieu of this annuity of £100 from lands in Devon and Cornwall not in the settlement.

One quarter of manor of Winfield and Stofford, in the county of wilts and all messuages, lands and tenements in Winfield an Stoffod in the said county of Wilts and Manor of Warleggan in Cornwall and other lands in Dorset, Wiltshire, Devon and Cornwall not in the settlement - to go to 'my kinsman' Henry Mitchell and John Bailward and their heirs to use of nephew James Tillie with redress as before [that is a line of inheritance that children of Mary Gotlie as set out above] with extra redress to Kinsman John Bailward and sons.

Downing in Mangotsfield, Gloucester to be settled by James Tillie etc on nephew William for life and William's heirs , charging the estate with £500 for daughters portions if William has no sons.

If brother William Woollie survived testator, then nephew James Tillie was to pay nephew William during father's lifetime the yearly sum of £20.

The Family Name

Persons enjoying the benefit of lands had to assume the surname of Tillie [note spelling of name].

Lease Management

Leases permitted but not of Pentillie Castle, barton of Pentillie, Penter, Horenford, barton of Bittleford, barton and tithes of Patrieda and tithes of west side of Lynher and of barton of Piend for 21 years without fine.

'.......now to the capital messuage Belle Cour, Southall and Winfield or any part thereof…[these].may be let'.

The 'Personal Estate'

To wife: 'In regard of her kindness to me whilst living and tenderness to my memory which I know she will have after my death … I bequeathe unto my said wife all her paraphernalia, apparell, jewills and ornaments of her person all the books china, portraits and toyes in her closet at Pentillie castle'.

She also received the Testator's coach chariot calash and set of 6 horses with choice of 2 other horses and cows and a further 100 guineas.

After wife's death to her grandchildren of Mary and Richard Gotley as she thought fit and in default to Albinia Tillie Gotley.

Wife to treat nephews kindly.

To Richard Gotlie, junior and Mary his wife for mourning £10 and for her separate use 100 guineas.

To Albinia Tillie Gotley £500 at day of her marriage with either one of my nephews but if she marries anyone else she is only to have £250.

To brother Woollie and my sister and 2 nephews and to Henry Mitchell, £20 to buy them mourning.

To John Bailward £50.

To cousin Mary Mattock: £50 on her marriage day. To marry any other than William Parkes. (If she does marry William Parkes the legacy is void).

To cousin Mary Love, daughter of Kinsman John Love £50 with interest from testator's death, the sum payable on the death of

Cecilia Love, widow, her mother, or on her marriage day.

To cousin Albinia Jones £30.

£50 to poor relations, 'that is to be at my sister's and my executors discretion bestow amongst those of my poor relations, cousin germans [more distant relatives] and strong cousins'

£50 to be 'distributed to such poor and religious and godly people as my said sister and brother Wooley shall judge to walk righteously, uprightly and truly morall in the sure Christian faith in which my dearest mother and brothers lived and dyed which is the same I have stedfastly believed in and in which I hope .... to die'.

To brother William Woollie, sister Mary, Henry Mitchell and John Bailward (trustees) household goods etc at Pentillie Castle (Inventory to be made and signed by testator's wife). Wife to have use of goods for life.

Goods in Wiltshire to go to person who has the inheritance of Pentillie Castle

Trustees [Brother Wooley, Sister Mary, Henry Mitchell and John Bailward] to `lock up preserve and keep all my records, writings writing books and papers' also printed books and papers.

The Funeral:

To wife £50 for funeral [costs]`desiring four of my ancientest Workmen may lay me in my Grave unto whom I give forty shillings each.'

To Other Staff:

- £10 to William Trenaman
- To honest Richard Lawrence in meat and drink for his own person to value of 2 shillings and 6 pence per week at Pentillie during his life.
- To domestic servants living with testator at death 40 shillings each.
- To Samuel Holman, his tools.
- To John Cory a joint of mutton weekly for his life as I have done.

The Residue

Residue of estate to be sold and an estate to be settled at Belle-Cour in Wiltshire.

Executors: William Woollie, Henry Mitchell and John Bailward.

Witnessed by Richard Lawrence, Samuel Holman, Henry Mitchell, David Davies[3].

The Later Codicil of 1713[2]

In 1713, the year of his death, he added the following in order to give his followers a clearer idea of his wishes.

'...Being now in the sixty seaventh year of my age since the Sixteenth of November last having thro' Mercy hitherto enjoyed a great Share of Health But Sensibly finding a great decay of Strengthtake this opportunity of settling my affairs myselfe to prevent suites in Law or that (called) Equity on my leaving This Troublesome World for that of a more peaceable. My Requests are but few and souch as tend to peace and love; I Desire as I have been punctual in payment soe such with the personall Estate I shall order be as Expeditiously in giving the like satisfaccon to the discharging those few Debts I shall leave Nor Imbo:(?) zelling the Assetts of one hand to purchase Mournings pride and vanities and there bye on the other hand grieve and weary the Honest Creditor.

Laying aside the pompous solemnity of a Funeral That by Its Extravagance would devour the Living, following the Methods herein prescribed, I Desire my servant Samuell [is this Samuel Holman, one of the witnesses to the earlier will?] may within fiftie Houres next after my Death Compose and make for me a Timber oake Chaire, and my Servant John Quilting a Crape or Flannel Lining therefore In which I may sit exactly fit Tight and Close Remaining in One of the little Roomes near Pentillie Library until the Lady Elizabeth Tillie my wife shall order above Fifteen and under Twenty Five of my Men Servants (not Gentlemen Pall-Bearers who make It their Imploy for Lucre not

A transcription of the first part of the Codicil: CRO CY/1678

Lovesake) To Carry and lay me in a Repository for that purpose to be made Either on that Eminence called Mount Arraret or Pisgah Giving unto Each of such my Men Servants a Gold Ring and a pair of Gloves'.

The codicil then goes on to cover the exchanges made in relation to those lands of his wife's dowry and lands she had inherited in her own right from her father Sir Richard Chiverton, which included lands in Quethiock and Is Ive, and £2000 given to her by her father. Sir James sets out his wishes in regard to this, again, I imagine, to reduce the possibility of dispute.

It was the codicil that changed the funeral arrangements from a 'private interment in Pentillie Castle', where he had built a chapel, (although that chapel may not have been licensed) to one where he was laid 'in a repository', or vault, on the hill where now stands the mausoleum. Although burial in a vault was of course common, building such a vault outside a church or church yard was still unusual[3].

Sadly, the codicil does not make clear whether the mausoleum tower already existed, but I am sure that it had already been built as some form of garden or folly tower, and that the vault was inserted into that building on his death, a view supported by the recent archaeological investigation of 2013.

It will be noted that the codicil makes no reference to the requirements for food to be supplied after his death, to the spire on the building or indeed to many of the 'facts' listed in the original note by Hals and later expanded by gossip.

In the event it seems that his instructions were carried out. The vault was built; the tower extended and altered. His staff carried out his instructions, which suggests that he was liked and respected.

I have always particularly admired the requirement that the funeral procession should be restricted to his men servants and should not include 'gentlemen pall bearers who make it their employ [to walk in funeral processions] for lucre not lovesake'.

Friends and Relations

There are a considerable number of names mentioned in the will of which we have no information elsewhere. Excluding those who were perhaps his staff, they hint at a considerable extended family. Although relationships are made difficult by the imprecise definition of 'brother' or cousin' and so on, and although these terms may have been used loosely and as a form of endearment, it still seems that Sir James Tillie had a number of relations. Clearly, of particular importance were Henry Mitchell and John Bailward, described as 'brothers' or 'kinsmen' who, even if not 'blood brothers', had appeared in Tillie related legal documents for some twenty years or more. Richard Gotley, his brother-in-law, is described as a brother, but there are also references to more distant relations.

Sir James Tillie's signature to the 1704 Will
CRO CY/1676

The will makes clear his devotion to Richard Gotley's daughter Albinia Tillie Gotley, Sir James' god daughter, who was the granddaughter of his wife, through her first marriage.

We do not, however know anything about his 'kinsman' John Love, his wife Cecilia Love or their daughter Mary, nor about Mary Mattock or Albinia Jones. Other names that are absent are those associated with other Tillie members like his brother Jonathan, a merchant in Bristol who is thought to have predeceased Sir James, but who should have left some family. Perhaps Sir James' sister Mary was his only surviving sibling.

Another family member mentioned is Richard Elletson, of the West Indies, who appears to have been married to Susanna, another niece of Sir James.

Another absentee is 'Stephen Tillie' who had appeared as a witness in many documents and might have been either a member of the Tillie family or an 'adopted' son. He is not however named in the will.

Lady Elizabeth Tillie

We know from a reference at Wingfield[4] that Pentillie Castle was boarded up and not lived in by 1718, and imagine that his widow Elizabeth may have moved almost immediately to one of the houses at Quethiock, perhaps Trehunnett. She is thought to have lived her last years in Quethiock, which had been owned by her Father, Sir Richard Chiverton, and which had then passed to her, as part of her marriage portion when she had married her first husband, Sir John Coryton. When her father died, it had then passed to her as co-heiress of her father's estate. She died[5.] at Quethiock some four years after her husband on 9 Sept 1717.

The impression left from reading the will is of a man trying to make sensible arrangements for his family and legatees and of someone who is anxious to avoid dispute about his will, and who wishes his wishes to be settled promptly. He gives the impression of a wealthy man who did not like waste, but was sufficiently proud of his life to make his death and burial an individual one.

The will and codicil do not support the wilder tales that have accumulated around the name of Sir James Tillie.

Endnotes

1 Will made 22 March 1703/1704 in third year of Queen Ann Proved: P.C.C. 18 March 1713/1714; The National Archives; Prerogative Court of Canterbury and related Probate Jurisdictions: Will Registers. Name of Register: Leeds Quire Numbers: 254 - 286. Will of Sir James Tillie of Pentillie Castle; 18 March 1714; PROB 11/537/279
Also: Cornwall Record Office CY/1676 Will of James Tillie, knight, Pentillie Castle, Pillaton 22 Mar 1704
2 The addendum to the will is under Cornwall Record Office reference CY/1678 Undated, but assumed from preliminaries to be 1713. The codicil text below continues after that section noted in the main text, as in the summary of the CRO. It gives an idea of the extent of Sir James Tillie's holdings and also introduces some new 'relatives'.

Recital wife Lady Elizabeth Tillie had conveyed to testator: capitol messuage and demesnes of Trehunsie in Quethiock formerly in possession of Sir Richard Chiverton, knight deceased with all other her lands in Quethiock and St Ive. Also £2000 given to her by her father Sir Richard Chiverton, knight deceased to Richard Winne and Robert Biddolph deceased in trust to uses. Testator in consideration of this resettled barton of Trehunsey and her other lands and tenements in Quethiock and St Ive on her as long as she remained a widow. Also settled on her - Pentillie Castle and manor of Pentillie. East, Middle and West Parks of Pentillie. Pentillie and Penters in Pillaton. Horenford alias Hornavers alias Higher Middle and Lower Horenford alias Hornafers. Township of Pentillie, Penchaufour Penters and Penters Cross. Great and small tithes under modus of 13 shillings and 4 pence and 4 shillings and 6 pence. Property in Callington, Liskeard and Saltash. Manor of West Dreynes, including West Dreynes, Dreynes Towne, Hiltown, Lower Trenant, Higher Trenant, Pellagenna, Reedhill, Dreynes Hill, Kellowham with Roses park with high, conventionary and improved rents. Barton of Piend in Stockley English, Devon. Spreetwell in Stockley English. Bamsdon in in Puddington. Property at Brownes, Pages and Mount Pleasant in Sandford, Devon. Patrieda in Linkinhorne with tithes including tithes of the Vicarage 'when Tilled by Lay Hands'. Tithes of rectory of Linkinhorne on west side of Lynher. Had also settled on wife, lordship of Softlie and tithes tenement called Civillie and one twelth, one third and one twelth of Great Common of Teasdale in Durham. All this sold and purchased instead Bittleford in Landulph, Jories, Penters Park alias Leribeaton, Hiltown in St Neot. These settled on wife. Above lands then bequeathed to wife by will under same conditions. Rest of lands: manor of Warleggan; in Plymouth; Cooknie in Whitchurch, Dorset. Kellowham woods and West Dreynes woods in St Neot - to Benjamin Dobbins of Mangotsfield, Gloucestershire, gentleman, Stephen Tillie, Pillaton, gentleman and Zacharias Shrapnell, Bradford, Wiltshire, clothier for life of nephew James Tillie to uses. With 99 years term (to trustees) or lives of Richard Elletson, esquire, former husband deceased of niece Susannah Tillie, Edmund Edlyn, Island of Jamaica, esquire and his wife Ann. Then 20 years term to trustees then to male heirs of nephew Jeremiah Tillie Elletson, son of Richard Elletson.

3 'At the time of the 1711 Act, [which provided for building 50 new churches in London, and instigated debate, as summarised by Vanrugh, about the desirability that churches 'may be freed from that inhumane custome of being made burial places for the dead'] just two years before Tillie's death, there were no freestanding mausolea in con-consecrated settings in England. Indeed there were hardly any mausolea at all'. Information from unpublished paper: 'Putting the Pentillie Mausoleum in Context' by Dr Kate Felus July 2011

4 In notes marked 'Rated in Winkfield', 1718, Edward Lisle was rated in Winfield for properties including Pombery, Hortonn, Notts Hall, and Belcour. These notes also said that 'Pentillie Castle is now in charge of a land agent and all view from the road of the Castle and Mount Ararat boarded up'.

5 Lady Elizabeth Tillie died in Quethiock Parish, Cornwall and was there buried on September 9th 1717. Bishops' transcripts Doc ref: BT/195, Quethiock.

Top: Collecting bodies during the Plague of London, 1665
Below: The great fire of London, on 4th Sept 1666,
with the highest flames around Old St Pauls.
Detail by unknown painter.

Chapter 7

A Brief Introduction to the Period

James Tillie was two years old when Charles I was beheaded in London, was fourteen years old when King Charles was restored in 1660 and died one year before the accession of George I in 1714. He lived through the reigns of four different monarchs and one 'protector' in Oliver Cromwell. This was the period when the country changed from one that could still appear late Tudor, to one that was very different, the world of the 18th century.

The Civil War, religious differences and changes in the way the country was governed had done much to alter the lives of a people who felt as though they lived in a different world. 100,000 had died in that war, and it might have been thought that after so many years of war the restoration of King Charles II in 1660 might have brought a period of peace. This was not the case.

England remained threatened or engaged, even if only indirectly, in war. This was not a period when life can have felt settled. Wars or armies were not distant, but a present, local threat. The French were always a threat; wars with the Dutch continued through the 60s, and during the second Dutch War of 1664-1667 they made their famous raid up the Thames and burnt the English fleet. There were wars within the kingdom itself. These included a rebellion led by Monmouth, an illegitimate son of Charles II, whose defeat at the battle of Sedgemoor resulted in the savage trials associated with the name Judge Jeffreys.

Despite James II's standing army, his daughter Ann's husband, William of Orange, arrived from the Netherlands to land in

Top: The Dutch burn the English fleet before Chatham, 20 June 1667
Painting by Peter van de Velde
Below: William Penn helped develop Pennsylvania in the Americas for quakers and others. The illustration picture shows him making a treaty with Indians in 1682.

the West Country. He invaded England with a largely mercenary army and James II fled to France. James returned in 1689 and attempted to recover his crown, invading Ireland with Catholic followers and French troops, but was defeated by William of Orange at the Battle of the Boyne in 1690.

William had spent much of his life resisting the armies and political machinations of the French and Spanish. These European disputes developed into the 'War of the Spanish Succession', sometimes called a first world war because of the countries, continents and numbers involved. For nine years England had an army stationed on the continent, in a war which provided great victories for the Duke of Marlborough, from the Battle of Blenheim in 1704 onwards, and which ended with the Treaty of Utrecht in 1713, the year of James Tillie's death.

At a time when the country longed for stability, rumours abounded. Religious differences caused conflict, dispute and uncertainty. A good example was the plot imagined or fermented by Titus Oates in 1678, which produced a public frenzy which could be compared to the McCarthy hatred of communists in 1950s America. Another plot, the Rye house Plot, was an attempt to murder both Charles II and his brother James in 1683, which resulted in the execution of those alleged to have taken part, since of course executions remained a factor of failure and were common throughout this period. They included Roman Catholics executed in 1678, those who had taken part in the Duke of Monmouth's rebellion, and so on. James Tillie himself married a girl whose father, Sir Henry Vane was, despite a pardon from Charles II, executed in 1662.

For the whole period of James Tillie's life there was no certain heir to the throne, but much debate about the succession to the Crown. Charles II had no legal heir and was succeeded by his brother, James II who, unlike his brother Charles II, a closet Catholic, was more open about his faith, producing fear that he would force Catholicism on the country.

The Execution of the 5 Iefuitts.

The late D of M beheaded on Tower Hill 15 july 1685

Left: Fear of catholics, treachery, and foreign spies led to the hysteria of the implausible plot against the King's Life, discovered and concocted by Titus Oates, 1678-1681. This led to the execution of 22 people.

Right: King Charles ll left no children save a number born out of wedlock. These included his son, the Duke of Monmouth, who invaded the West country in 1685, only to be defeated at Sedgemoor and executed six weeks after he landed. The defeat led to the notorious 'Bloody Assizes' of Judge Jeffreys.

It was the birth of a Catholic son to James II which brought matters to a head and led to his exile. The crown passed to his protestant daughter, Mary and so to William who was protestant, Dutch, James' son-in-law and a grandson of Charles I. William and Mary had no children who survived beyond childhood; Mary's sister Ann also had no surviving children. On her death in 1714, therefore, the crown went to a distant German cousin who spoke no English.

The exile of James II ensured that during the last 24 years of James Tillie's life there was always a 'King in Waiting'. This threat could not be dismissed since James' family did return in attempts to retake the crown in 1715, two years after James Tillie's death, and again in 1745.

Not only, therefore, was this a period of concern about wars and invasion, but it was also a period when the relationship between Crown and Parliament varied as Parliament was necessary to finance the Government. The power and relationship of Crown and ministers also changed, at the expense of the Crown. Disputes with Parliament meant that Charles II dissolved Parliament in 1681, as too did James II, who struggled to pay his standing army, a factor which led to him selling knighthoods, such as that gained by Sir James Tillie.

The second half of the 17th century saw changes in work and workplace for much of the population. In many ways the more settled agricultural life that had existed for 100 years, or even in 1660, when four fifths of the population were tilling the land, had been replaced by the poverty, struggle and squalor of people trying to make a living either in emerging industries or in the slums that were now surrounding towns. The growth of towns and the movement of large parts of the population from country to towns started after the Civil War and continued throughout this period. As the old order declined and the new order tried to establish itself, the status of merchants and traders also improved, particularly as Parliament needed money.

This was not just a time of commerce and new worlds but also of disease and disaster. The Great Plague of 1665 decimated the

William of Orange embarks from Hellesversluis for his invasion of England in 1688.
'Vertrek van zyn Koninglyke Hoogheid van Hellesversluis na Engeland: 19 Oct. 1688'.
Engraving by T (Thomas) Doesburgh, a Dutch engraver active 1683-1714,
after an oil painting attributed to Abraham Storck in the National Maritime Museum Greenwich.
From an original print in the possession of the author.

population of London and was really only stopped by the Great Fire of London the following year, which burnt out so much of the City. Mortality, disease and survival were an ever present issue. James Tillie's first wife was one of perhaps sixteen children, few of whom survived infancy, demonstrating that even for the rich, few children could survive. Death and the shortness of life were ever present concerns.

The poverty of many in the country was described in Daniel Defoe's "Tour Through The Whole Island Of Great Britain, 1724-7" which told of the country he had visited. One of the earliest writers to do so, Defoe described the conditions and difficulties of those he saw. Since Sir James Tillie had an interest in lead mines in Durham, Defoe's Letter VIII includes an appalling description of the life of some lead miners. He describes the horrific conditions, abject poverty, miserable life and poor life expectancy of those working lead mines by means of small drain like holes running 150 feet below ground.

This was also a period of religious change and fervour. Much of the country was anti Catholic, but there had been growth in other denominations, which included extremists such as the 'Diggers', puritan sects, dissenters, and Quakers. This was a period when the Quakers became a distinct body and disapproval of them contributed to the establishment of Quaker colonies in North America. Acceptance of differing doctrines became better established after the Toleration Act of 1689. However, views on religion, or even politics were often kept quiet and it seems possible that when James Tillie referred in his will to 'dying in the belief in which he had been brought up', this could be a reference to the fact that his mother was not in the established church. Despite such beliefs, this remained a country where the established church was in poor hands and little respected, where bribery and corruption and an immoral life were common and indeed taken for granted. There were many strict and honourable men, but the country continued, in essence, to run through corrupt transactions and cliques.

In the world of arts and society, the restoration of a court brought back patronage, but also hangers on. The last part of the 17th century has been called one of the most immoral of times for an older society, falling before new ways and fashions. Rochester's dissolute poems still shock us. Mohun's empty trial for murders seemed a waste of time, but time showed that that branch of society and type of behaviour was irrelevant. Those of more importance were the bureaucrats, merchants, diarists who were creating the world that would become the 18th century.

The most obvious survival of the period today is the architecture, which changed with the return of Charles II, who had spent much of his life in both France and the Low countries and brought with him different architectural and social habits. The arrival of William of Orange also brought Dutchmen, Dutch traditions and Dutch architecture. The building of much of London and its rebuilding in a largely different style remains one of the great achievements of the time. The Great Fire of London forced a considerable rebuilding

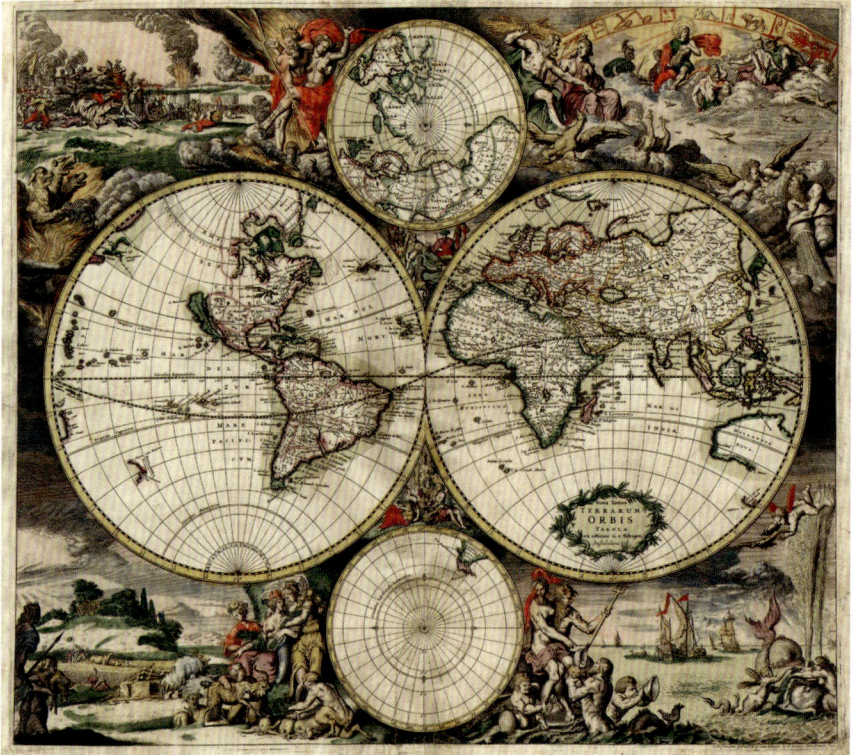

A map of the world in 1689 by Gerard Van Schagen

The map was produced in Amsterdam in 1689. Original size : 48.3 x 56.0 cm. Produced using copper engraving. This image is made up of six separate images downloaded from Helmink.com and stitched together. Public Domain

of the city, and many of the splendid new churches still stand today. The change in design sought by the merchant and professional classes for their houses brought new architectural style and habits to every parish in the country.

This growing middle class were merchants, traders, lawyers and even industrialists, who did not always have family homes or land. As their wealth increased, they wished to emulate a landowning gentry who were struggling with lack of funds and a system that no longer allowed them to rely on rents, privilege and court places. Sir James Tillie built himself a tower in Wiltshire so, it was rumoured, that he could consider the downfall of an old family at Farleigh Hungerford Castle; an instance of spectacular ruin for a family of old gentry, who had lent money to Charles II, gambled, spent, wasted money to such an extent that their great castle and family home had to be sold, while Tillie, a self-made man, was building up his own assets.

Fifty years before, travel around the country had been difficult. Decay of the roads had become so bad that much of the population were restricted to their immediate neighbourhood, but business and trade required road improvements. The first turnpikes were established in 1662. Transport and travel were still by pack horse for goods and horse for people, but the population was becoming more fluid and instead of people remaining all their lives near the village of their birthplace, they could consider moving to a town or to another part of the country. Sea travel was still the primary method for goods and persons, but despite the difficulties, Sir James Tillie was able to travel between Wiltshire and London, to distant Cornwall, and to the north of England, although the last two journeys could have been by sea.

Traders and professional classes moved to become pre-eminent in the business and life of the country. There were opportunities arising from the chaos caused by the civil war. For instance, disruption of mining and their workers offered new opportunities for a fresh start after the Restoration, and the same was true in other industries.

The principal opportunities were, however, overseas, and the sums to be made by those financing or taking part in such trades could be enormous. There was trade with the West Indies. Charles II himself helped set up the Hudson Bay Company in 1662. William Penn was given great swathes of land in 1682 which allowed him to establish what would become Pennsylvania, with the help of many who were, like him, Quakers. The East India Company continued to expand and make vast fortunes for those engaged in the trade with India. In medieval times the lending of money at interest had not been possible, but the availability of finance changed the business world. A growth in trade was accompanied by a need for finance. The need to finance a standing army, in particular, led to the beginning of the national debt in 1692 and in 1694 to the incorporation of the Bank of England.

However, there were also business failures. The most notable examples were when the moneyed class of Scotland got over excited by the Darien scheme, which by the 1690s had become so serious a failure that the poverty of Scotland led to the Act of Union in 1707. Although sharing a crown with England, Scotland was still an independent country, which was then rather unwillingly bailed out by England. Enthusiasm for overseas money ventures, trade, and the finding of quick wealth in the new worlds, also led at the end of James Tillie's life to such foreign ventures as the South Seas Company. This became an overinflated investment whose values crashed in 1720. However, the existence of such schemes illustrates the existence of a class of business men and rentiers interested in promoting and lending money on schemes carried out by others.

The wealth of merchants and of professional classes brought changes in the ownership of land. However, for many, such purchases were not investments but an attempt to buy into what they perceived as an upper class with influence over a neighbourhood. At the same time the traditional landowning gentry, with little other income save rent, were struggling. This produced conflict between the established small gentry and the 'arriveristes', but did not stop the advance of this new class to the top. The growing work of lawyers, of property and family disputes all show not only how fragile life was, but how devoted the entire country was to arguing about property and money.

Sir James Tillie's lifetime was one of change. It was one where people could consider a different career in town, when there was enormous growth and opportunity overseas, in America and in other continents, when there were discoveries in science. This was a period when changes in society could result in change in the status of the merchant and professional.

This was also the period which saw the growth of a leisured class, who had sufficient income to enable leisure to be enjoyed, a leisure that was not based entirely on country pursuits but on new activities and interests. This was also the time when the population started increasing, when towns grew in size and when a larger percentage of the population had funds or income. It was also a time when England could engage in a serious continental war, and rely on its ships for trade and defence.

Finally, the whole social and political background to the life of Sir James Tillie is put neatly in context by the minutes of the 'parliament' of the Middle Temple, who maintained meticulous minutes of their meetings and administered and ruled over several hundred students and lawyers. They ignored great events and concentrated on the minutiae of their life, a life that was essentially stable, improving and one that promised a future for professionals and a growing 'middle class'.

An engraving thought to be from 1692, the year of their marriage,shows proposals for building Pentillie Castle. It probably celebrated the marriage of Sir James to his wife Elizabeth, and signalled Sir James' intentions for a fine building. The print is in the style of Jan Kip and Leonard Knyff and may have been prepared from Sir James' ideas and sketches. It has the initals of Sir James and his wife in the top corners. *Private Collection.*

Chapter 8

Pentillie Castle

The Site and Early History

The land between the rivers Tamar and Lynher, north-west of Plymouth, was reasonably good agricultural land where the rivers had encouraged habitation and trade around the estuary and its inlets. Landing places and quays were possible up the many inlets of the estuary. The most important sites for the last 2,000 years have been those associated with trade. Landing places and later quays were in use at Cotehele, Burcomb (where a quay can still be found some way inland), and Halton, Hornifast, Pentearr, Clifton and many other inlets where boats could be drawn up at high tide.

There are early barrows and defended hill forts in the area, but the area defined by the hamlets, quays, many streams and inlets may once have been in the control of those who lived at Cadson Bury Fort, just south-west of Callington, below which was built the great house of Newton Ferrers. The land was part of the Hundred of Wivelshire, later divided into West and East Wivelshire. From the beginning of the medieval period this area west of the Tamar was a place of reasonable sized farms and wealth.

Pentillie Castle itself is built on a distinctive hill but no traces of Iron Age fortifications have been found either there, or in the grounds. It seems likely that early habitations were associated with Pentearr at the head of the little stream to the immediate south-west of Pentillie and with the valley and landing place immediately south of Pentillie.

The entrance drive to Pentillie now bypasses the site of the original farmstead at Pentearr, which lies off to the left and from which an earlier road led into Pentillie.

Pentearr and Paynters Cross

The track to Pentillie Castle starts from Paynters Cross (as spelt on the modern Ordnance Survey map). Three parishes, Pillaton, St Mellion and Landulph, meet close to Paynters Cross, a place once described as one of the only two hamlets in the parish of Pillaton. This important crossroads was where met the roads from Saltash to Callington and from Pillaton to Cargreen and was on the ridge way that wended its way north and south between the streams that led on the west to the Lynher and the east, to the Tamar. There is a possible Iron Age fort at the top of Paynters Cross; field layouts suggest another one on the next ridge north.

Paynters Cross was a settlement first recorded in 1200AD as 'Lirbeuston' a name which includes the Saxon word for farm, 'tun'. This became 'Loribeaton' in the earliest legal documents of the 17th century, and the name survived until 1801, when the place was referred to as 'Paynter's Park als. Lorybeaton'. Although the name itself is now lost, the settlement still survives as 'Paynter's Cross', a name which it adopted because the hamlet and crossroads were by Pentearr, an important farm or farm hamlet just east of the crossroads. It is not named, as has been suggested to me, after some early painting contractor, or a family called Painter. Variously spelt as Penters or Pentearr, this is similar to the not uncommon name Pentire, usually meaning a 'house by the headland'[1] and I believe that that was indeed the original name of this peninsula.

Pentearr was still shown as a place of substance on Joel Gascoyne's map, for which his survey may have started as early as 1693[2]. When it was published in 1699, the map showed a house called Pentearr on the north side of the stream to the south of Pentillie; A different entry was made for Pentarr (note spelling)Cross, marked on the site of what is now Paynters Cross. Pentillie Castle was shown with a symbol and as owned by Sir James Tilly, one of nearly 100 property owners marked in the county, all of whom are thought to have subscribed to the map to gain the mention of their name.

The family who had lived there must have fallen on hard times early in the 17thC, since such documents as we have suggest that the holding had become divided between numerous owners and tenants[3]. The hearth tax records for 1662/4 suggest that there was no sizeable holding which remained identifiable with Pentearr. One deed refers to Pentearr having rights of fishing on the Tamar[4], which suggests that there may have been a fishing village in the valley south of Pentillie, and another reason perhaps for the early medieval importance of the hamlet.

Pentearr farm was sited, as so many others in Cornwall, just below the ridge of ground some way up the slope from the stream and on the south slope. Here there was a building 'platte' and a well, both of which can still be seen. The road from Paynters Cross started to the south of Paynters Cross and led straight to this site. Below the house were other well sites and a road that led down the valley to the beach on the Tamar. It is usually possible to trace a Celtic or early

An enclosed spring and well head is all that is left
of the old hamlet of Pentearr.

medieval field pattern for most old farmsteads, but because of the
landscaping that started in Tillie's time, there seem to be few if any
old field boundaries. Interestingly, the field names given with the Tithe
Map of c 1841 show that there were no surviving old names, nor
names associated with agriculture. The failure of older farming names
to survive is usually evidence that farming failed before the start of
the 17th century, as seems to have been the case here, with Pentearr.

Assembling the Land

Sir James Tillie is thought to have bought Pentearr around
1680, and then purchased, piecemeal, the various parts of the holding.
These included 'Penters Park alias Leribeaton' and 'Penters in Pillaton'
and 'Penchaufour Penters and Penters Cross', which last is a duplication
in two languages of the same phrase. His purchase of the leases and
shares that made up this land is difficult to follow. Parts of the land
in Pillaton Parish were within a manor owned by the Corytons, but
they appear to have disposed of their interests before the civil war. In
another case, James Tillie is noted as the ultimate beneficiary, or third
in line of the right to some land, but is also, puzzlingly, the witness
to that deed. Other deeds are for the benefit of, or witnessed by, his
friends such as John Bailward, a Quaker business man, and Henry
Mitchell. Since much property conveyancing used methods such as
arranging transactions through a chain of third parties, leases with
a right to buy, or the commencing of law suits for possession which

would not be defended, (a system which allowed a swift and recorded inheritance in the days before land was registered), it is often difficult to follow what were the real intentions. The difficult issue is to decide how much of the Pentillie estate around Pentearr was bought by Tillie honestly, and how much finagled out of the Coryton Estate, or from the Chiverton Dowry of his wife, Elizabeth, who had been a Coryton. My own belief is that the Pentearr properties were properties of little value but held in complexity and divided ownership. These took time to sort out and assemble, but Tillie acted honestly in acquiring on his own behalf unwanted bits on the verge of or outside the great estates.

Assembling the estate took him some time, and he continued into old age gaining adjoining land at Bittleford, Tinnel, Hornavers and Halton. The importance to him of his Pentillie estate is evident from his will since, when he therein made plans for the property and acres he owned around the country, it was only the farms immediately around Pentillie that he wished to remain as one inviolate unit.

In papers dating from the early 1680s, before he was knighted, he had assembled sufficient land to be referred to as 'James Tillie of Pentillie Castle'. It is possible that he had by then already made a start on building a house at Pentillie. It is also clear that at the time of Gascoyne's map in the late 1690s the farmstead of Pentearr still stood.

Early writers tried to find a connection for the name Pentillie in the Cornish language and early place names. However, no such connection exists. The original name for the place was Pentearr; the name Pentillie does not appear in any records until the name was used by Sir James. The name Pentillie simply celebrates the surname of Sir James Tillie. It was chosen by him, and was intended to imply therefore, 'The Tillie Headland'.

The Design and Building of Pentillie Castle

In 1734 the great house he had built at Pentillie Castle was described as: 'This Pentilly is a new name given by himself to this his seat, from its situation on the side of a steep hill, having a pleasant

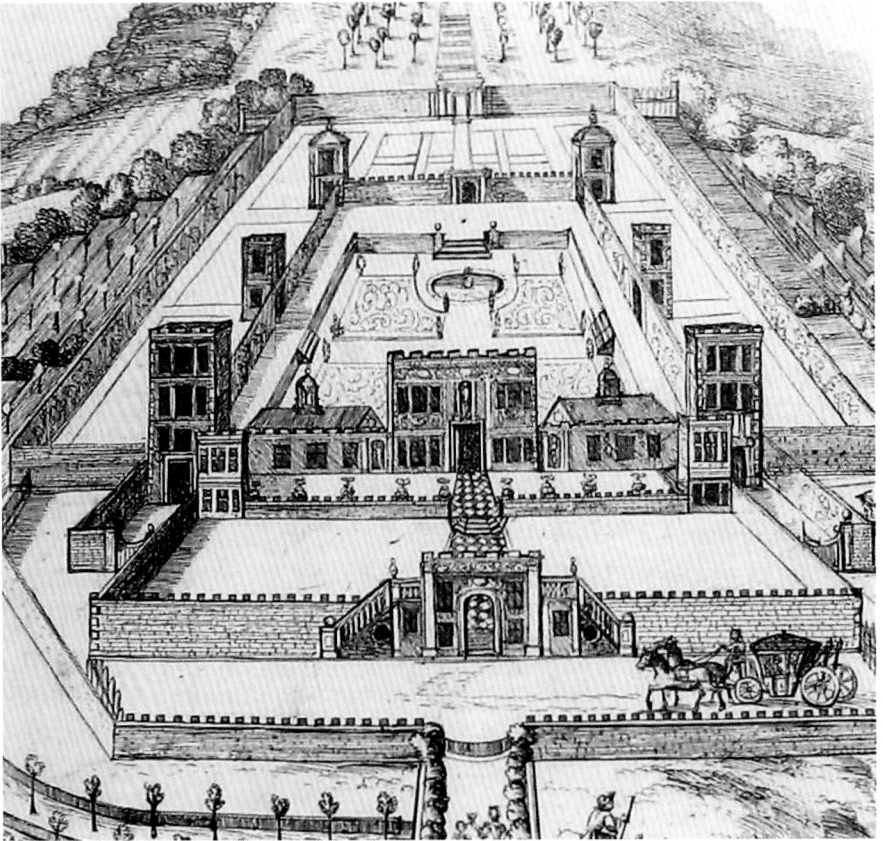

An enlarged section showing the house in the proposals for building Pentillie

prospect of the country round about. He has adorned it with fine new buildings, composed of several towers with gilded balls and several walks of lime trees on the side of the hill. All which together at a distance made a pretty show'[5]. This description makes it clear that the house was of some distinction and, for the time, unusual, with its towers and gilded balls. It also makes clear that there was not only a house at Pentillie, but also gardens with 'several walks of lime trees'.

Sir James Tillie was unusual in planning a house on an entirely new site. So far as we know there had never been a house at the end of this hill overlooking the Tamar. New house sites are rare in Cornwall and indeed, England, because most places with access to drinking water, transport and with protection from the weather had already been used. A house of status nearly always replaced or extended an earlier house on the same site.

At Pentillie, the earlier house was at Pentearr, which stood at the head of the harbour creek, some way inland, with shelter from the weather, good water wells and at the centre of the farm's field system. Pentearr is a site similar to those most other established farm sites of Cornwall.

We are not sure when Tillie started work. In the mid-1680s he was described as being 'of Pentillie Castle'. Either this was a statement of aggrandizement and hope, or he had already purchased Pentearr and started work on a building right on the headland.

A look at the surviving buildings, the cellars and at prints and drawings shows that the southeast corner of the building does not match the rest of the balanced design. Surviving plans and drawings suggest that this first stage had a hall or dwelling range running east to west, with a tower on the south east corner, (and perhpas an unfinished but buttressed gable to the west). This building, perhaps started in the 1680s, appears to have been in an earlier Jacobean style and can be seen on the right of the print of the west elevation dated 1770. The basement or half-hidden ground floor has windows which can never have been viable with present western ground levels, and some of the basement floor appears on a slightly different alignment at the southern end, which also appears of different work. The southern end had a different style to the remainder of the structure.

The suggestion that Pentillie was built in two phases is supported by the view expressed by Repton in 1809/10 that it looked as though the southern tower was of earlier construction[5]. He added that further investigation suggested the whole structure had been built about the same time. It seems probable that there were two phases marked by a material change in plan after work had started, with a plan for a grander building taking over from what had first been foreseen.

'Pentillie on the Banks of the Tamar', (part) by Edmund Prideaux: Drawn c.1717
Reproduced by permission Mr & Mrs P Prideaux-Brune

'A view of Pentily Castle in the County of Cornwall the Property of James Tilie esq. 1770'
The west front. *Reproduced by permission StAubyn Estates*

'Pentilly on the Tamar': Undated print. Tillie's domes can just be seen at the rear of the house.
Warehouses and landing places reflect the historic importance of the creek.

We can make assumptions about Sir James Tillie's design based on what we know of his life. He was the son of a copyhold farmer, and had risen high, consorting with the great, but had pretensions, ambition and a perhaps misplaced sense of grandeur. He wished not only 'to make a statement' but also to suggest a long established great house. He may also have been a person of genuinely old fashioned taste. For instance, the monument set up in the mausoleum has 'eared' strap-work in a Jacobean design more typical of the period before 1640. Comparison with the style and decoration on the monument in St Mellion of the lawyer Sir William Coryton emphasises the difference in taste and 'modernity' between the two lawyers of the same generation.

The evidence surviving from Pentillie suggests that his designs were indeed old fashioned. He was also, I think, careful with his money and did not throw the stuff around as was often the practice of his society clients. It is interesting that he seems to have re-used second-hand material such as the Tudor granite doorways in the basement and that the finished house was relatively small and only one room deep. Perhaps he valued a building budget.

Finally, he was no doubt affected by the practicalities of the site, the absence of level ground, the wish to impress a new wife and the magnificence of the chosen site.

It may have been his Cornish wife that prompted the move to Cornwall, rather than to Wiltshire, but we suppose that towards the end of the 1680s Sir James Tillie spent less time running his lawyer's business from London, and retired or planned to retire to Cornwall. This may have had much to do with the death of his client, Sir John Coryton, and Sir James' marriage two years later, in 1692, to Sir John's widow, Elizabeth. This marriage may have instigated, indeed helped finance the improved design and second phase of building.

It is to this marriage date that we ascribe the 'architects sketch' for the new building at Pentillie.

'A View of Pentillie on the Banks of the Tamar' *(part of highlighted engraving)*
Note battlements to East; 'Engrav'd for the European Magazine: Published by J.Sewell, Cornhill. October 1st 1785'

Above: The river or east elevation. *Below:* the west, courtyard view
Humphry Repton: The Red Book for Pentillie: 1810.
In his drawings you could lift a tab to show proposed changes. *Private collection*

A Baroque Palace?

A single copy of a 'bird's eye' view of Pentillie has survived from the end of the 17th century, when there was a fashion for realistic views of houses, first established by Hollar in the 1640s, and continued by Jan Siberects. Jan Kip and Leonard Knyff, both aged about 42 in 1692, specialised in the 'bird's eye' approach to representing buildings. Their drawings also included animals, coaches and horses and they illustrated garden plans with some care. They settled in London and are famous for producing large books of country house illustration, particularly the *Brittannia Illustrata*[7].

Sadly, the drawing of Pentillie has been cut down to fit a frame and so the edges and, more important, the dedication, title and author section are missing. Although we do not have their names on the drawing, it is possible that this proposal for the house at Pentillie was produced by Jan Kip and Leonard Knyff, in London. Tillie had had his own portrait done in January 1687 by Kneller[8], painter to the King. We can suppose therefore that, although other artists produced this type of representation, he was able to arrange for a drawing by the 'market leaders' Kip and Knyff around 1690. If it was they who prepared this bird's eye view of the house, it matches their earlier style when the title, now missing, was at the top, with a coat of arms in the centre. It appears to have been drawn without a visit to the site because, although quite accurate, details suggest that it was prepared in absentia and before construction was well advanced.

There is of course no coat of arms on this picture, because Tillie had lost the right to bear them; for this drawing they are replaced, unusually, by two cartouches. These were discussed earlier, but are the initials of both Sir John Tillie and his wife Elizabeth. I suppose therefore that this drawing may have been prepared for or about the date of their marriage in 1692, was intended to celebrate that, and to show how splendid would be the house at Pentillie. It may even have been the obtaining of her dowry that enabled Sir James to increase the budget and expand or extend the building.

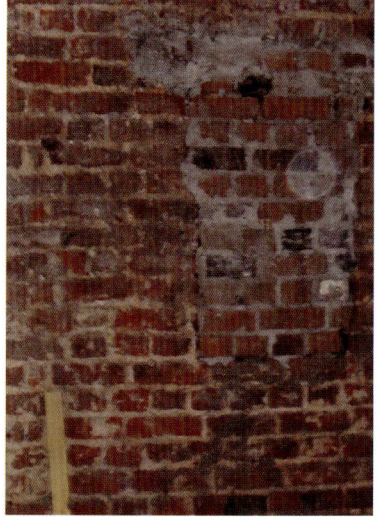

In 1966 much of Pentillie was demolished and reduced to a size closer to that built by Sir James Tillie. The forgotten pillars of the west Loggia were rediscovered. Their capitals supported the brickwork of that west front. An example, taken from the first floor interior, is to the right. This is an early example of brick use in Cornwall.

The West front still has the original Loggia pillars of Sir James Tillie's house. Although the towers mimic the original design they date from the 1967/8 rebuild.

The bird's eye view for Pentillie is fascinating, but clearly a design rather than a record of a completed building. Much is accurate in showing the site. Details of interest include the field layout on the way to Mount Ararat, the distant hills, the timber docks, the quarry, the lime kilns and the hint of the inlet to the south. The house has a walled garden to the west, and a row of pavilions running north to south, only one room thick, with towers at each end. The gardens and access roads reflect earlier roads in the valley and the difficulty of access on this steep promontory. Service and stable yards are detailed and indeed were eventually built in the positions shown. The design for the house and grounds uses the hill to make a magnificent estate.

The house design is unlike others of the time and the series of landscaped avenues and long views laid out in this picture are almost certainly the concept of Sir James Tillie himself.

It is the design of the house and its palatial ambitions that make Pentillie unusual. The pavilion style is similar to French hunting lodges and French designs of the earlier 17th century. These became better known in England both with the restoration of Charles ll, who had spent much time in exile in France, and when Versailles was visited after opening to the public from 1685. A French pavillion style seems the principal source for the architecture of Pentillie, but was unusual in England where the styles of the day looked for regular elevations and more concessions to comfort and changing social conditions. Such continental ideas may have been gained by Sir James in France if he did, as I suspect, spend time there as a young man.

The floor plan was old fashioned. The drawing shows a central one room deep pavilion with no internal corridor, standing over a raised basement with a single storey pavilion to each side. This side pavilion is separated from the central block by a corridor. Beyond that are flanking work units and towers included to add grandeur. To the west, away from the river, are a sunken garden, walkways and walled enclosures with more perimeter pavilion towers. The inclusion of a cow yard and other service areas suggests that the illustration is

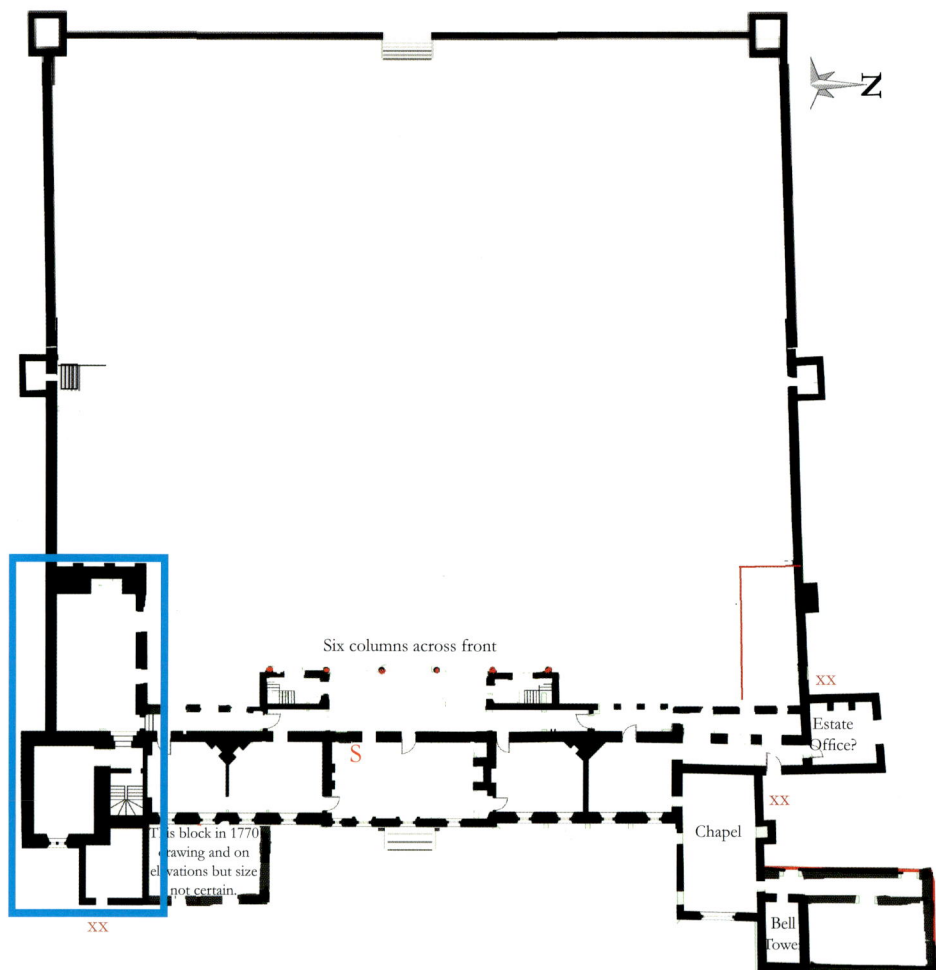

A conjectural plan of the Pentillie ground floor as first built.

The section outlined in blue was an earlier or first phase and may date from the 1680s or before. The cellars to this section are on a slightly different alignment. The west elevation of this wing had support piers to the gable. Buildings to the east and south east remain relatively untouched although the kitchen/bakehouse in the east corner of the garden yard is probably an early 18th century addition, as may also be the extension in the bottom right corner of this drawing.

As first built, baroque windows ran on both east and west to admit light to vaulted stores below. It is uncertain when these were blocked by raised ground levels. Note the cellar entrance for stores marked at XX. The design included for a formal enclosed garden with four garden towers. The remnants of two towers still stand. The walls had a walkway around them to allow views over them. Six pillars to the loggia of the original design can still be seen. It is not known where other pillars (of which parts survive) might have been used. It is guess work to suggest stairs were each side of the Loggia. Another possible site would be behind the second door from the Loggia, marked with an 'S'.

a practical guide for the buildings rather than an edited edition for show only. The main access proposed re-uses the older road in the valley, which was then extended to run round the hill and come up a ramp between the house and the river to a grand set of steps before a windowed lodge. The O.S. map from 1809, an illustration at the start of the next chapter, shows that the road network and sweeping east drive outlined in the drawing survived to the beginning of the 19th century.

Sir James Tillie was not interested either in a building with a pediment, or in a Palladian building similar to that erected by other lawyers, or his clients. This bird's eye view shows a building design unlike others of the time and unusual in England. It can with some justification be called a design for a palace with integral gardens and approaches, an architectural development not taken further in this form in England. It is unique.

Sir James Tillie's Pentillie[9]

House, gardens and landscape were the creation of Sir James Tillie. They remain one of the earliest surviving planned landscapes in Cornwall. Considerable alterations were made to the ground levels around the house and much was done to enhance viewing points.

It is surprising to find many similarities between the house as built and the bird's eye view or 'proposal' drawing. On a difficult site with steep hills and valleys, avenues were laid out and buildings erected. The plan provided for three areas. These were the walled gardens immediately by the house, a larger walled park area, and beyond that the landscaped drives for viewing the country.

The walled second area included gateways, a wall across the width of the headland, and towers. Legend suggests he was so unpopular with his neighbours that he had to defend himself from ruffian attack. This seems most unlikely. It is more likely that they are part of a romantic landscape, more garden ornament than defence. A first small entrance tower still stands north of the modern entrance.

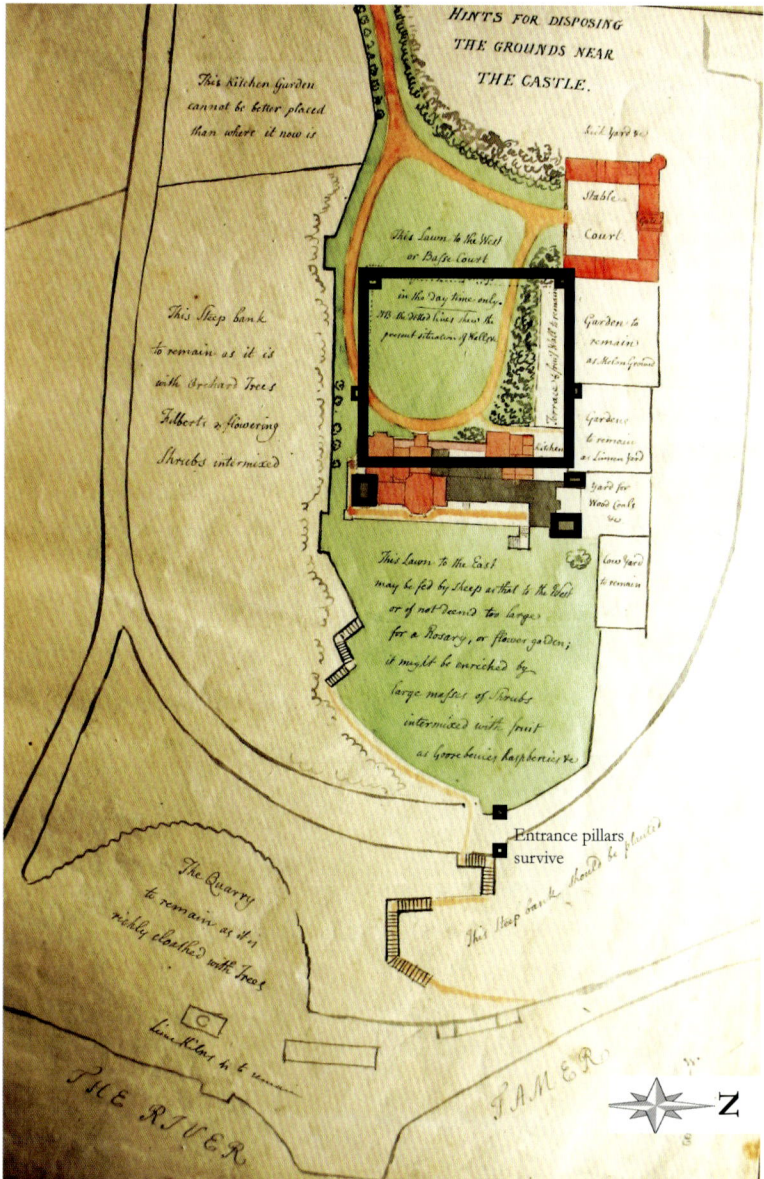

Proposed changes to the garden at Pentillie, from Repton's Red Book of 1810.
Repton's plan of the earlier courtyard included the positions of four towers, now outlined in
black. The original south carriage drive to the north stables is shown as in use.
Private collection: reproduced with permission

Remnants of a second tower stand just down the drive. Repton refers to another one, whose site cannot be clearly identified. It seems possible, therefore, that Sir James Tillie had planned a series of towers for the way to his house.

However, as mentioned, it appears that there was a change in design after work had started and that the southern section was an earlier phase perhaps dating from the 1680s. The northern basement, first intended as a semi-basement, is most interesting. It is at a slightly different angle to the southern wing, and there are signs of an earlier plan, and building. Three doors in the basement re-use granite openings of older style, recut to have the dates of construction, 1698 or 1699. The cellar had three ground level entries, two from the north, and a possibly older one from the south east. The entry ways from the north can still be seen, and are an indication of how the house must have been serviced.

In the cellars are windows, high in the wall, which were intended to be viewed from outside, now blocked by later terraces. These small delightful windows are in three shapes, square, oval and round, a 'Baroque edition' based on an earlier fashion. If they could still be viewed, the principal floor would stand slightly above the ground, giving it more importance. It might even have required steps up to the entrance on the inner or courtyard side. The small windows to the west appear to have been blocked earlier than those to the east, where the main floor must have been reached by steps until the rebuild of the early 19th century. Steps up to the perimeter of the walled west garden are shown in the 'birds eye' drawing, and although the 1770 print shows some vestigial walkways to the east, it seems likely that it was Sir James who changed his mind and that the ground was brought up to suggest that the west entrance was at ground level.

The main entrance was not, as today, from the west, but from the east, where the drive swept through fine gateways to steps to the house. If arriving on the west, you were faced by the blank castellated wall enclosing the courtyard, which can be seen in the print from 1770.

Three pictures show some of Tillie's original underlying structure and typical 17th century construction. Two of floors (The centre picture shows the main *Salon*; The third picture shows that the wall had a low chair rail with, probably, a wide chair rail.

The barrel vaulted ceilinig to the old 'chapel' may have had decoration like that of Wingfield Church, which appears of similar date.

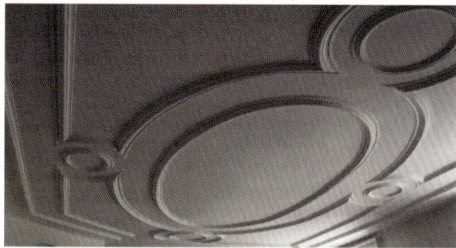

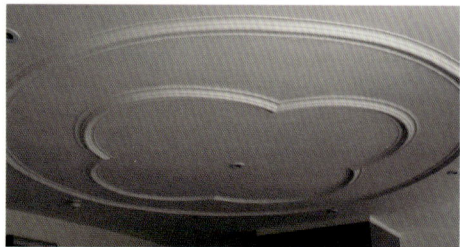

Surviving elements include the rustic quoins still to be seen towards the south end of the hall, which are in the 1770 print, and two 1690 style ceilings on the ground floor.

At the far end of the garden was a loggia of four and two half columns (of Elizabethan rather than classical design). Above, in a brick façade, was a niche with a statue of Tillie himself, a statue which survives today on its new site. In the grounds of modern Pentillie are pieces of another column so that it is possible that there was a further loggia or colonnade, or that this is a red herring. Although Henry Vlll had included internal corridors at Hampton Court in the 1540s, Pentillie was designed without them. One room led through to another unless one went outside to the colonnaded loggia. In 1810, Repton noted that with doors to both sides of a building a single room thick, the house was very cold.

The 1770 print has two entrance doors showing from the loggia, and it seems possible that the right hand one opened onto the stair case. The loggia formed the long entrance porch to the main hall or saloon which was heated by a large fireplace at one end and had windows looking over the river. To each side was a pair of saloons, each heated by an angled chimney stack. The east windows may have been large, divided by transoms and mullions, as in the Knyff drawing and in the style of the house at Belle Cour.

Above the entrance loggia an undivided 'long gallery' with three narrow windows ran between the towers, looking over the court. Parts of the west elevation used expensive, fashionable brick with a moulded string course. As was the case at Belle Cour, brick was reserved for buildings of high or higher status. It seems probable that the first phase of building was in stone. The second phase was in brick, an early use in Cornwall and intended to display wealth and status.

Further north were service buildings round a second court, with the bake house or kitchen. The present Estate Office had a large chimney so may have been an office or service room. The site of the kitchen is not certain. Further to the north were yards, gardens including fruit walls, melon gardens, a cow house, farm yard, barn, coach house and stables. Walls and pavilions separated the owner's area from the animals, services and supply routes to the basement.

The original design must have had much fine carved timber, of which these two wonderful pieces survive.

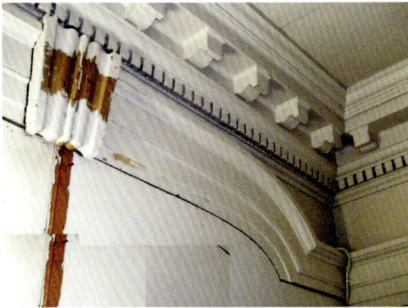

There are also remnants of original plasterwork and other possible early survivals like the shouldered door and some decoration to the right.

Left: A fireplace of 1690 design in the Quay House was perhaps reused from Pentillie.
Right: The roof structure to the present Estate office appears to be late 17th century.

There are several prints of the house dating from the 18th century, before the house was altered. Because of the financial turmoil that lasted through the 18th century, it seems likely that few alterations were made to Tillie's house during that time.

The first drawing of the house that survives is by Edmund Prideaux and dates from a tour he made in 1717, only 4 years after Tillie's death. This, and later prints, provide an outline which we can relate to the original 'bird's eye' view and to surviving detail. Two drawings of the west elevation, that of 1770 and one by Repton from around 1809 are also useful.

Repton produced coloured pictures of the west and east elevations as they were before alteration. The illustration of the west side shows the two 'Elizabethan' towers, perhaps in red brick, and the castellated wall to the courtyards. These 'pepper pot' towers with the supposed 'golden balls' were a great feature of the house, and quite unusual for 1700 and were described in the 18thC as old fashioned or Elizabethan. The second Repton picture shows the house from the river. The small brick wings at each end of the main facade are clearly shown. The steps in the centre of the eastern terrace suggest that the basement windows and entrances are already lost. The roof has lost the battlements shown in earlier drawings and the roof appears to over sail the walls. A sloping wall with arch supports (which survives today) marks the line of Sir James Tillie's great east entrance drive to gateway and stable yard.

The interior probably had much carved wood, of which only one or two examples survive. We can only surmise that the house must have had fine woodwork and heavy Jacobean stair cases. There is some surviving plasterwork to ceilings and heavy mouldings in the rear of the loggia and a heavy 'rustic' effect to door openings. Rooms were panelled to chair level height and the underlying structure for that panelling was found during renovation. Early floors have survived in the main saloon and have a typical 17thC construction of wide timbers. Door and architrave details are difficult to date precisely to 1700, but

The east front has been altered; the top terrace now blocks the small windows to the basement. An earlier access door to the cellars was off to the left and a flight of stairs to the saloon was nearer the house. The 'chapel' window is to the right.

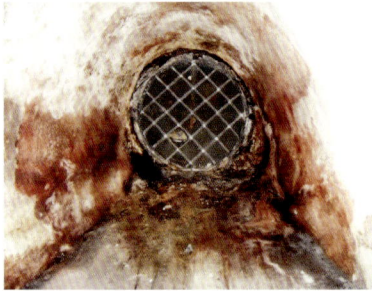

Eleven windows survive in the basement. They are in three different shapes, (square, round and oval). Three oval, four circular and one square light were arranged along the east, one or two retain their original glass. There remain three blocked oval openings to the west.

more seems to have survived than might have been expected, despite suggestions of an 18th century redecoration of the interior.

A barrel vault survives in what is thought to have been the chapel. This may have been decorated in the style shown by the barrel vault in the parish church of Wingfield in Wiltshire.

One uncertainty is the window glazing. Pictures of the east front appear to show these as both large and small openings To the west, the 1770 drawing shows the main windows with small panes to each casement, and no clear suggestion of 'modern' or sash openings. Windows to the side have a strange blocked section to each side of the lower half, so unusual as to suggest that it must be an accurate picture, but one that I cannot explain.

In examining the plan and surviving details of Sir James Tillie's house, we have plans prepared by Repton, the evidence on the ground and the illustrations. This chapter includes a reconstruction of the probable plan of the house at the time of his death. However, although we have dates for its start and we have dates on the chapel bells which may signal the end of the construction, we are not certain how much of the house, started in 1699, was finished when Sir James Tillie died in 1713. I assume that like many such a personal building project, work never really stopped. We can assume that it was fine enough for his wife to continue living there after his death.

The Pentillie of Sir James Tillie deserves further research and admiration.

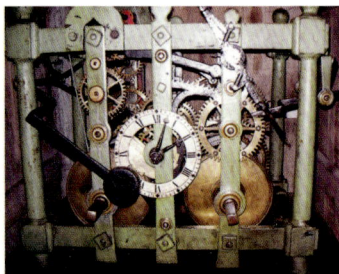

The clock and bell tower must have been a prized possession. Six of Sir James Tillie's bells, each of different size and tone, remain in store. A further bell is mounted on top of the Clock tower. The workings for the clock still tell the time. The bells each bear the name Sir James Tillie and dates which varys from 1705 to 1707. The bells are said to have been last re-hung and sounded for the marriage of William and Evelyn Coryton in 1887.

Endnotes

1.　'Cornish Place Name Elements' by O J Padel, 1985 notes two elements in the name: Pen and Tyr. Tyr is held to mean 'land', and may have come to mean 'holding', suggesting a meaning of 'holding on the headland, for Pentearr. 'Pen' has a number of uses, but usually meant 'the end', or 'head', or 'promontory.' Since there is a prominent headland with steep sides at the site, the use of Pen for Pentearr fits well with that suggestion. It is suggested that the combination of 'Pentyr' could refer to the headland alone rather than to the farmstead of Pentearr.

2.　'A map of the county of Cornwall newly surveyed by Joel Gascoyne'. Published Exon : Sam. Darker and Sam. Farley for Charles Yeo, 1699. Reprinted in facsimile with an introduction by W.L.D. Ravenhill and O.J. Padel: Devon & Cornwall Record Society, 1991.Exeter.
Review of Gascoyne's work in Cornwall over perhaps six years described in: 'The Lanhydrock Atlas': Cornwall Editions 2010; Edited Paul Holden PP16-17.

3.　The land at Pentearr hamlet and land around Painters Cross was in different occupations and appears to have been split up from 1620 onwards (CY452). In October 1626, William Coryton was agreeing to lease one third of Penters, and other properties, in a deal with Giles Inglett and Nicholas Hatherly where a lease for 99 years was given of one third of the interest in tenements including Penters, then occupied by John Tremanian, junior. Rents included a third of a capon (CY701). John Coryton seems to have bought back another third in 1640 (CY/718). Deeds of 1676 for Painters show great complexity of descent and interest of several parties with two thirds of Penters held for third parties and then, in the end, for a lease of 1000 years (CY/668). In 1685 'Painters alias Penters, Pentillie, with free fishery in the water of the Tamar', appears to be sold back to Sir John Coryton and his wife Elizabeth, who was to become Tillie's wife (CY/669). A deed of September 1686 for a tenement in Penters is passed around, but the deed is witnessed by John Lanyon and Henry Mitchell, both friends of Tillie (CY670). In July 1698 John Bailward of Winfield, one of Tillie's friends and representatives, takes a lease for 999 years at a peppercorn rent, of 7 acres called Penters, alias Penters Parkes, alias Lerribeaton in Penters, Pillaton, the land to be used as directed by James Tillie (CY/671). In March

The yard to the north shows what may have been an earlier ground level, with the entrances to the cellars. Most walling is from Tillie's build; one garden tower survives in the top right hand corner. Centre are the massive remnants of a bakehouse or kitchen chimney. The square building centre left is the modern estate office, which may have been its original purpose.

Left: The north east bell tower remains as built, save for lost render and the rendered mouldings to the string course; a relieving arch to the east suggests a large blocked window or opening to the stable yard. To its left is the altered gable end of the chapel, which once also had an entry, now blocked, to the service basement.

Right: Half way down the hill to the east can be found the original entrance pillars and curved stonework of Tillie's house. This was the main entrance that ran down the south valley to curve round the east end to the stables and service buildings to the north.

1704 another transaction appears to buy out the interests of a tenant, a package of land including '2 closes called Penters Parkes alias Lerribeaton, Pillaton'. Henry Mitchell was the witness to this document also. (CY/1809). All these documents survive because they were parts of the deeds and ownership of the Coryton estate, which eventually, in the 18th century, inherited all Tillie's interests.

4.	CY/669

5.	Gilbert, Davies The Parochial History of Cornwall (4 volumes) Nicholls, London. 1838. Volume 1 page 314. Gilbert is quoting a source of 1734.

6.	Humphry Repton (1752-1818)	Red Book for Pentillie 1810 Private Collection.

7.	'Britannia Illustrata: Or Views of Several of the Queen's Palaces, also of the Principal seats of the Nobility and Gentry of Great Britain, Curiously Engraved on 80 Copper Plates. London' (1707). The etchings by Kip, were from bird's eye views in the Dutch manner by Leonard Knyff (1650 - 1721), Dutch draughtsman and painter, and by others; eventually Kip did both drawing and etching. Johannes Kip (1653 - 1722) was a Dutch draughtsman, engraver, and print dealer who was active in England, after producing works for the court of William of Orange in Amsterdam.

8.	Sir Godfrey Kneller, 1752-1818. Court painter and Principal Painter to the Crown from 1680.

9.	Pictures tell a thousand words, and there are a number of illustrations with details of the early house in this chapter which are not further detailed and which it is hoped are self-explanatory.

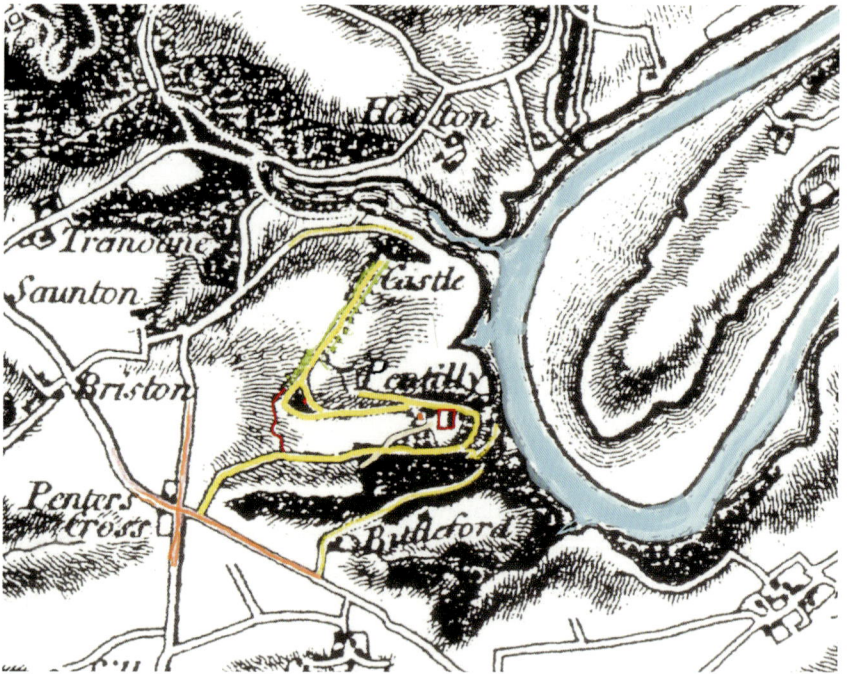

Pentillie in 1809

The O.S (Old Series) map 1809 shows the layout of the grounds much as they may have been left by Sir James Tillie, and before the 19th century alterations. Colours added for effect. Note that the main drive still goes round to the south of the building, through the second gateway to the service buildings to the north.

A drive continues on the north to a far corner of the garden where there is a right turn to the long tree lined avenue to the north and to the Tower, here called 'The Castle', surrounded by trees. A second walk or drive leads past the well or grotto in the corner.

Outlined in red is the wall to the West boundary where an exhedra, a semi circular arbour or viewing point is shown. This plan does not show all the drives believed to have been designed and executed by Sir James Tillie.

Chapter 9

Gardens and Grounds at Pentillie

The house has approximately 55 acres of garden, with a further two hundred acres landscaped to create views, drives and walks, extensive and beautiful woodlands and a setting for the house. Service buildings include stables, cow byres, staff cottages, sawmills, and many others. Splendid as is Pentillie, few now recall that it was first laid out around 1700, with designs, curiosities, avenues and spectacular effect. This was an early example of garden planning on a new site.

In the centuries since Sir James first laid out the gardens, they have been altered and extended, and although it is tempting to describe the gardens as they are now, or list the ornamental garden follies and estate buildings, which once totalled some 100, it is more interesting to trace Sir James' design and follow his garden plan, walkways, even his walling and garden buildings which, despite two centuries of change, can still be followed in much of the garden. Such inspection shows the scope and extent of that original scheme, for which Sir James Tillie deserves greater recognition as a design on what was a green field site.

Before looking at Pentillie itself, a garden design should be put in the context of other gardens of the time. What might Sir James have had in mind for the design of his gardens, avenues and walks?

Garden Design at the end of the 17th century

The sixteenth century had seen an increased interest in the design and layout of pleasure gardens, although such gardens were designed not so much for the growing of plants but rather for walking and leisure activities such as bowling. A Jacobean garden would normally have one smaller enclosed area for use by the family and women. A second larger area, still with a formal layout, was intended for visitors and would have terraces, walks and a bowling green. Both areas could be walled or enclosed and were usually on different sides of the house. In Cornwall, examples of such features can be traced at Trewinnard, Caerhays, Godolphin and many other houses of the time.

Towards the end of the century formal French or Dutch inspired gardens became popular, with examples in Cornwall at Mount Edgcumbe and Rosteague in Roseland. The restoration of Charles II brought to England many who had spent time either visiting or in exile on the continent, and who were influenced by the baroque fashions of the time. André Le Nôtre had provided the most influential of Baroque gardens at Versailles, where perfect symmetry, an axial layout, radiating walks, parterres, fountains and a principal axis had their place. This transferred to England with the development of a formal and private garden, which was a mixture of axial and impressive design, and of smaller, enclosed spaces with beds which might be called a development of the medieval herb garden, although by now, with hedges and displays, looking quite different. The end of the century also saw an undoubted Dutch influence, with the arrival of Dutch trade, and then a Dutch king, William of Orange. The designs of Le Nôtre had spread around the continent, and were amended in Holland, where William of Orange's new garden at Het Loo, designed by Le Nôtre's follower Claude DesGotz, displayed a leader's, a king's preference. Although still formal with perfect symmetry and organisation, that garden is not intended to dominate the landscape but instead has simpler squared beds in an enclosed area and raised walks around the edge, the whole idea being that the garden was for private pleasure rather than public display. Outside the central formal garden there were scenic avenues, but these were intended for meandering in a carriage or on horse rather than to provide views.

In Cornwall, the rebuilding of the great house of the Corytons at Newton Ferrers was started by John Coryton, the first husband of

Elizabeth Tillie, and was finished by Sir William Coryton, Tillie's friend and client. The gardens here have a series of descending terraces, with walls, ballustrades and lots of decorative ball finials. There was a separate walled section and a rumour that 'an Italian' had been involved in the design. The gardens were started around 1685 and probably finished by 1695 and therefore an example which Tillie could have followed in either architecture or garden design. Newton Ferrers is sometimes called the earliest of the classical houses to be built in Cornwall. Another great house of the time was Stowe, Kilkhampton, built by John Grenville, whose gardens were also walled, divided and largely private. This house built in 1680 was demolished only 59 years later in 1739, but was another example of what Tillie might have emulated.

The new house at Pentillie Castle, begun in the 1690s, had courtyard gardens laid out with corner and intermediate viewing towers in a rather old fashioned style, but with long rides set out beyond the enclosed space. This design looked back to the grand French designs of mid-century France, where Sir James may have spent some time. The design reflects a formal approach to pleasure with raised walks and towers, and in some ways imitates the earlier 16th century fashion for gardens and pleasure rooms. At Pentillie the garden is also divided into two, one at the front for public arrival and view and one at the back for private use. Although the site may have restricted placing gardens to the side, such side gardens were probably not considered.

The design did not reflect a changing taste which, with the turn of the century, became in the early 18th century a love of scenery, of views, of a more informal approach, or of 'scene-painting'.

From around 1700 there was a general change in the design of gardens and although John Kemp designed an exceptionally small patterned garden within a walled garden at Rosteague, such designs and the influence of Dutch horticulture resulted in such enclosures being included within larger schemes, which by the middle of the 18thC had become a very different concept. There are many examples

From Top: Stowe, Kilkhamton;   Newton Ferrers; Bake had a late 17th century garden
These three pictures by Edmund Prideaux c 1717. Reproduced with permission
Bottom: Menabilly had a formal walled garden of around 1700, with parterres, separate walled
sections and a viewing mount (bottom left). *Private collection. Reproduced with permission.*

in Cornwall of the changing taste in garden design that took place after 1700, and it is perhaps of interest that several houses where work started before, around or just after the time of Sir James Tillie's death show that change in taste. This does not appear to be reflected in the garden of Sir James, as that must have been worked on in the first 13 years of the new century.

Antony, rebuilt around 1722, included a formal garden and decorative corner towers as an entrance court with landscaped areas which stretched beyond the walled enclosures. Others combined a new garden and style with a new style or façade to the house. Thus, at Bake, a Prideaux drawing shows the old formal garden by the earlier house, to which was attached a new house, façade and garden. At Pencarrow new façades and gardens were built away from the earliest house and new approach roads provided. At Menabilly, a new prestigious façade was provided with a new formal large walled garden, complete with mounded lookout point and walks or rides in the areas beyond the walls. This was also an example of the common raising of a garden so that you could enter it directly from the original first floor of a house. At Prideaux Place similar changes in layout can still be traced. Even a less wealthy gentry house, such as that at Harlyn, was altered from 1690 by Gregory Peter with a new wing and façade and formal gardens with a 'viewing point', which at Harlyn included an exhedra.

At Caerhays, a walled garden was added c.1720 on a different site to the earlier Tudor enclosure with its terraces, walks, bowling green and ponds. The new walled garden was provided with an octagonal banqueting house, viewing mounds and two turrets from which to admire the scenery. Beyond the walled gardens perhaps a further 50 acres or so was laid out with walks and in particular tree plantations. This area was described in an inventory of 1753 as including *'the flower garden, spalier hedge garden and kitchen garden, the new wilderness, malt house grove and John Eddy's orchards, nursery near John Eddy's orchards, cherry garden, garden top the orchard meadow, garden above the ash hill in the Grove, the orchard beyond the ash hill neat Lower White Stiles, the new orchard including the nursery, the nursery near the White Style stable, the Nursery in the Helland stable, Gidle Orchard, Park Grove as far as the gate into Churchtown field, the present park Lawns....'.*

The Pendarves family built a new house, Pendarves, outside Camborne with an open area in front of the house. This was bounded by what was perhaps the earliest ha-ha in Cornwall with at its centre an exhedra decorated with statues of classical figures. This early 18thC garden was evidence of the changing taste and a wish to show an interest and knowledge of 'classical' culture.

By 1750 gardens had become important in the social status of owners. Rather than small inward looking gardens for retreat or terraces for walking and sport, or avenues, gardens opened up to views and larger areas of scene painting. One of the most telling examples of the new 'garden' is demonstrated by a guidebook of 1749 for the great gardens of Stowe. This publication, intended for gentry visitors, lists 77 monuments for the walker to look at. However, it does not mention a single shrub, tree or flower. Whilst this may be an extreme example of garden description, it does suggest that gardens were intended to give vistas, views and provide opportunities for walking and travel.

In Cornwall there are several examples of the changed approach to gardens. At house after house, a new façade was built to face away from the original working side of an earlier house, and the 'new' side often provided with a new style garden.

However, the design for Sir James Tillie's garden seems, like the design for his house at Pentillie, to have looked back rather than forward and to have been intended to reflect French and Dutch influence, and provide an area for private enjoyment. However, this opinion must be modified by his design of rides and walks and indeed by his use at both Pentillie and Belle Cour of distant towers, intended for quiet seclusion and thought. As in other aspects of his life, Sir James Tillie appears to have been a mixture of the conservative and the imaginative, or an individual whose designs fit uneasily in any established historic pattern.

Surviving Evidence

Splendid as they are now, and splendid as they have been for two hundred years, it is notable that at the end of the 18thC the gardens were already recognised as special. Such reports must be accepted as recognition of the achievement of Sir James Tillie since it would seem that little alteration was made to the gardens during the 18th century.

Immediately after the death of Sir James in 1713 the house was boarded up[1], and his descendants were occupied elsewhere, and in particular with court cases. Not only were the Tillie (formerly Woolley) family occupied with law suits, but so were the Coryton family. Peter Coryton, (formerly Goodall), lived at Crocadon, fought many legal disputes, including one with his relations, the Hellyars, who claimed much of what had been the Coryton estate. This suit dragged on from 1740 to 1772, and like many such a legal affair, must have drained the Coryton family's resources. Peter's son, John Coryton (1740-1803) married into the Tillie (formerly Woolley) family and it was this marriage to Mary Jemima Tillie that brought Pentillie castle into the Coryton family. It was only in 1809 after family deaths that their son could move into Pentillie, following what was said to have been a period of neglect lasting several decades.

During the 18th century, there was a long period when Pentillie was either empty, let, or in the possession of owners dogged by law suits and was followed by forty years of inactivity and decay at Pentillie. Such a century of inactivity and lack of interest is important, because it suggests that the 18th century at Pentillie was one when little money was spent and that therefore few changes will have been made to the house and gardens after the death of Sir James Tillie in 1713.

Sir James Tillie's Design for the Gardens

It is unusual that we have for Pentillie a drawing which may represent Sir James' dream for the site. The first drawing of the garden is that which I believe was prepared around 1692, more as a proposal of what was intended than as a record of what already existed.

An engraving thought to be from 1692 shows proposals for Pentillie Castle and the layout of the gardens. The print is in the style of Jan Kip and Leonard Knyff and may have been prepared from Sir James' ideas and sketches. *Private Collection.*

This wonderful bird's eye sketch, illustrated in full earlier, has a number of terraces along the slopes of the hill, on two sides, each lined with trees. Walks and steps on formal axis lead from one part of the gardens to another. The house has a grand entrance courtyard to one side, with to the rear, or west, a formal walled garden. This garden is lowered below a walkway which is itself surrounded by a wall with six observation towers. Outside this wall is a second walled garden laid out to formal squared beds, a walled garden that entirely surrounds the central garden. Beyond that second garden to the west are further straight avenues and trees. It also shows a separate drive to a separated commercial area of wharfs and riverside activity, and a separated area for stables and services. The thrust of the whole design is a straight line from the steps to the wharf up the hill through the house, the west gardens to a further avenue extending into the distance. This drawing may therefore represent Sir James Tillie's ideas and scheme for the garden in 1692, although in the next few years he must have changed his plans to add extended drives and features outside the central site. Such extended landscapes were often drawn on bird's eye views like those promoted by Kip and Knyff, but are not shown on the drawing for Pentillie, so it may be that he did not then consider such a wider landscape.

Apart from the evidence on the ground, the evidence for the extent and layout of Sir James Tillie's grounds is to be found in a few 18th century prints and illustrations, some written sources and from the drawings of those early 19th century garden designers who made proposals for change.

The 18th century evidence tends, perhaps in accordance with the preferences of the time, to emphasize the trees and landscape rather than west gardens. A drawing by Prideaux done in 1717 shows the eastern tree covered slope to the river with planted Conifers close to the house, and other plantings of trees. A 1734 source quoted by Gilbert[2], recorded that *This Pentilly is a new name given by himself to this his seat, from its situation on the side of a steep hill, having a pleasant prospect of the country round about. He has adorned it with fine new buildings, composed of several towers with gilded balls, and several walks of lime trees on the side of the hill. All which together at a distance make a pretty show.* A print dated 1770 shows a formal courtyard garden of hedge edged beds surrounded beyond the buildings by luxuriant trees. In another print of 1785 the trees remain the dominant factor.

Gilbert, in his book published in 1838, also reported that Sir James had *'laid out the hill slopes and avenues long before landscape gardening was thought of. One splendid avenue of his planting remains'*. I am not certain to which avenue this remark refers, although it supports the idea that Sir James must have laid out more than one such avenue.

Several writers made references to the splendour of the

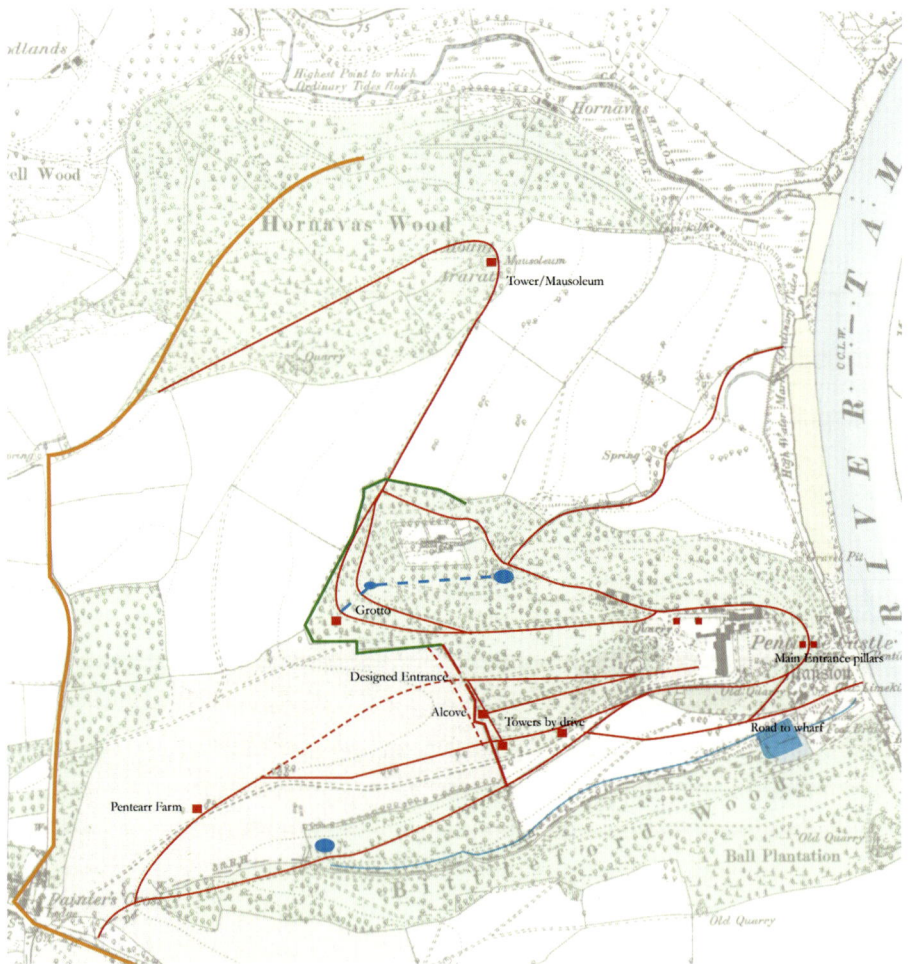

A map of Pentillie with some of the features, walks, drives and towers
of Sir James Tillie's landscape plan

grounds and site and among such visitors was John Swete[3] who, writing in the 1790s, spoke of the *'rich and noble woods,'* the *fine situation and that the 'beautiful woods which overspread the rising hills are surrounded…..by the circumfluent waters and in every point of view appear the most pictoresque beauty'*. W G Maton writing in 1794[4] commented on the view of Pentillie as *'highly beautiful and luxuriant'* views, and on what appears to have been unchecked and abundant growth.

The first Ordnance Survey map for this area, published on 11 October 1809 and presumably surveyed some time earlier, predates the alterations to house and garden at Pentillie as proposed by William Wilkins, Repton, Lewis Kennedy and Elizabeth Coryton. The 1809 Ordnance Survey shows several drives around the grounds, garden areas, a semi-circular walled exhedra to the west boundary and an avenue of trees leading to the Mausoleum (here noted as the 'castle'). Then, from 1809, the proposals of alteration prepared by Repton for the Corytons give further clues as to what still remained of Sir James' layout. These were first set out by Repton in his 'Red Book'[5]. This includes his drawings of the earlier building, and parts of the earlier garden. Additional ideas and designs by Lewis Kennedy, set out in his 'Green Book' of 1813[6], include illustrations which show that two of Tillie's entrance towers still stood along the drive, as must much of the original layout. Thus, although work had probably already started on the grounds by then, a comment from 1820 suggested that *'the remains of the gardens and shrubberies show them to have been very extensive…'*

By 1822 the garden was listed by J C Loudon as one of the most important of Cornish gardens a comment that must reflect the considerable extent of surviving older gardens.

Sir James Tillie's Garden Plan.

An illustration of the conjectured layout of the grounds in 1710 gives an idea of his work. In addition to the walled garden to the west, the steps and terraces to the east, and the drives, there was also a series of walled gardens such as 'the melon ground', a long south

Left: The restored tower that was to the right of the earlier entrance drive can be compared with a similar tower, *right,* although it has lost one storey, in the garden at Caerhays.

The modern drive entrance

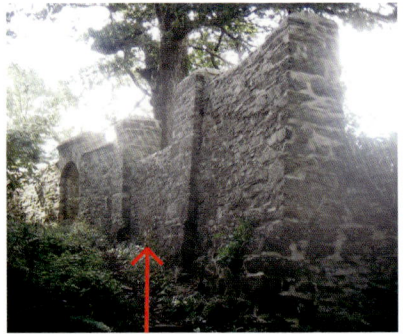

Left: A restored alcove set in the west of James Tillie's boundary wall.
Right: Further north there is another pedestrian entrance, on the left of the photograph, and then the blocked gateway that once formed part of the geometrically planned drive to Pentillie Castle. The red arrow marks the entrance between the early gate piers.

facing wall for the growing of fruit, vegetable gardens, and so on. His effects included stone arbours and other curios.

One of the intriguing elements of research at Pentillie is the sheer quantity of well-cut stone, roll-moulded door jambs, columns, window mullions, sills, fireplaces, and so on. They not only fill the gardens but can be seen throughout the buildings of the estate. In just four lesser buildings I counted some 15 granite doorways from the early 16thC and 13 mullioned stone windows. The steps in the garden themselves are re-used sections from a once high-status build.

We know that Sir James Tillie started re-building his house by using three stone doorways from another house, cutting his own name and date into the stone above the decoration. It is possible that re-use, an honourable and sensible habit, extended to the gardens where there is still plenty of quality stone, some of which may have come from the houses that Sir James demolished and reused. We know that the old house at Pentearr near the outer gates was demolished. However, the date for such reuse is confused by later demolitions such as those in the early 19thC of the mansions at Clifton and at Crocadon. Some stones may also have come from demolition when the 1810 wing was built at Pentillie, or from the demolition of that wing in 1978. The 'spare' stones in the garden include parts of a Tillie column whose original position was unknown.

One notable red herring is at the entrance to the Lime Avenue, where a date-stone reads NLEL 1628. These initials probably refer to the marriage in 1628 of Sir Nicholas Lower and Elizabeth Lower who lived at Clifton, south of Pentillie, on the edge of the river. This was a substantial mansion, with medieval quay, halls and a private chapel which, in the mid 19thC, was bought, demolished and replaced by a new farmhouse.

Another puzzle are the lime kilns towards the river. On Repton's plan, it is suggested that these should remain as curios. There remains today a kiln with Tudor doorway, but whether this, with its recut and dated lintel, was built by Sir James remains conjecture.

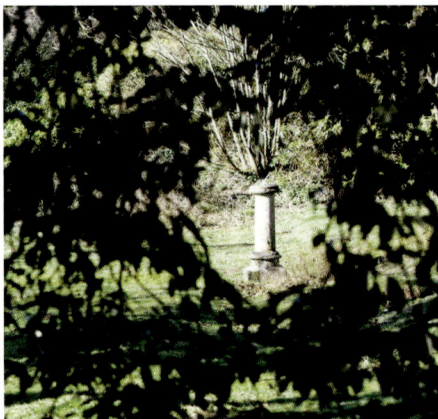

The grounds have much intersting stone work.

The left hand picture shows the view through Tillie's original park entrance.
The picture on the right shows some of the massive walls of his service buildings.

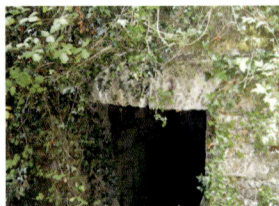

From Left to Right: Garden stonework from Tillie's time; A lime kiln with reused doorway;
A grotto.

Nearer the house, more remains of the original than might be expected. For instance, one of the original courtyard towers is still in place, with walls stretching west to the remains of the outer little tower on that garden corner. To the north much of the walling and service buildings remain. Even the present estate office appears to have been built by Sir James. Other details of his garden are shown on Repton's plan. His vegetable garden appears to have been to the south west on a slope, but other gardens and walled enclosures stretched beyond the enclosed space. To the north and north-west were a stable court, kitchen court, cow yard and rick yard, all of which can still be traced on the ground and of which considerable parts still exist. The layout of the yard for the terraced fruit wall is still respected, and can still be traced in the courtyard south of the present estate office, despite two hundred years of alteration.

Beyond the formal gardens round the house, there were avenues and the plan gives some idea of those. The most confusing matter for a modern visitor is the site of the early drives. The modern entrance drive comes in just south of an older road that ran through the settlement of Pentearr, is still marked by a line of trees, and then entered north of the small entrance turret, before going along a ridge past a second small tower, whose ground plan is shown on a drawing by Lewis Kennedy, and then down to the south west corner of the house. However, another route had been intended as the access and this appears to have been placed in accordance with the axial designs shown in the 1692 bird's eye view. This provided for a drive that ran straight from the west entrance of the house to the western boundary wall, parts of which still remain, high and buttressed. and in which are two gate piers through which once ran a track. However, such a route provided no easy access to anywhere and appears to have been blocked. Although it met the requirements of a geometric plan, I am not sure it was ever put into use, because the route between that gateway and the house was over difficult and steep ground.

Another and older route ran from Painters Cross along the

north side of the valley south of Pentillie to the bay below Pentillie, and this must have formed for some time the convenient access to the headland on which was built Pentillie. It must also have provided the easiest access to the east and entrance front, since it is shown on designs and plans and the gateway sides to the east. The valley route was then the principal route to Pentillie, with a main road down to the commercial wharves or bay, and with side steps to the house above. Other routes are thought to have existed running north west around features and along avenues, including a tree lined avenue that stretched from the northwest corner of the enclosed boundary, towards the tower on the hill to the north.

Surviving stonework includes the two towers on the west drive, and a wall that runs from the outer tower north. Here the earliest plan shows a bow going out to the west, perhaps an exhedra, viewing point or arbour. This arbour with a fine arch, pinacle and ball and early use of brick, appears to date from 1700, and is in the western boundary wall. Other puzzles include a grotto or hut, whose original purpose remains a bit of a mystery. I am inclined to think that it was intended either as an object of interest on a walk or that it was a spring and basin to provide water flow to the areas lower down the hill, rather like the similar construction above the walled garden at Caerhays.

The most outstanding landscape feature must be the tower on the hill, which is discussed below. Like the tower that Sir James built at Belle Cour, I believe this was a place to which he could go for the pleasure of the journey and to walk, the equivalent if you like of the garden shed, club, or moored boat to which men so often retreat.

A study of Sir James' work to the gardens and grounds of Pentillie remains to be undertaken. There is so much that survives from his designs and building that such research would seem worthwhile and should help to establish Sir James Tillie's garden scheme as not just interesting but innovative, striking, worthy of retention and deserving of greater attention.

Endnotes

1. 1718: A reference to Pentillie being boarded up following the death of Lady Elizabeth Tillie found in a Wiltshire assessment for rates due on Belle Cour

2. Gilbert D 1838 Parochial History of Cornwall Vol 1 p 314

3. Quotation from 'Travels in Georgian Devon: The Illustrated Journals of the Reverend John Swete (1789-1800)' by Todd Gray. Four Volumes edited and published 1997, pp 137-138. John Swete, born John Tripe, (1752-1821) is best known for his 'Picturesque Sketches of Devon'. His MS Journals are at the Devon County Record Office

4. W G Maton writing in 1794, quoted in 'Report on Pentillie AD 2000'. Nicholas Pearson Associates Ltd

5. Humphrey Repton (1752-1818): Red Book for Pentillie 1810 Private Collection, Reproduced with permission

6. Lewis Kennedy (1799-1877): Proposals for Pentillie 1813 Private Collection Reproduced with permission

7. John Claudius Loudon 1783-1843 wrote and encouraged horticulture and landscape gardening and may even have been the first person to coin and use the phrase 'landscape gardener'. One of his many works included 'An Encyclopaedia of Gardening' published in 1822.

'Cemetery at Pentillie'
An engraving from a drawing by Ricahrd Brown done c 1823

Chapter 10

The Castle on Mount Ararat

Most of the stories that surround the life of Sir James originate with the tower on a hill north of Pentillie. Inside the tower, the decaying statue of a man seated in a chair, shrouded in ferns, could be glimpsed through a slot in the entrance. It was this statue that, with the addition of a few scandalous suggestions about his life, formed the basis for stories of Sir James Tillie.

Early History

For some two hundred and fifty years, the tower has been an object of rumour and confusion as to its purpose and build. For much of that time, the entrance had been blocked, with only a small window available through which to spy the decaying statue of Sir James Tillie sitting on his chair and looking over the Tamar. The mausoleum was frequently mentioned by travellers and antiquarians and the stories about Sir James repeated.

With the arrival of interest in romantic landscape and gothic fantasy the interest in the tower increased. In 1790, the Revd John Swete repeated a version of Sir James Tillie's death and described the impressive mausoleum[1]. A typical response was that summarised in a letter about Pentillie from Robert Clutterbuck[2], dated Sunday August 28th 1796:

'On a hill contiguous further to the North stands a square Brick Building firmly closed and barred, divided into two apartments; in the Lower of which is a monument erected to the memory of Sir James Tilly, an ancestor of the present

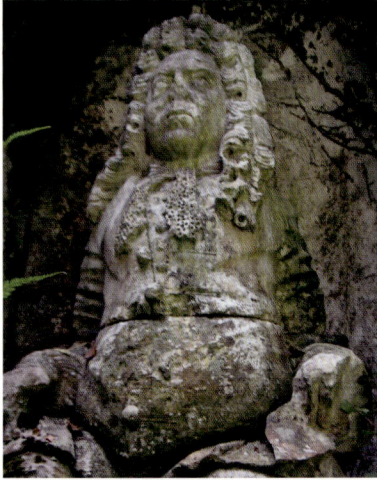

A view of the statue in the tower as
glimpsed through the grille in 2009.

Climbing the steps to the look at the statue.
A picture taken before recent renovation.

possessor, of which we obtained an indistinct Sight, thro' an aperture in the Window: the effigy is represented sitting in an erect posture much mutilated and mouldering fast to decay. In a vault below, the body of Sir James, dressed in the cloaths he usually wore, and in the Chair in which he usually sat, was placed soon after his death. Who from a strong aversion to interment ordered his body to be disposed in that manner'.

Clutterbuck went on to say that *'The house is apparently of great antiquity and is the supposed place of rendezvous of all the fancied evil genii of the Neighborhood'* and referred to the *'plausible and horrifying narrative of the tourist Gilpin'* in support of his stories. It is interesting that Clutterbuck correctly refers to the existence of the vault below the tower, a vault whose existence became forgotten over the centuries.

The 1807 ordnance survey shows the mausoleum approached by a tree lined avenue, which existed before the changes suggested by Repton or the Coryton family had been carried out, and which was therefore probably one of Sir James' original tree lined avenues.

Repairs and alteration to the tower were carried out early in the 19th century by John Tillie Coryton (1773-1843). The works included inspection of the burial vault, after which its existence seems to have been forgotten. John Tillie Coryton's son Augustus reported that the vault contained the bones of Sir James and that he had been interred in a sitting posture, within a coffin. The works to the tower gained enormous interest and it was said that crowds came out from Plymouth to admire the mausoleum and hear the story of the eccentric Tillie. The excavations appear to have given rise to the story that the body had then been reburied in St Mellion churchyard. The whereabouts of the body became a mystery with stories varying as to when and where it had been moved. In recent years, a diviner stated with confidence that the body was buried in St Pillaton. The body became confused with the statue and perhaps because the world loves a good story, the facts became forgotten.

A newspaper article[3] summarised the stories of Sir James Tillie's burial and recited the rumours that he had been set in a *'Chair in*

Pentillie with the tower in the distance. Repton's painting shows proposals to add landscape trees and a look-out stair turret to the tower: c1809

The Tower from the north east, in a photograph from 2009

this tower with a table in front of him on which were to be placed bottles and glasses, pipes and tobacco, as emblems of a sensual life.. This was not done however. Some years ago the father of the present owner of Pentillie Castle opened the vault and found there the remains of his ancestor, in a sitting position indeed, but enclosed in a coffin"

A much used reference book of the mid-19th century, Lake's Parochial History[4] noted that the Mausoleum was of two stories, and that it was in the upper room that was placed the effigy in marble, suggesting an awareness of the forgotten vault.

There were further repairs and clearance of undergrowth in 1906-7. These repairs included alterations to the roof, possibly because it had collapsed, and it was probably then that the flat roof was replaced by an inverted v shape with a drain that ran through into the porch. There are reports of a tree growing in the tower[5], of the reopening of the original doorway and that the statue was damaged by leaks. Repair, replacement and some alteration does not, however, appear to have extended to once more re-opening the vault. It may have been the arrival of tourists a century earlier that had caused the entrance to the tower to be blocked, the side windows blocked and the entrance restricted so that the statue could be seen only through a small window.

Baring Gould[6] wrote in 1909 of the repairs and the tower and mentioned that the tower had great notoriety and that many visitors from Plymouth came to the mausoleum. However, Baring Gould did not know of the vault below the floor, saying that the ground floor was the intended vault. He also said that the portraits in the upper chamber had been removed to Pentillie Castle. I doubt whether they had stayed in place until his time and suspect this was rumour rather than researched fact[7].

In the early years of the 21st century, paths were cleared for the walk up to the tower. Through a grill it was now possible to make out the life size statue of Sir James Tillie, sitting in a chair and dressed in clothes called old fashioned for the time.

186

The statue in the tower:
A plate taken by Sidney Wright when the roof was off the Mausoleum: 1906
Cornwall Record office archive AD 1848 Reproduced with permission.

A Description of the Building

In 1692 the drawing for Pentillie Castle showed the hill north of Pentillie as bare save for a knob like projection on the summit. By 1716, the date of a drawing by Prideaux, it is shown surrounded by fields, but is also shown as a tower, much as it stands today, rather than as a squat building.

Some have suggested that there may have been some ancient encampment or tower on the hill here, but although there are tracks, ditches and other vestiges of what might have been ancient use, recent archaeological investigation confirms that the tower appears to have been entirely the work of Sir James Tillie, who built the platform and provided the ditch to the rear, building over boundary hedges which had run from the hill top.

Since his will of 1704 does not mention the tower[8] , I believe it was probably built after 1704 and before 1712. It is a square tower some 9.4 metres high standing on a rock platform which is itself about 1.5 metres above the surrounding land. From the track on the east there are therefore ten stone steps up to a two storey porch[9].

This narrow porch was built at the same time as the tower and has niches, perhaps for busts, on each side. It leads to what was once an arched doorway to the single room on the ground floor. Above this entrance door, it is probable that there was once some inscription. The ground floor room had two big arched windows and a high barrel vault or semi-circular ceiling and a floor of stone flags. There was also a niche opposite the front door, which is supposed might have held a portrait. There is some scribed beaded plaster remaining to the door, and plastered reveals to the windows suggesting that this lower room was fully plastered and of good standard. Outside the windows are lead-filled holes which probably held the hinges of external shutters.

This room had good light, grandeur and is thought to have been the study or retreat of Sir James Tillie.

One puzzle is that, unlike the similar tower retreat at his other house of Belle Cour, there does not seem to have been any allowance for a fireplace which, unless it was always considered a summer retreat, would ensure that this was often a chilly place to use. Above this room and its barrel vault was a further floor which, since there are no signs of windows can only have been a store or throughway reached from a ladder or internal stair, of which all trace has gone. Above that in turn was probably a flat roof which, if accessible, could also only have been reached from an internal stair. The apparent lack of access and use for the first floor remains a puzzle, and I think it must be assumed arises from Sir James Tillie's wish to have a high, recognizable tower of distinction.

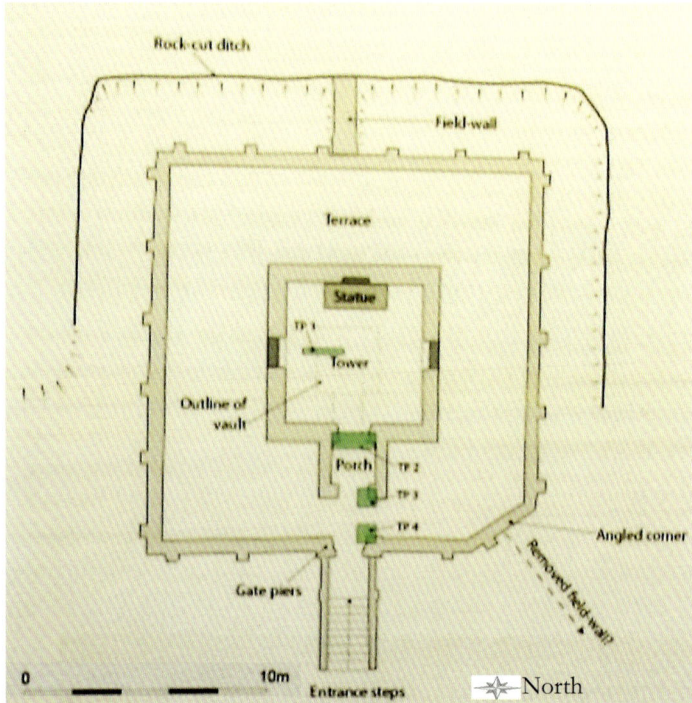

A plan shows the outline of the tower, the porch, wall and ditch.
Green marks the site of investigation trenches and access to the vault.
Plan: Jessop Consultancy.

Outside, the battlemented porch, the deep ditch cut into the rock, and the surrounding stone wall give the tower some distinction. The construction is of high quality. The three decorative string courses are laid on full lead, and the merlons on the roof were carefully constructed. Although it has been suggested that such fine design 'with an underlying geometry' must be the hand of a master architect, I suggest that it was the work of a competent, experienced and clever master mason rather than designer, since the design appears to be in the accepted and usual traditions of carpenters and masons in using geometric layout.

Originally, the walls probably had a lime render since the alternating decorative dark headers of the arches stand proud of the stonework. If so limed, this would have been a white tower which would have stood out. Late 20th century renovations elsewhere have shown how splendid a white limed render can appear[10].

There is also, on the north east, a raked or slanted corner, whose purpose is unclear. There is a similar raking corner to the south east of the house enclosure on the 1692 drawing proposal for Pentillie. Although it would be amusing to suppose that such raking corners had ritual significance, it is going too far to suggest any reason other than that of improving the drive so that a carriage could drive past the tower and return home.

Then, in front of the tower to the east, appears to be a landscaped and bounded area, with a semi-circular enclosure and terrace which could be another exhedra. This would have provided space for enjoyment, for admiring the really splendid view and would have provided an objective for the walk or drive to the tower.

The building was already standing before Sir James Tillie decided to use it for his mausoleum. This is evident from looking at the tower and from the recent investigation of construction phases. On the north side, the stone below the arched window had been removed after the building of the tower, which was probably made to give the men digging the vault sufficient space and access for the excavation below the ground floor, presumably in 1713. Once the vault was finished, the interior clear and the stone slab floor reinstated, the stonework was replaced below the window.

This vault has eight steps, with a shaped bottom step, which descend from the access porch, in which the main door was altered slightly to receive the stairs. The vault is 2.5 metres square with a vaulted brick ceiling, a stone floor and lime plastered walls. The vault is not quite in line with the main building, and appears to have been dug to fit in, with no apparent geometric design or proportion. It is brick lined, as is common for vaults, and was a material of status preference for Tillie himself, although the use of brick was at this time still relatively uncommon in Cornwall.

The statue pictured in 2009, before restoration..

Recent Investigation

When I first wrote on the history of this monument much was still uncertain, hidden behind a couple of centuries of rumour and imaginative tales. All this was changed with the carrying out of an archaeological investigation in 2013. The drama and attention received by the mausoleum is summarised by an article in the Daily Mail newspaper of 12 February 2013:

Human remains discovered at a stately home are believed to be those of the man who built it and ordered that he be buried in his best clothes with his pipe as he waited for the afterlife. An excavation of a mausoleum in the grounds of Pentillie Castle in Saltash, Cornwall, is thought to have uncovered the body of Sir James Tillie, who built the home in 1698 and died in 1713. He asked that on his deathbed he should not be buried, but dressed in his best clothes, bound to a stout chair and placed with his books, wine and pipe in his favourite folly to await resurrection. His servants are believed to have brought him wine for two years until, unable to bear their macabre orders any longer, the remains were interred and a marble statue built in his place.

Mystery has long surrounded his final resting place - but recent renovations of the mausoleum uncovered a brick chamber under granite floor slabs, in which human remains were found. It had been long assumed his remains were moved to a church. Archaeologist Oliver Jessop, who was recording the historic fabric of the building, and surveyor Richard Glover, were delighted.

In 2012 Ted Coryton, the owner of Pentillie, had set about arranging for restoration. With the help of a grant from the Country Houses Foundation, this work was completed in April 2013. In the course of restoration, and once burial and exhumation licenses had been obtained from the Ministry of Justice, the brick built vault below the raised ground floor was inspected. When the vault was opened it was possible to see the rotting remains of the covered chair, the body and of other materials.

A note from Ted Coryton reported that *'we opened the vault under the mausoleum on Monday, [February 4 2015]. Within were the*

The restored and repaired statue in 2014
Reproduced with permission.

remains of a leather chair on which someone had been sitting when it collapsed. We ....left [the skeleton] sitting there. It is nice to confirm that the story is true and that his wishes were fulfilled. He was alone.'

Propped against the rear west wall were the remains of two wooden planks with metal studs arranged as letters. More rotten planks were on the floor and human remains beneath them. The planks appeared to have been covered with a material which was perhaps wool or velvet, the cloth held in place with studs, some of which were laid in a decorative pattern and some spelling out the name of Tillie and the date of his death. The coffin furniture and coffin are a valuable addition to study of 17th century practice, but also confirm that this was, as the codicil to the will had suggested, an oak coffin built in the shape of a chair; Sir James had indeed been buried in a sitting position. The metal fittings for the chair, for holding the planks together for carrying and for the other boxes said to have contained papers and materials have survived in sufficient detail to be analysed.

The report also mentions in passing that there appears to be a 'healed blunt force injury in the centre right hand side of the skull'. Although the skull could not be further investigated, this suggests that at some time Sir James had either fallen or been hit with considerable force, an intriguing bit of information to add to speculation on his life.

There is no doubt that there is a public fascination with this discovery, and the detailed reports are frankly rather gruesome. Such details may be of interest and delight to admirers of modern detective thrillers, but I think it entirely right that they should be glossed over. Reports of the investigation are both detailed and thorough, and any one writing on Sir James Tillie in the future can refer to them carefully. It seems right that the Corytons investigated no further and that, save for a time capsule left in the vault, the remains have been left undisturbed.

Much new information has therefore turned up in recent years. In the vault of the mausoleum is indeed the body of Sir James Tillie placed as stories had suggested by his loyal servants directly below the

The moment of discovery: A slab is lifted and Sarah Coryton, the châtelaine of Pentillie, peers into the vault for the first time.

Left: Two of the coffin planks were reconstructed. *Right:* The panel as it might have been, with decorative studs and part of an inscription: *Sr I* (for J) *T Obijt. Novr*

Reproduced with permission: The Jessup Consultancy

statue that stands on the ground floor. The statue and its base are of Beer Limestone, the canopy is of Bath limestone and the inscription panel on Ashburton 'marble'. The statue too has now been restored with remodelled nose hands and feet and remains a magnificent example of a rather backward looking restoration style. The sculptured chair has Jacobean strap-work decoration and is itself a fine artefact. Below the chair was written:

This monument is erected in memory of Sir James Tillie Knt who dyed ye 15th day of Novmbr Anno Dom 1713 and in ye 67th year of his life.

The Mausoleum Tower at Pentillie remains a splendid folly, an object of admiration, an objective for walks or exercise and a famous landmark in the Tamar valley.

A Retreat and Mausoleum

However, the tower at Pentillie was not built as a mausoleum. Its design and use should be considered in the light of recent research of the similar tower built by Sir James at Belle Cour, his other country house in Wiltshire.

It seems clear that Sir James wished to establish not only that he came from an armigerous family and was of high status but to show the world that he was a man of importance who had 'made it'. He started assembling the lands that eventually formed Belle Cour in 1673, and although he continued assembling land in Wiltshire for thirty years, it is not clear when he started building his house there. In a deed of 1695 he acquired a freehold which says a house had been built but was in the possession of Sir James' not the vendor, suggesting Sir James had built the house.

At Pentillie in Cornwall, it seems probable that some building work had started in the 1680s, although the main building phase started in the 1690s. Although there is no clear evidence of the dates, I am inclined to think that the works at Belle Cour precede the very splendid work at Pentillie and also think that the 'castle' or tower at Belle Cour almost certainly predated the tower at Pentillie.

A colourful monument in St Mellion Church, near Pentillie, to Sir William Coryton,(d.1711) and his first wife Susannah (d.1695) is a magnificent construction with coats of arms, blazons and decorations. The married couple, in the costume of the day, kneel each side of a prie-dieu. It is interesting that, presumably for reasons of dynastic pride, Sir William chose to be remembered with his first rather than second wife. This monument, a public statement of power and family, erected at a similar time to that for Sir James Tillie, is very different to the monument for Sir James, which does not even mention his wife.

The pillars stand on a deep decorated base which was obscured and does not therefore show in the photograph.

The tower at Belle Cour was just beyond the walled gardens of the mansion at the southern boundary of his property, With a pitched roof and of two storeys, it had an outside stair to the study on the first floor which had windows to three sides. It also had, built into the wall, a fireplace set across the south west corner of the first floor. The building is of good quality, with late Jacobean style hooded and moulded mullioned windows and fine mouldings to the door.

There is one string course just below the level of the first floor joists and another one tight to the eaves. The pitched roof carries a fine stone roof, but the almost hidden eaves course suggests a third storey was possible, perhaps with a battlemented lookout. However, the roof, which I have not seen close to or from the interior, appears of good age and could retain the original 17th cenury structure. The name of the tower, which was long known as the 'Castle', suggests that it may once have had a battlemented storey. The name 'Castle', stuck to it for centuries and is, I imagine, Sir James' name for it when first built, perhaps with some irony. It is still obviously a tower, although of modest proportions, and now masked by surrounding buildings.

One story of the tower says that Tillie built the tower in this place so that he could look over the fields and valley to the north-west to the great castle of the Farley Hungerford family. Its owners, seriously wealthy and long established, gambled furiously, ran out of money, had to sell up, and then sold the castle to be demolished for the salvage funds. I like to imagine that Tillie got some satisfaction from making the point that he, who had started as the son of a copyholder farmer, now had a tower looking over the site of one of the greatest castles of the area. However, although this is a nice story, it is not credible, and it seems more likely that the tower was built as a study and retreat for Tillie.

Wiltshire was the county of his childhood and remained the home of many of his friends and business contacts and was close to the trading centre of Bristol. As he retreated from London, particularly after his defeat in the Court of Chivalry, one can surmise that a country house and base in Wiltshire was an attractive proposition.

The earlier fashion for separate buildings in a garden was for their use as a belvedere, to watch sports, pause during exercise or find refreshments and social gatherings. Before 1700, there were many small corner towers, hunting lodges, gatehouses with first floors in which to banquet or picnic, but few, if any, buildings built away from a house intended for work, study or contemplation.

John Evelyn, whose mid-17th century writing on gardens is as important as his better known diaries, is one of the few who mentioned the importance in a garden of 'solitudes and retirements'[11]. John Evelyn provided designs for many garden buildings, and most of decorative or unusual appearance. They included aviaries, decorative beehives, music machines a rabbit warren 'tower'[12] but, as far as I know, no buildings in a garden for a man to enjoy.

When Sir James Tillie was planning his towers in the 1690s, the concept of a tower or any other garden building as being for 'other solitudes and retirements' was relatively new.

Throughout history, humans have sought a retreat or change

of place, whether this was found in a garden shed, a local pub, the kennels, falconry or some other hobby or activity. However, such retreat is only possible for an 'upper' or leisured class, a class for whom every day is not filled with labour, a class who are able to live off or control the work of others. The 17th century had seen the creation of such a class of merchants, traders and professionals, a class of whom Sir James Tillie was a prime example.

Although a castle or tower was, for Sir James, a sign of status and a sign that he had 'arrived', an isolated building may have been designed to provide a study and retreat, a place to store papers, even a secure place for deeds. In Sir James' case I believe it was also to provide a place where he could be alone, and high up. At Belle Cour the study was on the first floor. At Pentillie the tower was high above the surrounding ground, built on a stub of rock on a hill top.

17th Century Death and Burial.

Many stories of Sir James had emphasised that he was an irreligious heretic, and that his burial and mausoleum was the act of a pagan. However, while it is certain that his burial plans were eccentric, they should also be seen against the problems of getting and staying buried that were affecting the country in the late 17th century.

The difficulties arose from plague, the great plague, disease, an enormously expanding population and the growth of towns and cities with churchyards intended for villages, and the difficulty of finding a place for a coffin in a restricted parish graveyard. The churches themselves had gone through a 'de-frocking' in the civil war, from which they had not recovered. Leadership and vicars were held in poor repute and lost the social support that had financed churches and maintenance. This in turn had meant a loss of respect for churches and their churchyards which had often become playgrounds. The graveyards piled high, filled with 'scattered bones' and re-dug frequently, were notorious for the disturbance done to recent burials and bodies. In London there were also the difficulties of grave and tooth robbers;

even memorial stones and grave goods could not be relied upon to endure. The difficulties of disease and of bodies not being buried led to the suggestion that, as had happened in the Roman Empire, burials should take place outside towns and away from population centres. Evelyn wrote of churchyards:[13] *'I observed that most of the church-yards (tho' some of them large enough) were filled up with earth, or rather the congestion of dead bodys one upon another, for want of earth, even to the very top of the walls, and some above the walls so as the Churches seemed to be built in pitts.'*

The matter had become so serious that there was debate and even, from the start of the 18th century[14], Acts of Parliament intended to regulate the problem.

Although the great and noble had long had vaults beneath or in churches and although there had been many small chapels or vaults attached to churches, the first and only mausoleum built before 1700 was erected within a graveyard[15]. The first of the great mausolea of the 18th century is usually considered to be that built at Castle Howard in 1722[16].

Sir James Tillie, who had lived and practised in London was right to be concerned about his grave and concerned that it should stay undisturbed. However this was in tune with general practice, and the habits of his Quaker and Wiltshire merchant connections would also have been helpful to him.

There was at this time public debate about burial, and given Sir James' concern that his dynasty and record should endure, it was unusual but acceptable for him to be buried in a building outside consecrated ground. A separate and strong building must have seemed a sensible precaution and may have been why he was neither in a vault at Pentillie, or in the chapel he built there. His wish was for security, and was not unchristian.

However in the process he established what appears to have been the first mausoleum in England built outside un-consecrated ground, which, even if this was a re-used tower, was itself another 'first' for remote buildings of contemplation.

Top: The renovated Mausoleum from the east in 2014
Bottom: A view down the north side of the tower towards the Tamar,
past the terrace before the tower.

At Pentillie the tower was built for his pleasure, with a room which gave stunning views over the Tamar; I think it can be surmised that it was an improved version of the earlier tower built at Belle Cour. It was only in the year of his death that the tower at Pentillie was adapted as his mausoleum, although we cannot be certain when the east window was broken open to the ground to allow builders in. I believe that, although work may have started on the vault shortly before his death, the vault was created in the tower as the site for his coffin and that, as his codicil suggested, he was 'stored' in the coffin in a room at Pentillie whilst a vault was prepared.

Despite the legends that have accumulated, it is therefore his will that sets out the sequence of events for its change of use to a mausoleum. In the will of 1704, he had requested:

'And I do desire my body may have a private interrment at and in such place at Pentillie Castle as I have acquainted my dearest wife the Lady Elizabeth Tillie with and to have such Monument erected and Inscription thereon made as I have desired of my said dearest wife'. It has been suggested that since some maps call the tower 'Pentillie Castle', it was that distant tower to which he referred. However, he had long referred to the house at Pentillie as his 'castle'. I think that when he made this will he had some place at Pentillie in mind, although this was not necessarily the chapel he had built there.

In 1713, the codicil to his will, written in the year of his death, changed his instructions and he wrote that [they should] '*.... Carry and lay me in a Repository for that purpose to be made Either on that Eminence called Mount Arraret or Pisgah...'*

The area around the Mausoleum has continued to be known as Mount Arrarat. Although Mount Arrarat and Pisgah could have been two different locations, there is no anecdotal evidence for any other hill being called Pisgah or that differing names were given to different parts of the same hill. The force of the 'either' in this codicil cannot be reconciled with the geography, so we can only assume that Sir James used both names for the hill on which he had built a tower.

Both Arrarat and Pisgah are names that suggest a height from which one can gaze at a promised land which assures a good future for oneself and one's descendants. Mount Ararat[17] was where Noah's Ark landed after the great flood and the name implies that the hill was a place from which, following the flood, man could go down to re-establish himself. Pisgah[18] was the mountain from which Moses could see all the land promised by God to him as land for his people 'and their seed' or descendants for ever. Both names fit well with Sir James Tillie's enthusiasm for his own importance and his dynasty.

Sir James is usually described as an eccentric and that seems fair, but then what becomes the norm is often considered as eccentric when first mooted and Sir James' buildings establish Tillie as among the earliest of those who built on their estates either buildings for pleasure or mausoleums.

Tillie's two towers of Pentillie and Belle Cour are among the earliest examples in England of buildings conceived as a retreat, a study, a landscape feature. These became more common later in the 18th century but were a relatively new concept at the end of the 17th century.

Used by him for study, it seems likely that they were examples of his attempt to stress his ancient nobility and social importance. It is interesting that both had the name 'Castle' applied to them, a title that lasted down to modern times and must surely reflect his own name for the towers. As towers, they deserve further study in the history and development of the English country estate.

At Pentillie the conversion of a tower to become a mausoleum also represents one of the earliest examples in England of any mausoleum built outside a churchyard. Although altered to become a mausoleum, it still may be the earliest example of such buildings in England.

Endnotes

1   The 1704 will asks that burial take place at Pentillie Castle and it has been suggested that since the Tower was colloquially called the Castle and so named on the early O.S. map, the tower was meant by that reference in the will. I think this most unlikely, particularly since Tillie had referred to the main house as a Castle since first assembling the patchwork of lands, and starting work there in the 1680s. The house was built with a chapel, although there is no record of it having been consecrated.

2   Review of the construction of the tower has been amended by the considerable work and research carried out in 2013 as part of an archaeological investigation. This chapter owes a debt therefore to the Jessop Consultancy and their associates, whose views are reflected by some changes to earlier research. Their extensive reports and archaeological analysis are only briefly mentioned here.

Jessop Consultancy: Pentillie Mausoleum; Historic Building Survey and Investigation of Burial Vault: Unpublished paper by Oliver Jessop, September 2013.

Associated papers and reports by Dr Kate Felus, John Phibbs, Richard Glover MRICS

Felus, Dr Kate: 'Putting the Pentillie Mausoleum in Context'. Unpublished paper; July 2011.

Glover Richard, MRICS: Unpublished papers on the Mausoleum at Pentillie and its restoration 2011-2013

3   Examples of recent rendering can be seen at Manorbier Church, near Tenby, in Wales and at the chapel of Winchester College, Hampshire. Both medieval buildings and towers appear splendid in differing from the usual plain stone.

4   John Swete, born John Tripe, (1752-1821) is best known for his 'Picturesque Sketches of Devon'. His MS Journals are at the Devon County Record Office

5   Clutterbuck, Robert: Journal of a Tour through the Western Counties of England during the Summer of 1796 pp 305-7, MS3 277 Cardiff University Library

6   JLS: June 1 1861

7   Baring-Gould, S Cornish Characters and Strange Events; Two Vols, 1908: chapter on Sir James Tillie

8   Western Morning News 13 August 1938

9   There is one portrait alleged to be of Sir James Tillie, now at Pentillie, which has been damaged around the lower face, and it is possible that this could be a portrait once intended for the tower. This is, however, pure speculation.

10   Lake's Parochial History of Cornwall: by Joseph Polsue c 1865-1872, 4 vols

11   John Evelyn was in his early 20s, and building a garden for his brother at Wooton, Surrey. He wrote that 'I built... a study, made a fishpond, an island and some other solitudes and retirements'.   E. S. DeBeer, ed., The Diary of John Evelyn, 6 vols., Oxford, 1955, II, 81.

In 1653, Evelyn included a 'banqueting house' in the garden he designed at Sayes Court, Kent.

12   Elysium Britannicum," 217. British Library, London

13   Memoirs illustrative of the Life and Writings of John Evelyn, comprising his Diary from 1641 to 1705/6, and a Selection of his Familiar Letters.   Edited by William Bray, published 1818. Extract from 2nd Edition, London, 1819. Volume 1 PP445-6, referring to Norwich, 17 October 1671

14   At the time of the 1711 Act, [which provided for building 50 new churches in London, and instigated debate, as summarised by Vanbrugh, about the desirability that churches 'may be freed from that inhumane custom of being made burial places for the dead'] just two years before Tillie's death, there were no freestanding mausolea in con-consecrated settings in England. Felus, Dr Kate: 'Putting the Pentillie Mausoleum in Context

15   Ailesbury Mausoleum in the churchyard of Maulden Bedfordshire by Thomas Birne, 1st earl of Elgin in memory of his 2nd wife.

16   The high baroque, dramatic architecture of Vanbrugh (1664-1726) really only became established after the turn of the century. He was only in his twenties when work started at Belle Cour and Pentillie; his earlier landscape ornaments such as the Great Obelisk at Castle Howard of 1714 and the Belvedere at Claremont of 1715 are later than the work at Pentillie.

17   Genesis 8:   Verses 1-6 in the King James Version

        'And God remembered Noah, and every living thing, and all the cattle that was with him in the ark: and God made a wind to pass over the earth, and the waters assuaged; The fountains also of the deep and the windows of heaven were stopped, and the rain from heaven was restrained; And the waters returned from off the earth continually: and after the end of the hundred and fifty days the waters were abated. And the ark rested in the seventh month, on the seventeenth day of the month, upon the mountains of Ararat. And the waters decreased continually until the tenth month: in the tenth month, on the first day of the month, were the tops of the mountains seen. And it came to pass at the end of forty days, that Noah opened the window of the ark which he had made'.

18   Deuteronomy 34: verses 1-5 in the King James Version.

'And Moses went up from the plains of Moab unto the mountain of Nebo, to the top of Pisgah, that is over against Jericho. And the Lord shewed him all the land of Gilead, unto Dan, And all Naphtali, and the land of Ephraim, and Manasseh, and all the land of Judah, unto the utmost sea, And the south, and the plain of the valley of Jericho, the city of palm trees, unto Zoar. And the Lord said unto him, This is the land which I sware unto Abraham, unto Isaac, and unto Jacob, saying, I will give it unto thy seed: I have caused thee to see it with thine eyes, but thou shalt not go over thither. So Moses the servant of the Lord died there in the land of Moab, according to the word of the Lord'.

Belle Cour: the tower as a barn
*Wiltshire Farm Buildings 1500-1900, Pamela M Slocombe
1989; Published Wiltshire Buildings Record, Devizes Books
Press and Studio 108, Corsham, Wiltshire.*

Chapter 11
The Building of Belle Cour

Sir James Tillie and Wingfield in Wiltshire

Sir James Tillie has long been associated with the house he built and named after himself at Pentillie, but it had been forgotten that he built another mansion in the village where he had grown up. Contrary to stories about his birthplace, Sir James Tillie was born in Wingfield, Wiltshire, as was recorded not only on the engraving of a painting of him by Kneller but also on an inscription on the Church at Wingfield. This was added, just beside the south porch, shortly after he had been made a knight by King James ll in January 1687.

Although this plaque was erected in 'memory of his ancestors', it seems more likely that it was intended to boast of his new knighthood and record how far he had come since his upbringing on a small holding in the village. The plaque which he erected by the south porch is still there today.

Opposite the porch are two fine tombs, each of different design, whose inscriptions are so worn as to be illegible. These are believed to be the two tombs referred to in the inscription. Sir James must have had some influence with the Priest and church wardens to be able to erect these tombs, and the inscription in such a prestigious place, and we can wonder whether he may also have made a donation to the church fabric, or financed repairs such as the church barrel roof.

Born on November 16 1647, he spent his early years in Wingfield, where his father was a small farmer or copyholder[1] as had been his grandfather. This was therefore the village where he grew up. Although he seems to have had relatives and friends of merchant class,

These are believed to be the two tombs erected in 1687 for his grandfather, and father with their wives and family, respectively. No inscription is legible, but the older John Tillie with wife and children is on the right and the younger John Tillie, Sir James' father, with wife and children to the left. Note the fine baroque carving, including cupids and swages of fruit and flowers and the differences in design for each tomb.

Erected Anno Dom: 1687
By Sr: Iames Tillie Kt:
To the Memory of his Ancestors who
in this Parish lived vertuously & died
Piously and lie interred under the Two
Opposite Tombstones viz Under the
Nearest Stone John Tillie the elder
and Mary his Wife and Severall of
their Children
And under the remotest Stone
John Tillie the Younger and Susanna
his wife and Severall of their
Children.

The 1687 inscription in memory of his ancestors was placed by Sir James Tillie on the wall west of the Porch at Wingfield Church; a fine piece of slate below a baroque stone moulding.

and his brother Jeremiah also became a merchant, we do not know where he went to school. However, he retained friendships he had made in Wiltshire all his life, including some who were Quakers.

In 1791, the Vicar of the parish wrote that: 'The descendants of Sir James have yet an estate here, which is said to have been purchased by that gentleman from an attachment to the original residence of his ancestors. There was till lately a house upon it which bore evident marks of that singularity of character which discovered itself upon other occasions'[2]. Wingfield was therefore the hamlet in which James Tillie had grown up and the parish in which he built himself a fine and perhaps unusual house.

Early History

Wingfield hamlet with its church and church farm is off to the east of the north-south road through the valley. The River Frome runs on the west of the parish through a valley before joining the Avon at Bristol.

There is a cross roads where the main north south road joined the east road which at Farleigh Hungerford guarded the river crossing. Until this cross roads was improved when toll roads were put through, Wingfield had been a small hamlet and parish with one or two big farms and cottages straggling along the east-west lane between the church and Pomeroy Manor, once one of the most important houses of the parish. Even before the black death of the mid-14th century this hamlet had never been of great size or importance. The land was largely wood with much common and some scattered small-holdings, with commons which stretched west and east of the north-south road through the parish and which were edged by more small holdings. This was land of relative unimportance which had, until the dissolution of 1539 been owned by the church[3]. Wingfield was a small settlement set in woodland with some fairly poor quality land, a great common and a population only just in the hundreds, most of which had developed around the edges of the common.

Winfield or Winckfield
From two sheets of: *Andrews and Drury: Map of Wiltshire 1773*

'Wingfield Inclosure Award' *From the enclosure map of 1822*

The first draft of the Tithe Apportionment, 1838; the red
box marks a smudged erasure thought to be the demolished
cellars. *Wiltshire Buildings Record*

The name itself has varied in spelling through the years, and had usually been written as Winfield, or occasionally 'Winckfield'. From the 19th century, Wingfield became usual and is used here[4].

Rumours

Like other sites associated with Sir James, Belle Cour has accumulated its own legends. There are many stories of the origins of Belle Cour, none substantiated. The forgotten site was said to be a castle or a nunnery. The existing late 17th century farmhouse was thought to be the original house and all that was left of that nunnery. The tower that is now in separate ownership, and was once a folly retreat and study, was known locally as 'the castle', giving rise to rumours of some great building that had stood south of the farm. The persistent rumours for the existence of a nunnery probably originated with the arcaded well court of the farm, said to be cloisters, and because the land around Belle Cour and Pomeroy was, until the dissolution, the property of an Abbess. There is no evidence for any such building, although of course land could be owned and managed by religious orders, including nuns. Support for the story of a religious foundation may have come from the existence of 'Chapel field', south west of Pomeroy Manor, although this field name is because it was close to the medieval manor chapel there. Another close, a couple of hundred yards to the south east and east of Pomeroy Farm on the lane to the church and purchased by Tillie to become part of Belle Cour, was known as Monk's, presumably because of an earlier ownership, and this too may have contributed to the legends.

Such stories have persisted. Even in 2015, I was told firmly that Belle Cour was the site of a nunnery and that that indeed was why the place was called 'Belle Coeur'. This last word, the French for heart, was thought to have survived from the naming of the nunnery, perhaps in a Marian tradition or connection with 'sacred heart'.

The spelling and legend of the farm as 'Belle Coeur' has persisted. Although every old legal document, maps such as the

The area around Belle Cour, Wingfield,
as shown in the map for the Tithe apportionment of 1842

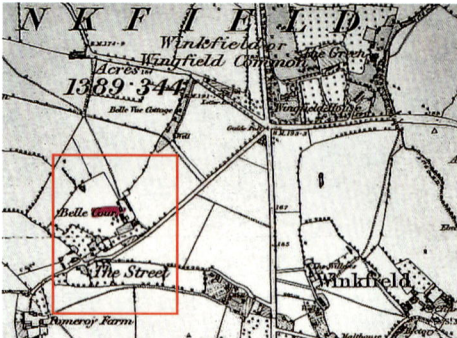

Above: Belle Cour: aerial photo of 1945.
Left: Belle Cour: from the Ordnance
Survey map 6" of 1884/5

1838/1842 tithe map which use both Belle Coure and Belle Cour and the OS map of 1884-6 recorded the name of the farm as Belle Cour, the modern OS map sadly and mistakenly records the farm as 'Belle Coeur', giving credence to stories of a religious site. It should still be known as Belle Cour.

Assembling the Land

James Tillie started assembling land in Wingfield in 1673 when he was only 26 or so. Although we cannot tell when the purchase and swapping of land became a project for a small estate rather than assistance for his father, surviving deeds show lists of fields, cottages and odd corners of land assembled over a considerable period. These transactions seem complex and frankly confusing, and involved not only other members of his family, such as his brother Jeremiah, described as a merchant of Bristol, but also trusted friends like John Bailward or Henry Mitchell.

The transactions were for small pieces, leases, cottages, fields, rationalisation and swaps such as that with the Vicar for Glebe land. There were also transactions where it appears Tillie did not wish to disclose his interest. Although the estate came to include land around this and other parishes, the main focus was on land to the west of the Common, an area which included fields which may have been those leased by his forebears. A reference in the Somerset Archive gives 1693 as a date by when he was recorded as owning Belle Cour in Wingfield. This suggests that the house was already built and that it was under his control. However, he does not appear to have completed the purchase of Belle Cour until 1695, which year is the first time that the name occurs in surviving Wiltshire related deeds[5].

In 1695, and to 'retain an attachment to the original home of his ancestors', he finally bought the estate in Wingfield called Belle-Cour from Walter Long. It might be suggested that this transaction was for a house built by Walter Long. However, given that the Vendor Walter Long is described in the deed as in 'possession', rather than

Red Dotted line suggests site of
house with blue lines marking
demolition 'smudge' marked on
1838 Tithe plan and blue pond
shown on 1841 Tithe map.
'Pond' was larger eastwards in
1884 OS map.

N

Farm yard

Arcaded well court yard
Well

This field to the
east was still
Common Land
until 1822, al-
though used by
Tillie and then
Coryton.

Edge of yard and freehold property

Staff wing

Door central to
dwelling not build-
ing

Coach House doors

"The Castle"
the Tower
built by Sir
James Tillie

Buttress of old stone
presumed later addition

Walled Garden as marked
on earliest maps. Walls of
brick

Use of this area uncertain,
since much changed by sub-
division and small hodlings
etc noted in Tithe map.

Purple shows
dry summer
marks

This kink
marked on earliest plans.

Dash marks land drain

Route of right of way allocated
in enclosure of 1822

Hard road past Tillie's

Part of Common Land transferred to Tillie in 1822 enclosure act

This area becomes a dwelling/
smallholding: suggests not in
Tillie ownership

Lane beyond not
existing until 1822

'The Street' or or old road from Pomeroy to Wingfield Church

Tillie's Access drive??

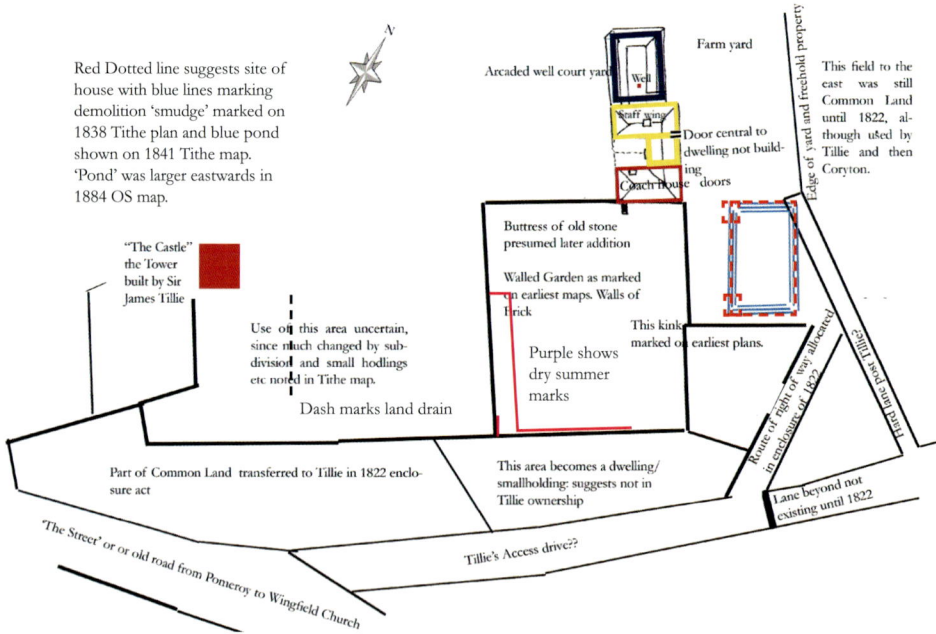

The area of Belle Cour, Wingfield,
based on the map for the Tithe Apportionment, 1842

'occupation' of the house occupied by Sir James, and given that much surrounding land had been acquired over the years, I believe that Sir James had built the house on leased land and that the deed therefore formalised his ownership. The last of his acquisitions in Wingfield seems to have been in 1704, when Sir James Tillie also acquired the residue of a lease to an estate called South Cross in Wingfield:

It is possible that, excluding plots of land not immediately near Belle Cour, Tillie had owned 160 acres around Belle Cour. Details of the holding were set out in the documents of his ultimate heirs, the Coryton family, who continued to own Belle Cour. They managed it until the main farm at Belle Cour was sold by the Coryton family in 1828[6].

The Site

The land where Belle Cour now stands was either part of or on the edge of the large common of Wingfield, and was only a short way from what had once been a great house at Pomeroy. This is still a fine farmhouse, although there is little sign of the medieval manor, which was then reached by a track running west from the church hamlet. The road pattern of the Parish was altered by the arrival of toll roads running both east-west and north-south. Today, and imagining that the 1822 enclosure road from Belle Cour north east to the cross roads did not exist, Belle Cour seems remote and difficult of access. However, it was but a short track from 'The Street', the main east-west route of the hamlet between church and Pomeroy. In addition, a further track led north-west from 'The Street' towards Farleigh Hungerford.

The fields of Pomeroy stretch around its farmhouse, save for the northwest corner which was bounded by the road that ran east to the church. The line of this road was still marked on the 1884/6 OS map as called 'The Street'. North of this road was common land, and in the waste or small land between common and Pomeroy it seems that there were small holders and small holdings of a few acres each. It was on the land to the west and south of the common that Sir James Tillie

A photograph of the west side of Belle Cour, thought to date from before 1914,
shows the farmhouse before 20th century alterations.

The arcaded well court at Belle Cour
Left: An undated picture showing the well in use   *Right:* The yard in January 2010

assembled a number of plots, fields and one or two cottages, in order to obtain a site of some size, and one on which he could build a house.

This appears to have been a green field site, on which there had been no previous dwelling. He named the house Belle Cour, or 'beautiful court' or place. The name first appears on deeds in April 1695, when Walter Green transferred to 'Sir James Tilley of Belle-Cour, Winfield, Kt' the *capital messuage or mansion called Belle-Cour, with terrace walk, green court etc., ponds, orchs. etc. in front between house and Easthills close, ... Also ponds, commons etc. between plantation gdns. etc. of Sir James Tilley and Redmans close*[7].

This was an unusual site for a mansion, and so may have been chosen because it really was the 'place of his ancestors'. The area appears to have been on the edge of the common, although since it is so close to Pomeroy, it is possible that some land in this corner had been purchased from that farm. Maps suggest that Belle Cour had been artificially fitted into the old field system and surrounding plots. The enclosure plan of 1822 shows common between the track to Pomeroy and what was then the boundary of Belle Cour, which was set back from the boundary. The siting of the farmhouse and mansion away from a track and not in the centre of a field system supports the view that this was a genuine 'greenfield' site. We believe that Sir James Tillie was already the occupier and builder of the main house, which he had himself named and built. I have not found any reference to a building on the site dating to before Sir James' time.

It might be suggested that the present farmhouse, or its predecessor was already on the site. However, this service building and courtyard is a considerable distance from the track. Its door faces away from the road and it has a rectangular yard inserted into the field pattern. It is away from the common and beyond or behind the site of the mansion house. There is no obvious geographic or boundary reason to have sited a dwelling so far from the boundary, suggesting that the present farmhouse and its well court cannot be older than the mansion which it serviced[8].

The farmhouse at Bellecour is of 17th century build. The well court is to the right.
The original staff or front door, now blocked, is behind the wall plant.
The stable door, still there in living memory, is outlined in red.

From Left: Two gate posts;
a buttress of dressed stone;
fine stone on a farm building.

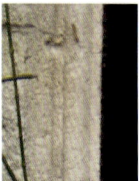

Left: A cut, angled moulded garden ornament may be a string course. The Tower House has
a door frame with finely etched moulding and four stone cross mullion windows still in situ.
Right: The stone roof to the well yard and the mouldling to the Tillie church plaque hint at
other design elements.

Creating an Ancestral Home

It is probable that Belle Cour Mansion was already built and long occupied by the time of the transfer of 1695, which notes that the house at Belle Cour was already standing. It seems probable that the house was built either before 1690, perhaps started after the grant of his knighthood in 1687 or even earlier. In any event, Belle Cour was finished before work was well advanced at his other site of Pentillie, but not before work on that much larger place had started. The description of Belle Cour in the 1695 transfer refers to the site as though it were a considerable gentry house. The definition of a mansion was usually that it was a house where lived someone who earned his income either from rents or from business elsewhere, and was neither tradesman nor farmer. Belle Cour was described as a mansion, with outbuildings and the 'terrace walk, green court etc., ponds, orchs' which suggests a house of some status, and with gardens which were already laid out.

The Farmhouse at Belle Cour

The surviving dwelling at Belle Cour is now a farmhouse. Save for brickwork to the south elevation, the building is of roughly coursed rubble stone. The brickwork which faced the immediate garden of the mansion, was used because it was a material of higher status than the stone of which the remainder of this building was built and because it fitted with the brick walled gardens of the mansion. Belle Cour has the same mixture of brick and stone as Pentillie, the brick being used for the higher status walls. Like the garden walls, this brickwork is in English garden wall bond. The existing farmhouse was designed as a manager or staff dwelling of no great size, and is fascinating because it is still possible to trace the original layout and function.

Despite much recent modernisation, the essential 17th century building remains intact with its original roof structure, a turning stair to the attic and much to delight the building enthusiast.

The southern end and wing of the building was a coach house and the outline of its east doors is still visible. It is possible that the

Belle Cour farmhouse has many examples of reused or original material including:
From top left: The 17th Century steep roof with through purlin, raftered structure; two panel door; winding attic stair; quoins to stable opening; fine stone fireplace; larger finely moulded fireplace typical of 1690.

In the garden are further pieces of the demolished house:
From left: A baroque door frame reused in a garden wall; A selection of cut stone, door mouldings and other cut stone, including a 'gothic' window, which may come from another site; A gate pillar appears to reuse an old capping; the rusticated pier could also be from the earlier house; A pier, (not shown) uses fine cut stone; fine quoins also suggest a quality building.

west end of this wing held stables. The remainder of the north-south wing had a central door with a room each side, and a service room or kitchen in the north-west wing behind.

Following the demolition of Belle Cour, some fine materials were reused. For instance there is a good scribed fireplace (and bread oven) in the main room and a small bolection moulded fireplace now moved from the first floor to the south ground floor. To the rear and west there is still a kitchen with a large fireplace, and to the north of the whole building was the well courtyard.

An earlier report wrote: *'Some parts of the building are obviously very old, such as the well which is now closed up. Until the turn of the century, the ground floor was all paved in Blue Green slabs, the main fireplace erected centrally about three quarters up one end of the building, attached to this building the cloistered yard.'* (Somerset Archives). This well courtyard is an arcaded cloister very much in a style Sir James Tillie favoured, since such arcades exist also at Pentillie. The well was placed in the centre of the yard. The surrounding arches are little altered and retain many of their earliest features. They remain one of the most unusual features of the Belle Cour site.

The Grounds

A plan of the gardens relies on examination of the ground, the earliest maps and the description. Today, much has gone, but a fine walled garden remains, which includes a doorway taken from the demolished mansion which has been inserted into the wall. According to tradition there were larger courtyards to the south, and in a very dry summer the lines of such walls could still be seen[9]. The surviving garden walls are of high status brick, and meant to be viewed, the brickwork even continuing along the blank gable end of the service wing to the north. The brickwork is in English garden wall bond, which is three rows of stretchers with a single row of headers, a style rare at the time outside the north of England.

Beyond the walled garden was the tower, which served as a

Mathews Farm, Pomeroy Lane, Wingfield

This house appears to have been built between 1785 and 1822, and to have reused much stonework from the demolished Belle Cour. Easy to identify are three square windows, whose single mullions were only recently removed; two windows like those of the Tower, though probably turned to lie on their side; two oeil de boeuf oval windows; a stone door frame with baroque hood mould, and a fireplace of fine grained stone. The well cut quoins, perhaps the string course too, were also reused items. The front door has a hooded and chamfered oolite stone surround.

study and retreat for Sir James.

The description of the house and gardens refers to walks, terraces, to ponds and to orchards. Of these we only know that orchards survived in quantity around the house even in the 1841 tithe map. However, there is no evidence of the ponds, and as yet no working layout which included terraces and walks. The garden layout must have been more extensive than that apparent today and deserves further study as a rare example of a planned late 17th century garden.

The Mansion at Belle Cour

A position for the house site is gained from examining the field plans, the siting of the service block and old coach house, the surviving walled garden, other landscape features and the survival of a presumed basement, which became a pond. The site of the mansion can be traced on the ground and fits well within old and present boundary lines. There are no clues as to the aspect of the house, but it seems likely that there was either, or both, a garden front facing south west and an entrance front facing the entrance track. The plan may have included stub or full wings to the rear and may have included a broken principal elevation with projecting stub wings.

The filled in pond suggests that, as at Pentillie Castle, there was a store below the ground floor so that the ground or principal floor over the basement was reached by a flight of some 8 steps.

The list of elements surviving from the demolished mansion is considerable and includes windows in two different styles, elliptical oeil de boeuf windows, moulded doorways, a possible porch, some five fireplaces, much ashlar stone work, pieces of moulded string course and other moulded stone. With so much material it is possible to guess at possible reconstruction[10].

The ground floor plan could have been similar to that at Medford House, Mickleton, which is also similar to that at Pentillie. A ground floor layout was therefore likely to have had one room each side of a central hall, in a building only one bay deep, with a service

Pomeroy Farm, Pomeroy Lane, Wingfield

Pomeroy, too, seems to have benefited from reused demolition materials. Both house and outbuildings have fine stone used freely on insignificant walls, outbuildings and the main housewhere it has been inserted into the earlier structure.

The entrance porch appears to be a late 17th C reused item with fine mouldings. The rear porch, (pictured) is of the same stone. Other pieces include: A fine fireplace (north ground floor) which has been inserted in a gable wall which, outside has squared ashlar blocks to the gable with an ashlar chimney above. Ashlar blocks have been used for garden walls, repairs in the hall and an 18th C partition. Another fireplace with decorated mouldings in the early hall has been altered more recently with the insertion of a welsh shield, but is also an insertion and may be the principle Belle Cour hearth. Windows are puzzling and may include reused material. The quantity of reused stone suggests the quality of the demolished house.

block to the rear or side. However, such a reconstruction is beset with difficulties. Was the building of stone, rather than brick? How much brick was used, rather than square cut ashlar? Was the window style closer to that of those reused at Pomeroy Farm, or did it include the smaller lights reused down the lane at Mathews Farm, perhaps because they were demolished first as being at the top or back of the house?

Windows at the garden tower were, like those at Mathews, stone cross mullioned, although there are some larger stone windows at Pomeroy which might have been from the ground floor. There are several doorways in finely moulded stone, some having an unhooded ledged moulding over the top like that attached to Tillie's plaque at Wingfield Church. There is so much fine ashlar bath or other oolite free stone, like that reused and still standing as the raking support of fine stone standing to the south of the new porch on the south east elevation of the farmhouse, that it is difficult to believe that the entire building was not built of such fine ashlar, rather than brick.

Where and how many were the oculus or oeil de boeuf windows used? Were there statue niches cut in to the front elevation, as at Pentillie Castle, and as perhaps re-used at Wingfield House? Above all, how does any design reflect what was described at the time as 'a house ….which bore evident marks of that singularity of character?'[2]. There is no evidence of stone columns or of pillars that might have been used. I suspect the walls were of rubble stonework (as is the farmhouse) but finished with fine grained ashlar to the main and side elevations under a stone roof, the whole having three string courses across each elevation.

The reconstruction sketch shown in this chapter does not show that the house 'bore marks suggestive of a singularity of character', but provides a basis for debate, although since it is unlikely that we shall ever find a picture of the house as erected; this debate may remain inconclusive.

Belle Cour: the tower as a barn
Wiltshire Farm Buildings 1500-1900, Pamela M Slocombe 1989; reproduced by permission.

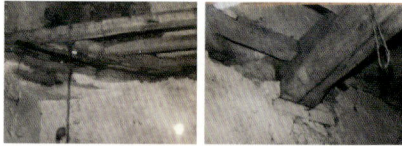

The Tower House, Belle Cour
Middle: Timber details, *Photographs taken in 1981   Left & centre*; South east elevation.
Right: First floor south west; detail door jamb. *Photographs 2010*

The Castle

It would be nice to suppose that the title 'The Castle', which was the old name for the tower and remained used locally, had survived because it was the name given it by Sir James Tillie. It is perhaps no coincidence that his other tower in Cornwall was also called 'The Castle'.

Like other Tillie buildings, it has accumulated stories of its own, including one that it was built so that Sir James could sit at the top and look over towards Farleigh Hungerford Castle. There are even stories of a tunnel that ran to Farleigh, despite a river ravine being in the way.

For the last two hundred years or so it has been a farm building, more recently known as a granary. After being given permission for conversion and extension in 1980, it was considerably extended and is now known as 'The Tower House'. Local building histories had called it a stable with a room for a groom above. This seems very unlikely, if only because the standard of stonework seems high for a stable, and because the door width of the ground floor is for persons rather than horses. Early maps and traces of foundations suggest that there had been other buildings and walls by the tower both before and after the time of Sir James Tillie. By the time of the 1822 land enclosure, the tower already had a range of open fronted barns attached to the north, a range that is said to have blocked the outside stair that once reached the first floor. Recent alteration and extension make it more difficult to imagine this as an isolated tower, connected perhaps only by walled garden areas to the main house.

It is my view that it was placed at the end of the gardens of Belle Cour and stood alone, having been built as a folly and study tower, where Sir James could, as his will suggested he enjoyed, work with his papers and books.

This tower was, like the service buildings at Belle Cour, built of rubble stone rather than of the higher status brick used for the main house and garden walls. However, it had fine stone quoins,

Left: A window in situ on the tower suggests how windows at Belle Cour may have looked. *Right,* a reused window, rotated, from Mathews Farm, Pomeroy Lane.

Wingfield House was erected about the time that Belle Cour is thought to have been demolished. However, save for the two intriguing niches in this elevation, there is no evidence to suggest that any element from Belle Cour was reused.

Once it is realised that bits of the demolished Belle Cour could be scattered throughout the neighborhood, there is a danger that such remnants will be found or imagined everywhere, and, like the ships timbers of the Tudor navy, become a feature of every house, no mattter how unlikely this might be. There are several Wingfield houses with parts which might match those of Belle Cour, but not only must these attributions be treated with care, but, save for the alleged individuality of Sir James Tillie's approach, examples of a late 17th century style are to be expected on many houses.

window and door surrounds of good quality, indeed of better quality than those surviving at other service buildings. Surviving stonework, all of which appears to be in situ, is of that local oolite limestone, of which Bath stone is a type. This stonework therefore could provide the pattern and material for the stones, doors and quoins of the house at Belle Cour.

There was a door on both the west and east (and perhaps one to the south) with a fine cross mullioned window to the south east or road side. The first floor had windows on three sides, with a doorway to the outside and an outside stair, to the north, later blocked or obscured by a cart-shed range.

The first floor was, therefore, well lit, with three windows. It was also heated by a fire place built across the south west corner with a chimney built into that corner. A survey[11] recorded the fine roof timbers under a stone covering, with good and a massive central floor beam with a 3½" chamfer and ogee stops in 16th century fashion. The roof then appeared of early date, but given both the absent chimney and that the top string course appears hidden at the eaves, it is possible that the roof is an 18th century replacement, and that the roof, as might be expected of a Tillie design, had a flat battlemented roof or third viewing storey.

Before conversion, the windows had been blocked with early handmade brick, perhaps from the house or gardens at Belle Cour. The stair must have allowed access direct from the walled gardens of Belle Cour. The tower was so sited that it was both visible from the house, but off by itself, and with fine views to the west.

It must have given Sir James much pleasure to visit and work there. Like the tower at Pentillie, which it predates, this is thought to be one of the earliest, if not the earliest, retreat tower of this type built in England.

Medford House, Mickleton, Gloucestershire, built around 1694, shows the standard shallow three bay house of the time, in fine warm stone. It also has two *oeil de boef* windows, and could have been an appropriate or admired style for the new house at Belle Cour. Medford's floor plan fireplaces and joinery fit well with the remnants and site at Belle Cour

A mid 17th century house in Maiden Bradley, Wilts., shows the admired elevation of the time. The porch has a fine lined mould-ing similar to that thought to have been at Belle Cour.

The Demolition of Belle Cour

After the death of Sir James Tillie in 1713, the holdings in Wiltshire were subsidiary to the other interests of his heirs, so it seems likely that after a period of vacancy the property was tenanted. The present farm building was only a service wing and coach house for the mansion built by Sir James. The house was that awkward commodity, a fine building for a gentleman but one where neither the main building nor the service wing and coach house were obviously suitable for a tenant farmer. The house was therefore a problem case, a house that was not needed by any member of the family, too fine to throw away, and difficult to let.

We can speculate that, although they continued to hold the house, and even add to the acreage, the family interest was not in the Wiltshire estate. Early in the century, and before the marriage of Tillie to Coryton, family relationships, friendships and business interests must have ensured they retained an interest in Wiltshire. However, with time the house probably became an overlooked secondary interest, likely to have become neglected and to have deteriorated. I imagine it made sense to knock the house down, particularly if it was both expensive to maintain, and difficult to let or sell.

Although the site of the house had been forgotten, we have some records to bracket the years of that demolition. First, demolition is unlikely to have been before the death of James Tillie lll in 1772. It was only a few years later that the vicar of Winkfield wrote that on the site of Sir James Tillie's estate at Belle Cour: 'There was till lately a house upon it…'[2]. This confirms that the house had only been demolished in the years immediately before 1781, the date of the letter.

A second record puts an end date on the demolition since in 1838 it was said that "the remains of a cross and a few stones of its basement were removed from their ancient site in a lane near Belle Cour". This suggests that the basement was the last part of the building structure to go. The first draft of the Tithe map, dated 1838, also suggests that something was removed around that year, because

A sketch of how Belle Cour might have looked when first built, save that this does not show a building that might be described as showing 'singularity of character'. The plot size was probably 48ft or 56 ft across this front.

this draft has an erasure smudge, a blob, to show that a building had gone. When the tithe map was redrawn and reissued in 1841, the blob had become a small pond, which it seems possible had been a semi basement. By the end of the 19th century this pond had become a larger horse pond. This horse pond is on a level site filled by no obvious pond or stream, again suggesting that it arose from use of a dug basement. Filled in in the late 20th century, it is still possible to trace its site, and ground level changes may be the remains of the building. Demolition is likely to have taken place between say 1775 and 1838, when the last stones were removed.

Such a date agrees with the dates for new building and renovations that took place in the immediate neighbourhood of Belle Cour.

Several sites are thought to have re-used material from the mansion at Belle Cour. First, of course, the present farmhouse has some splendid fireplaces and other artefacts which appear to have come from the mansion, together with re-used stone and cut stone in other farm buildings. Other houses where demolition material appears include Mathews Farm down Pomeroy Lane, Pomeroy Farm itself and perhaps others such as Wingfield House. Mathews Farm is recorded on the 1822 Enclosure map, and the building would appear to have been built around 1800. Considerable surviving material from Belle Cour appears at Pomeroy Farm, a much older house, altered or improved around 1800[12].

The mansion at Belle Cour therefore had a relatively short life, and probably lasted under a hundred years, that is from say 1688 to 1775. The remains of this project, which include the name Belle Cour, a fine and rare tower which may be the earliest study retreat built for that purpose in England, the remnants of a garden, a distinguished service block and the arched or cloistered well court, all suggest that the name of Sir James Tillie should be better known now and should be remembered in Wiltshire in the future.

Endnotes

1.   Copyholders were occupiers with a form of permanent tenancy which had rights of succession on the land of a manor, with some form of ground rent or duty being paid to the manor. Like a long lease, it was possible for some copyholders to sell or transfer the occupied land for money, and be sure of the manor's agreement, although some copyholders held under a term for 'three lives'. The system gave rise to complex land transactions and multiple agreements to organise a transfer.

2.   The Gentleman's Magazine for September 1791 includes a letter of August 18 to Mr Urban, (editor) from 'E.S.', The Rev Edward Spencer of Winkfield.

3.   Sometime after 1086 the land at Wingfield was held by the church. By 1400 The Manor of Wingfield, together with Pomeroy and the manor of Stoford had come to the Abbess of Keynsham and continued to be held by the Abbess until the dissolution of 1539. After 1539 Wingfield was granted to Thomas Bayley by the King and stayed in this family, by descent, until 1647 when it passed to the Ashe family who sold it in 1683 to Walter Greene. The names of both Bayley and Greene figure in the legal documents recording Tillie's assembling of land and Greene in particular transfers land to Sir James Tillie.

Information sources include those mentioned at end of foot notes and the Victoria History of the County of Wiltshire: Volume 7 pp69-76; 1953; Ed R. B. Pugh & Elizabeth Crittall; H. F. Chettle, W. R. Powell, P. A. Spalding, P. M. Tillott.

4.   The earliest records of the name are as follows:

Winfeld: c.1200-1286;   Wynfeld: c. 1200-1286;   Wintfeld: 13th century;   Winefeld: 1249-1286; Wynefeld: 1249-1286; Wynchefeld: 1276; Wyndeselde: 1535; Winfield: 1675.

Winfield, spelt without either a 'g' or 'k' was used in the legal deeds of the late 17th century. In 1791 (see reference to Gentleman's Magazine for September 1791), the vicar of the parish spelt the name with a 'k': Winkfield. The addition of a g between the syllables is more modern. The Ordnance Survey first edition 1" of 1817 records Winfield for the hamlet at the cross roads north of the church hamlet although calling that church hamlet Wingfield. The Ordnance Survey map 6" Ist edition of 1884/6 records the parish as Wingfield, the name almost always in use in the later part of the 19th century.

5. Records of transactions that allowed Sir James Tillie to assemble land in Wingfield are found in the Coryton archives in the Cornwall Record Office, to whom his papers eventually descended when the Corytons inherited all his holdings. However, the archive appears to have gaps and so may be incomplete so far as it relates to Wingfield. Since many small plots, cottages and owners are mentioned, research on the sites and owners of the various fields and field names of Wingfield could provide constructive analysis of the smallholders of Wingfield in the mid 17thCentury, but is beyond the scope of this writing.

The first transaction of James Tillie [referred to as 'of Mellin', that is St Mellion in Cornwall] was when, in 1673, aged about 26, he renewed a lease of two enclosures in Wingfield which his father, John Tillie the younger, had taken in 1666 (per Ken Rogers), although it seems that his father continued to occupy them.

By March 1675, James Tillie was acquiring and swapping land once held by his grandfather, and then held by his father. In that March he purchased for £29 some pieces of land and a messuage, (a word that usually meant a dwelling with its outbuildings garden and land) which had once been in the possession of his grandfather John Tillie the older. The other pieces of land included another messuage called 'Threshholds' with a half-acre and another four or so acres in small pieces. The transaction included a land swap with the parson of Wingfield and appears to have been not only a sort out, but perhaps rationalisation of land once held by his grandfather. It also included the purchase of land now occupied by his father and Robert Howell. Since the parson still had Glebe land due north of Belle Cour and west of the old Common in the early 19th century, it seems likely that some of the land swap involved land around Belle Cour.

It was another five years before we know of another transaction, when in June 1680 it seems that James Tillie got hold of further lands in Wingfield, perhaps in partnership with his brother Jeremiah, who is shown as a merchant from Bristol. The two Tillies sell some newly enclosed land to Walter Green, who was one of the larger landowners and, from 1683, owner of the manor. This was land which was then, and which continued to be, leased and occupied by James Tillie. The year after, and as was the custom in land transfers, his father surrendered his leasehold interest under the 1666 lease to his son James in 1681. The system avoided costs by leasing a property for a year under an agreement that allowed the tenant to purchase at the end of the period, which he usually did.

Then there is a series of transactions in relation to the same land, which was now back in the hands of the two brothers James and Jeremiah Tillie. In 1683 they granted a lease (signed by Jeremiah Tillie on behalf of both brothers) of the land, which included other bits towards Westwood. This was then sold to Walter Green a year later in 1684.

However, at the same time in 1684 Walter Green sold land to Henry Mitchell, 'citizen and fruiterer of London', who we know to have been a kinsman and trusted friend of James Tillie. This land was some pieces of land, a few acres which ran up to and was on the 'backside' of the copyhold messuage of John Tillie.

Simultaneously there was another land swap in 1684 involving the manor, the parson, and John Tillie and his two sons James and Jeremiah, proprietors of a copyhold estate. The transaction again involved the swapping, gaining and surrender of land. Then Walter Green transferred quite a list of fields and property, which had been occupied by John Tillie, to Henry Mitchell, who promptly, a couple of weeks later, transferred the whole lot to James Tillie of Middle Temple esquire.

Then in April 1695 Walter Green transferred to Sir James Tilley 'of Belle-Cour, Winfield,Kt, the *'capital messuage or mansion called Belle-Cour, with terrace walk, green court etc., ponds, orchs. etc. in front between house and Easthills close (which had been in the inheritance of Sir Walt. Long, then in poss. of Wm. and Jn. Seele). Also ponds, commons etc. between plantation gdns. etc. of Sir James Tilley and Redmans close. With the pound or pinfold. - Close called Five Acres adjoining Sloughes closes. - messuage called Notts. [Notts may also have been known as the house called South Cross] - closes called Kinges, Redmans, Marscroft, Pitmans Marscroft, Pease Close, The Home Mead, Green Close, Pombrie Croft, Parsons Close, Great Hitch, Little Hitch 60a. in Winfield, Stowford, Westwood, Hungerford Farleigh, Wilts.'* The area of land is said to have been about 65 acres [per Ken Rogers].

Finally in August 1704, Sir James and his friend John Bailward, gentleman of Rowlie in the Parish of Farleigh, acting in trust for Sir James, purchase for £161.5s 0d more land once held by John Nott being South Cross alias Sons Cross and 'Monckes' together amounting to some three acres. Moncks turns out to be plot number 37 on the Tithe map, to the south east of Belle Cour. This legal transactions include some other land, and it is difficult to track down the lands and what was going on, but included some land occupied by Sir James. The documents above can be found in the Cornwall Record Office:

CY/1216,1217,1218,1219,1220,1221,1222,1223,1224,1225,1226,
1227,1228,1229,1230,1231,3803. C54/4936, no. 1.

6   Despite what are understood to have been some disposals, the land at Wingfield held by Sir James Tillie was similar in extent to that held by the Corytons many years and generations later. In 1752, the place was referred to as 'The farm called Bellecour and Nothall', which covered areas around and to the north of Belle Cour.

In 1808, John Tillie Coryton who had inherited the Tillie property at Wingfield, purchased the manor of Wingfield and then combined it with Belle Cour. In 1815 Mrs. Tillie was being rated for Belle Cour and other places. In 1823 John Tillie Coryton of Pentillie Castle, Cornwall, took over, under the Awards of Common Lands, two parcels of land, now in Belle Cour farm. He was also awarded rights of way over traditional paths and tracks, including what was probably the original route to the church, past Monk's field.

In 1828, the whole of the Tillie/Coryton interests were sold to John Houlton of Farleigh Castle 'By the heiress of the Tillie Family, Belle Cur came to John Tilly Coryton Esq. who sold it to John Houlton Esq. of Farleigh Castle'.

1841 In the Tithe Apportionment of 1841, the map being dated 1838, the following occupied sites at Belle Cour.

Plot	Description	Owner	Occupier
90	Grove or Nut Close (Pasture)	John Houlton	Samuel Rudman
91	Orchard	John Houlton	Samuel Rudman
95	House,Yard,Buildings, Orchard and Garden	John Houlton	Samuel Rudman
96	Homestead	John Houlton	Samuel Rudman
98	Allotment (arable)	Joseph Houlton	Samuel Rudman
92	Orchard	Louisa Timbrell	James Reynolds
93	Cottage and Garden	Louisa Timbrell	Joshua Beaven
94	Cottage and Garden	Louisa Timbrell	Mary Cook
94	Cottage and Garden	Louisa Timbrell	Daniel Couch
97	Cottage and Garden	Joseph Chambury	'Himself'
99	Allotment and Roadway	Elizabeth Abigail Could	Joseph Gibbs

The owner was shown as John Houlton. Samuel Rudman had a tenanted farm, which appears to equate to Belle Cour, of some 64 acres. Coryton was listed as still owning some small pieces of land some distance from Belle Cour itself.

1875 "Thomas Rumming, a local farmer, had apparently acquired such manorial rights as still existed, there is no reference to the Lordship after this date".

Information sources include:

Victoria History of the County of Wiltshire: Volume 7 pp69-76; 1953; Ed R. B. Pugh & Elizabeth Crittall; H. F. Chettle, W. R. Powell, P. A. Spalding, P. M. Tillott

7   Cornwall Record Office reference CY/1227

8   Belle Vue: a few hundred yards north of Belle Cour is a building called Belle Vue, shown on the 1822 plan. This was the earliest building on a lane which ran down the west side of the old common, and looks as though it was once a small holding. However, the present house is not early 18th century but of later date. The medieval road layout, the common, its position between the common and glebe land, a well and site suggest that this may have been a farmstead or late 16th century squatter dwelling on the edge of the common, by an earlier track to Belle Cour. Of course the name may be an entire red herring, but one can speculate that the house, which has a 'beautiful view' of very little save Belle Cour, was named because it had been at some time part of Tillie's purchases. I hope some research enthusiast will be able to tell me the real story.

9   Anecdotal evidence recorded in conversation R & B Harvey 25 October 1984. I have heard stories similar to this and had the outlines described to me by two different people.

10   A full schedule of surviving worked stone doors, windows, fireplaces and much other material is held in the archive of SCSTyrrell. Recording of reused material at Pomeroy Farm, Mathews Farm and elsewhere is based on visits, records and photographs taken by SCSTyrrell. The list of surviving quality material is considerable and gives some concept of the design and fitting out of the mansion.

11   Harvey R & B: Survey: Belle Cour and 'Old Granary' tower 25 Oct. 1984 Ref B467.

         Slocombe, Pamela M: Plans photographs and reports May 1981

         Slocombe, Pamela M: Wiltshire Farm Buildings 1500-1900: Wiltshire Buildings Record, Devizes Books Press & Studio 108, Corsham, 1989

12   A cautionary note should be expressed about the demolition of Farleigh Hungerford Castle, which following the gambling, overspending and financial failure of Sir Edward Hungerford was sold in 1686. It was sold for demolition materials from 1705 until 1730 when demolition was over. The enormous amount of material, of cut and fine stone that was not only sold, but at one time made available to those who would carry it away, could have been a source for materials not only at Belle Cour, but in other houses at Wingfield. However the date of demolition does not agree with the suggested timeline and I believe that the story of re-used demolition

material at Farleigh Hungerford is a red herring. It is however possible that some pieces from Farley Hungerford may have turned up in the 19th century, when the Houlton family, who had bought Farley Hungerford in 1730, were also owners of land at Belle Cour (tithe map 1841).

This chapter would not have been possible without the help of the following,

• Gray, Mrs R. Wingfield Parish: A Chronological Record of Wingfield Parish. Unpublished typescript Pages 30 and 31 in particular. Complied by 1963, from research in the "Record Office, Trowbridge; Histories of Wiltshire; Notes by Wingfield rectors in 19th century. Notes and transcripts of many lost parish and church records. Folklore"

• Rogers, Ken Published and unpublished material by the former County Archivist of Wiltshire, Wiltshire historian and editor for the Friends of Trowbridge Museum. Includes: 'Some Wingfield Houses' Trowbridge History No 2, 1994

• Wiltshire Buildings Record, Wiltshire & Swindon History Centre, Cocklebury Rd, Chippenham, SN15 3QN

Dorothy Treasure, Principal Buildings Historian, provided much help.

Andrews and Drury: Map of Wiltshire 1773

Enclosure award for Wingfield Common 1822, dated 1 Nov. 1823

Wingfield Tithe Map dated 1838, approved Dec. 1840 and Award of 1841.

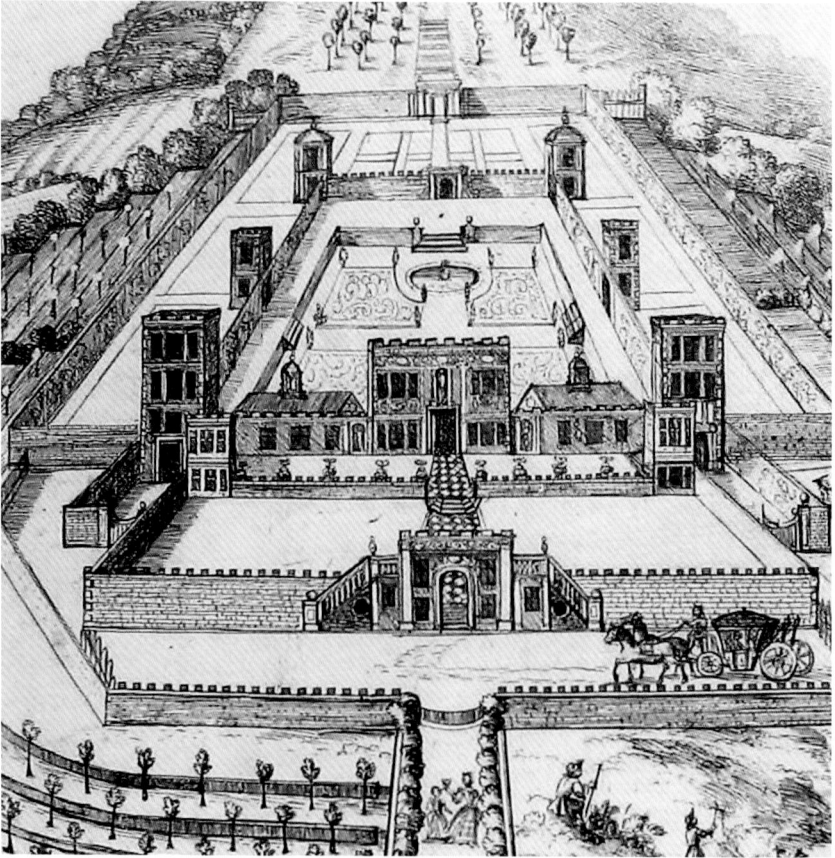

An enlarged section showing the house in the proposals for building Pentillie

Chapter 12

Comparative Architecture and the Design of Pentillie

In the 1690s the concept of the architect had not yet taken hold. Wren had certainly designed in accordance with what we would call architectural principle. However, he was 'The King's Surveyor' following classical fashions. Vanbrugh had started life as a stage set designer. Most designs were probably still carried out by a master craftsman according to established traditions, occasional pattern books and the whims of the client.

It is a mistake to consider the buildings of Cornwall as isolated from fashions prevailing in the rest of the country. Fashion works by imitation 'downward' from the centre of power and wealth. The restoration had meant many country gentry, particularly former royalists, had perforce to visit London and the disproportionate number of members of Parliament to Cornwall assured London connexions. Solicitors and businessmen found fortune and work in London and it was in London that the upper gentry could make contacts, seek office, or learn of new fashions in Dutch or French architecture.

Because the building at Pentillie as shown in the 1692 drawing is so unusual, we should first consider why this is so untypical a scheme and what sort of design Sir James Tillie might have considered.

The first half of the 17thC has been called 'The Great Rebuild' in Cornwall, a period when there was relative calm and wealth in the country before the Civil War, and when most houses of status were rebuilt. Such Jacobean houses were a development of the architecture

Ince Castle, c 1640-50
in a drawing by Edmund Prideaux

Newton Ferrers, Cornwall is sometimes described as the first palladian house in Cornwall and was finished by Sir James Tillie's friend and patron Sir William Coryton. This was the house to emulate. *Drawing by Edmund Prideaux c 1717.*

Anthony, in Cornwall

of an earlier period and often retained the courtyard houses of that time. After the Civil War the influence of the continent, where King and courtiers had been living for fourteen years, changed the view on building, and brought what can be called a new Baroque fashion to architecture. One could also describe it as showy, and although it had some pretensions to classical orders, buildings were erected without, generally, the actual knowledge of continental designs, of classical architecture which would help order the buildings. This Baroque fashion lasted but a short time, and was also associated with a different sort of house - the villa or multi-roomed residence - different from the sprawling homesteads usual earlier in the century.

Sir James Tillie had his offices in the Temple, London, and we can assume would have been familiar with the new buildings being erected in London, and the new fashions in country houses, which in the 1680s and '90s were either grandiose or imitated the simple classicism of Inigo Jones, the tastes of Europe and particularly Holland (whence came the reigning monarch in 1689). Nevertheless, he chose at Pentillie to design a building that looked back in style and appearance. Although he called it a castle, it was in fact a villa with extensive outbuildings and a garden whose design also looked back to older fashions rather than forward to the more open grounds then becoming considered.

Great houses such as Belton in Lincolnshire, built in an H shape and surrounded by formal gardens and avenues, might have been a fashionable example to follow. Even the Dutch gables of Montacute, built some 80 years earlier, may have been a likely guide.

Ince Castle, built of brick arobably round 1640, with patterned brickworks, corner towers and a first floor hall, has some similarities to Pentillie, which had first floor saloons, towers and castellated walls. Interestingly, Sir James Tillie's house at Pentillie was set up, as in the traditions of a century earlier, so that the hall or living accommodation and saloons were on the first floor over a basement. The existing cellar's windows, clearly intended to provide light, are now hidden

Stow, Kilkhampton 1685
in a drawing by Edmund Prideaux, c 1717

Trewinnard Manor, St Erth, as it might have appeared as
first built in the 1690s.

Left: Rosteague, the Roseland, a typical gentry house, had a new facade built on the earlier
building c 1700. *Right:* Lancarff, Bodmin is another house given a new facade around 1680.

by raised ground levels and terracing, but it seems possible that Sir James envisaged a raised first floor. There are some former openings in the cellar to the west or higher ground, although it must be doubted whether this could ever have worked unless they were to be used in conjunction with the lowered garden and raised walkways.

Sir James was seeking a castle, a status building which reflected his own sense of importance. I suspect he thought old fashioned tastes better suggested an established family. He did not want to look 'up and coming'. Pentillie therefore suggests a building of an older fashion, with a colonnade and towers.

Both Glynn, south of Bodmin, and Antony have small corner pavilions to the courtyard that reflect the tradition of Montacute. Such features were an important part of the design at Pentillie.
The garden was laid out as the formal gardens of an earlier period, and with the garden towers associated with an earlier architecture.

Pentillie does not reflect the fashions or designs for new houses elsewhere, and his designs seem to fit neither the Baroque of the period or the 'new wave' of William and Mary or Queen Anne. This new style was clearly not of interest to Sir James.

Some idea of the originality or strangeness of Sir James Tillie's design is gained by looking at other houses built around that time in Cornwall, some of which followed the fashions prevalent in the rest of the country.

Examples from larger houses include Newton Ferrers, the former home of his new wife, which was built by Sir William Coryton between 1685 and 1695, just as Sir James Tillie was considering the work at Pentillie. Since Sir James Tillie was the Coryton steward for some of this time it is probable that he also had some responsibility for this work, carried out to a very different design to that at Pentillie. Newton Ferrers is described as one of the earliest buildings in Cornwall to abandon Tudor precedent for classical design. Even the stables at Newton Ferrers, dated 1688, were of classical design with a projecting central break front.

Croan, west of Bodmin, had a single room depth wing added in front of the earlier house by Edward Hoblyn, a lawyer around 1696.

Trereife, Penzance had a new single room depth wing built in front of the earlier house by John Nichols, a successful lawyer, around 1710.

Rosemerryn, Budock had a single room depth extension built onto the original house by the Mason family around 1720.

Tregassow was extended and rebuilt from 1692 by Thomas Coke, whose family had become rich on fraudulent tin dealing. Never finished, the owner died in a puddle, seeking more money to satisfy a demanding wife.

Great Treverran, Tywardreath. A small two room and stair hall extension was added by John Thomas in 1704, combining late 17thC design with eccentricity.

Glebe House, Philleigh: A new wing was added on an old house c.1730

A selection of houses built or renovated at about the same time as the building of Pentillie Castle, show the pre-Georgian architectural fashion of the times. Examples shown include three seven-bay houses, and three five-bay designs from the same period.

Most new designs of the time had a more classical two storey façade, and by 1690 a simpler façade was already conventional; the illustrations give examples of some houses built about that time in Cornwall.

Two more modest houses are among the earliest of their type in the county. Tregassow, St Erme, was built in 1692 by a man also seeking status and the latest fashion and has a charming façade, although old fashioned in interior detail. Tregassow was unusual in being modern in outlook, but retaining features, such as chimneys, appropriate for use and style 100 years earlier. It too had gardens formed when the ground level was raised around an old house to provide prospects and garden entrance to the main or first floor. Trewinnard, St Erth, is a good example of a new house built in 1693 away from the medieval mansion, but built as a statement of status and position for wealthy and up and coming lawyers, the Hawkins family. This house, like many others of that period, had good quality rooms under a single pitch with a stair tower to the rear, with service and kitchen rooms in the older buildings or in separate wings. Thomas Hawkins' Trewinnard was at the forefront of new designs in Cornwall, only Tregassow appearing to have been started as early.

Other houses of similar design built in Cornwall about the turn of the 18thC century, include Trereife, near Penzance, or Croan, near Wadebridge, both built by lawyers like Thomas Hawkins, or Rosemerryn in Budock. Great Treverran, northwest of Fowey, built in 1704, has wonderful half engaged columns and pretensions to be 'modern', but it is only one room thick with a small right angled service wing.

This pre-Georgian period of English Baroque continued not only in the middle gentry but among the wealthiest of owners, and examples of building design taste can include Harlyn, near Padstow, from 1690, to which a plain new-style wing was added, Menabilly, which had a new 'classical' wing and façade between 1710 and 1715, Antony in the 1720s and Boconnoc and Port Eliot from the 1720s; Bake, near St Germans, had a new house built in front of the old ranges, but

The entrance front at Godolphin

The entrance loggia at Penheale

Examples of Columned Loggias:
Top: Penheale, Tregembo. *Lower:* Godolphin, Pendeen, Pentillie.

retained its old fashioned garden. All these houses had renovations which began before the arrival of a more mannered 'Georgian' style and when houses were refaced or rebuilt in styles to which Pentillie has little relation.

Tillie's designs for Pentillie were determinedly old fashioned and different.

The Pillared Loggia

One feature unusual for a building of 1690 is the colonnade. The use of a colonnade as a loggia or entrance area was rare in Cornwall and only a few examples of pillared loggias survive there, where such columns seem to have been a short lived fashion in the two decades before the Civil War.

An earlier example of such pillars was at the great house at Hardwick Hall, built at the end of the 16th century by a woman who hoped a relative might become queen. This has a central entrance colonnade or loggia flanked by two accommodation towers. Other examples from around 1620 include Hambledon Hall in Leicestershire. This house was built with a pillared loggia between the two side wings, as was also Houghton Conquest, Bedfordshire, where it was suggested that the loggia may have been designed by Inigo Jones, around 1615.

Examples from Cornwall include the north front at Godolphin, which had a colonnade and entrance of six columns and two half engaged columns to the exterior, and a second colonnade in the entry court. These were added around 1634 to fit between two earlier defensive towers. This loggia is similar to the west front of Pentillie, assuming two fewer pillars and differently roofed towers. There were also rooms over the entrance and, at Godolphin, a second colonnade was intended to run round the internal courtyard.

There is also a magnificent colonnade at Penheale, erected in 1636, where the columns, including capital and base are 9ft high, and where the entrance loggia has four full and two half engaged columns, as at Pentillie. This colonnade at Penheale appears, however, to have once continued around other sides of the courtyard.

Pendeen in south west Cornwall has a colonnade built within the main courtyard of the medieval house, perhaps to allow access to new guest chambers. Only two of the pillars survive, and they are in a simple and unmoulded style.

The columns at Tregembo, near Penzance, are more like those of Pentillie and Penheale, and once provided a grand entrance to the house. By the end of the 17th century or the beginning of the next, and in reaction to the old style, the house was turned round, given a more modern facade and the colonnade removed and used elsewhere.

Columns were used to provide cover and status. The remodelling in 1637 of the medieval hospital or alms-houses in Moretonhamstead, Devon, provided a magnificent Loggia that was not only practical, but also signalled the status of the town and donors.

Columns were also used to support covered entrance towers or porches for a relatively short lived fashion during the first half of the 17th century. Examples from Cornwall include Dinham on the Camel Estuary, (c.1635), the old Custom House, in Falmouth and Keigwin in Mousehole, which is earlier and has pillars rather more like those which give authority to the main porch at Godolphin.

The columns at Pentillie therefore reflect a style of which few other examples survive in the West Country as built after the restoration in 1660, and is an example of his 'backward looking architectural design'.

It has been suggested that Sir James Tillie might have used his contacts in London to help in the design of his houses and that the Mausoleum is so carefully designed that the hand of a master designer must have been present. I do not think that this is likely. Building and architecture were still the province of the master craftsman and most of the country 'architects' were still closer to site supervisors than designers. Traditionally a master mason or master carpenter was in charge of the works and capable of laying out complex geometric patterns. Moreover, most works were devised and roughly designed by a client giving instructions as to what was required, such instructions then being carried out by a trade master.

At Pentillie it seems likely that there was an earlier phase which was to the south of the site, where the first building phase probably had a traditional wing, with a tower beyond. This phase may have been shown as unfinished in the print dated 1770, since the gable is supported by buttresses to the west. This suggests that Sir James first started building with no clear idea of his eventual grand concept. Although it is clear that Sir James obtained a dramatic view of his proposed castle at Pentillie, drawn by an established draftsman and artist, this picture is an artist's visualisation and bird's eye view of what might be possible, rather than a detailed building design.

I suspect that building proceeded in accordance with his own direction of the craftsmen on site.

Although we have no evidence for the appearance of the main house at Belle Cour, which is reviewed in the chapter on Belle Cour, the surviving or re-used material, the garden plan, the colonnaded service courtyard, and the staff wing and coach house block, suggest that Belle Cour may also have been 'eccentric'. At Belle Cour, too, still stands the tower, itself of early 17th century in design and appearance.

The house at Pentillie reflected Sir James' wish to suggest a long established and traditional house; Belle Cour may have been more 'modern', but still used some relatively 'old fashioned' elements, and may have deserved the attribution of eccentricity.

Endnotes

1 See Pevsner, as noted in sources and references
2 Dr Kate Felus

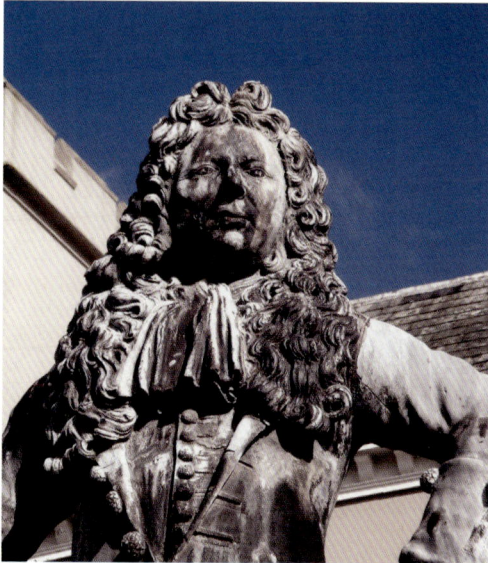

The Lead Statue of Sir James Tillie
Photograph taken in 2008, before restoration

Conclusion

Much of what we have learnt about Sir James Tillie suggests that he was not as unusual as he was portrayed, was not an evil man or thief and was certainly not irreligious.

However, we should not make the mistake of becoming apologists for a man whose life has been reviewed over the years in the light not of his own, but of a later morality. In the practice of the time, James Tilley probably took advantage in law cases, mortgages and actions and charged commissions when he could. This was the normal method of conducting affairs and I have seen no evidence of the outright theft or removal of assets so common amongst other businessmen and ministers of state. I have found him, rather, as of reasonable behaviour.

It is not certain how he made his money. Calculations of a fair commission on the rents that probably went through his hands produce a significant figure. He may have done exceptionally well from his interest in a lead mine. There are some activities he does not seem to have considered, such as a court place, local dignatory, politics, or advance in the law. He may have been just too sensible and practical to consider that. I suspect that his chief business was as a money lender and mortgage taker, who took land when repayment failed.

He can certainly be called an ambitious eccentric, but the last years of his life show him as a sensible retiring man who enjoyed his solitude and his studies in what may have been the first two study-towers in the country. He also seems to have been a somewhat old fashioned man. The designs and architecture of his house and mausoleum confirm that he was a man who looked back to days before the civil war, rather than forward to the changing architecture of the next century.

Much of Sir James' building at Pentillie Castle remains, despite the alterations that have taken place over the last 300 years. Now smaller than when first built, it is difficult to imagine how unusual was its plan and design. It is sad to read from 'Notes of rates collected in Winkfield' in 1718, that 'Belcour and Pentillie Castle is now in charge of a land agent and all view from the road of the Castle and Mount Ararat boarded up', following the death of Dame Elizabeth Tillie.

The manner of his burial in 1713, and the tower to which he used to take regular drives to sit and admire the view, contributed to legends. However, though eccentric, his will is quite sensible, and without the stipulations that later legend suggested. His wishes were carried out after his death, which itself suggests that these wishes were regarded with respect and he, with affection. There is no evidence that he was 'irreligious', but rather that the building of his chapel and the wishes of his will suggest the opposite.

Sir James Tillie was a competent, if perhaps sentimental man, who had wanted to leave his mark on the world. Although it is clear that he had wished to found a dynasty with a lineage more ancient and important than that he actually possessed, to be a gentleman with lands, castle and family tree and that he had hoped to start his own dynasty, he married someone for love. He looked after his extensive family of relations and carefully provided not only for his eventual heir, a nephew, but made provision for other members of his Wiltshire family. The extent of his friendships, his Quaker connections with their reputation for honest business and the fact that life-long friends still acted for him at the end as at the beginning of his life, attest to a worthy man.

Today, Sir James Tillie needs re-assesment not only to reverse the damage done by the scurrilous tales of Hals, but also to establish him as an original in the history of English architecture, and a man whose designs and buildings need much greater consideration.

Sir James was certainly ambitious, a self-made man who had done well. He must have been popular with women to have won two such wealthy wives, and liked by men to have been successful in business. He was a man who wanted to rise and indeed did so. He may have had a touch of the 'Del Boy' and been a man who sought advantage, but this was in an age when this was the only way in which business or social life was conducted.

Although he remains a character of legend and notoriety, I do not believe he deserves to be remembered as he has been in the past, but consider that, despite a wish to make more of himself, he would today be called an attractive character and good company. I would like to have met him and shared his enthusiasm for buildings and grounds.

A drawing of the Mausoleum, decorated for Christmas.
From an original sketch by S.C.S.Tyrrell, 2009

Sources & Acknowledgements

The endnotes to each chapter provide a guide to many sources.
Those of interest are listed below.

Baring-Gould, S   Cornish Characters and Strange Events; 1908/1925: 2nd Series pp 25 et seq.

Beacham, Peter & Nikolaus Pevsner The Buildings of England: Cornwall   Yale 2014

Cliveden Conservation, Bath   Restoration of the Statue in the Mausoleum at Pentillie 2013

Clutterbuck, Robert   Journal of a Tour through the Western Counties of England during the
                        Summer of 1796 pp 305-7, MS3 277 Cardiff University Library

Cornwall Record Office: Coryton papers, wills, deeds & Archivists summary & introduction.

Eveline Cruickshanks: History of Parliament: The House of Commons;
                        D Hayton, E Cruickshanks, S Handley 2002

Devonshire & Cornwall Illustrated, with historical and topographical descriptions
                        J. Britton & E.W. Brayley. Drawings by T. Allom, W.H. Bartlett, &c.   1832

Felus, Dr Kate   'Putting the Pentillie Mausoleum in Context' Unpublished paper; July 2011

Gentleman's Magazine for September 1791   Includes letter of August 18 to Mr Urban, (editor)
                        from 'E.S.' The Rev Edward Spencer of Winkfield [Note 'k' in village name]

Gilbert, C.S.   An Historical Survey of Cornwall, Ackerman, London. 2 vols. 1817 & 1820

Gilbert, Davies.   The Parochial History of Cornwall (4 volumes) Nicholls, London. 1838
                        Includes historical notes by Hals and Tonkin

Glover Richard, MRICS Unpublished papers: The Mausoleum at Pentillie and restoration 2011-2013

Gough Richard (1735-1809) Translated/extended version Camden's Britannia (3 vols. 1789; 4 in 1806)
                        together with personal papers now in the Bodleian Library Oxford

Granger Rev. J and Noble, Rev. Mark   Biographical History of England, London 1806

Gray, Mrs R   Wingfield Parish: A Chronological Record of Wingfield Parish.
                        Unpublished typescript compiled by 1963, Pages 30 and 31 in particular.
                        Sources included: Record Office, Trowbridge. Histories of Wiltshire. Notes by
                        Wingfield rectors in 19th century. Notes and transcripts of many lost parish and
                        church records. Folklore

Gray, T. Editor, 1997   Travels in Georgian Devon.
                        Illustrated Journals of Rev'd John Swete 1789-1800 pp137-8

Hals, William (1655-1737) Parochial Histories unpublished 1737

Harper, Charles G.   The Cornish Coast, (South) and the Isles of Scilly   Chapman & Hall, 1910

Henderson, Charles   1.   Royal Institution of Cornwall: Henderson Papers
                       2. Essays in Cornish History, Clarendon, Oxford. 1935

Hitchins, Fortescue, ed Drew, Samuel. The History of Cornwall, Helston. 1824. Vol 2 pp 559-563

Jessop Consultancy   Pentillie Mausoleum; Historic Building Survey and Investigation of Burial Vault
Unpublished paper by Oliver Jessop, September 2013,
Associated papers: Dr Kate Felus, John Phibbs, Richard Glover MRICS

Kennedy, Lewis   Proposals for Pentillie (1813) Private Collection

Lake's Parochial History of Cornwall: by Joseph Polsue   c 1865-1872, 4 vols
This includes: William Hals (1655-1737) Parochial Histories, unpublished 1737
& Thomas Tonkin, (1680-1742), unpublished 1742

Lyson's, D & S   Parochial History Cornwall (Volume lll for Cornwall)   1814

Mitchell, Andrew   Restoration of a life size lead sculpture of Sir James Tillie: 2008 : unpublished.

Moule, Thomas   English Counties Delineated or A Topographical Description of England,1838

National Archives   A2A National Archives; Kew, Richmond, Surrey

Nicholas Pearson Associates   Historic Landscape Survey and Management Plan: Tiverton 2000

Noble, Revd. Mark   Biographical History of England [after] Rev. J Grainger, consisting of anecdotes
and memoirs of a great number of persons. Vol 1 London 1806

Owen, Clare   Curator, Raby Castle Staindrop Darlington DL2 3AH

O'Donoghue, Peter   Armorial Affairs Sir James Tillie: Report by Bluemantle Puirsuivant 20.07.2009

Pentillie Estate: Papers and records, estate papers, photograph albums and family collections

Perrin, Richard   A Perrin History [re Wiltshire Quakers] 4th/web ed. 2014; Richard Perrin 2014;

Pett, Douglas Ellory   Parks and Gardens of Cornwall, Alison Hodge, Penzance.1998

Polwhele, Revd. Richard   History of Cornwall…Enlarged Seven Vols, 1816 inc Suppl. pp 44/45

Prideaux Edmund (1693-1745) Topographical Drawings: by permission Mr & Mrs P Prideaux-Brune

Repton, Humphry   Red Book for Pentillie 1810 Private Collection

Rogers, Ken   Published and unpublished material. Former County Archivist of Wiltshire,
Wiltshire historian and editor for the Friends of Trowbridge Museum.
Includes: 'Some Wingfield Houses' Trowbridge History No 2, 1994

Slocombe, Pamela M   Wiltshire Farm Buildings 1500-1900, Devizes Books Press, Corsham, 1989

Tyrrell SCS   Personal papers, records and photographs

Tyrrell, Stephen   Pentillie Castle: An Introduction to the History, Architecture and
Eccentric Owners of Pentillie Castle. Pasticcio 2009

Victoria History   History of the County of Wiltshire: Volume 7 pp69-76; 1953; Ed R. B. Pugh &
Elizabeth Crittall; H. F. Chettle, W. R. Powell, P. A. Spalding, P. M. Tillott.

Wiltshire Buildings Record, Wiltshire & Swindon History Centre, Cocklebury Rd, Chippenham,
Dorothy Treasure, Principal Buildings Historian, provided much help.
Andrews and Drury: Map of Wiltshire 1773
Enclosure award for Wingfield Common 1822, dated 1 Nov. 1823
Wingfield Tithe Map dated 1838, signed/approved Dec. 1840 & Award 1841.
Survey: Belle Cour & 'Old Granary' tower: R & B Harvey 25.10.1984 Ref B467

Wingfield Residents   The following provided information, records and recollections
Mr and Mrs Vigar: Belle Cour.
Mr and Mrs Lee and Kate Hatfield. Belle Cour
Mr and Mrs Priscilla Lawson, Mathews Farm 65 Pomeroy Lane Wingfield
Mr. & Mrs Ken & Wendy Fuller, Late of Church Farm Wingfield.
Dr Simon Young for his reminiscences of the Tower House, Wingfield.
Mr Andrew Daniels, Pomeroy Lane
Mr and Mrs David & Jacqueline Browne, Pomeroy Farm

Woodley, George   Cornubia, a Poem in five cantos descriptive of the most interesting scenery, natural and artificial in the County of Cornwall, interspersed with historical Anecdotes and Legendary tales, London and Truro 1819

- Thanks are given to all those mentioned above for the information they have provided, with particular thanks to Mr and Mrs Ted Coryton and family, of Pentillie Castle.
- I am indebted to Alison Spence, Principal Archivist, Cornwall Record Office, for her assistance in deciphering documents relating to the 1702 case of Lord Barnard and Sir James Tillie.
- Restoration of the Mausoleum was carried out with help from Natural England, English Heritage, and with financial assistance from Natural England and the Country Houses Foundation.

Illustration Credits:

- Where requested, the origin of a particular picture has been noted alongside the illustration.
- Photographs of items in the Cornish Record Office were taken by the author with permission.
- We have tried to trace the origin and owners of all photographs used, crediting the owner where possible. Some pictures have been provided from sources said to be available for copyright free use. We apologise for omissions or inaccuracies.
- Ted Coryton and the Pentillie Castle Estate, have provided many photographs, not only of the house and estate, but taken from records and reports made available to them or within their collections. These are used with their permission.
- Many photographs without attribution were taken by SCS Tyrrell from original documents, records or on location.